Orchids at Kew

THE · ROYAL · BOTANIC · GARDENS · KEW

Orchids at Kew

Edited by Joyce Stewart

LONDON: HMSO

© The Board of Trustees of The Royal Botanic Gardens, Kew, 1992
First published 1992

Applications for reproduction should be made to HMSO

ISBN 0 11 250007 2

British Library Cataloguing in Publication Data

A CIP catalogue record for this book is available from the British Library

Design: HMSO Graphic Design, Dee Slater

Frontispiece
Lemboglossum cervantesii from Mexico. RBG, Kew

Title page
Euanthe sanderiana, from a painting in John Day's scrapbooks in the archives at Kew. RBG, Kew

Illustrations next to chapter headings etc. listed below are taken from paintings published in *Curtis's Botanical Magazine* (reproduced with permission of the Trustees and Director, Royal Botanic Gardens, Kew).

HMSO publications are available from:

HMSO Publications Centre
(Mail, fax and telephone orders only)
PO Box 276, London, SW8 5DT
Telephone orders 071-873 9090
General enquiries 071-873 0011
(queuing system in operation for both numbers)
Fax orders 071-873 8200

HMSO Bookshops
49 High Holborn, London, WC1V 6HB   071-873 0011 (Counter service only)
258 Broad Street, Birmingham, B1 2HE   021-643 3740
Southey House, 33 Wine Street, Bristol, BS1 2BQ   0272-264306
9–21 Princess Street, Manchester, M60 8AS   061-834 7201
80 Chichester Street, Belfast, BT1 4JY   0232-238451
71 Lothian Road, Edinburgh, EH3 9AZ   031-228 4181

HMSO's Accredited Agents
(see Yellow Pages)

and through good booksellers

Printed in the Republic of Singapore for HMSO Dd 291785   C50   5/92

Contents

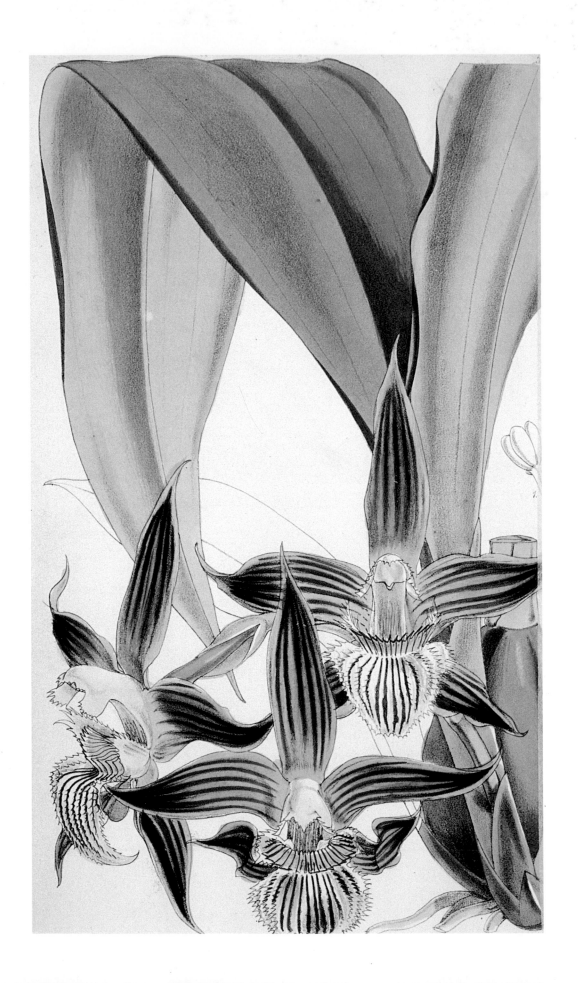

Contributors

Editor
Joyce Stewart

Contributors

Sandra Bell, Supervisor, Orchid Unit, Living
    Collections Department

Peter Brandham, Cytology Section, Jodrell Laboratory

Sean Clifford, postgraduate student, Anatomy Section,
    Jodrell Laboratory

Phillip Cribb, Assistant Keeper, Herbarium, and
    Curator of the Orchid Herbarium

David Cutler, Deputy Keeper, Jodrell Laboratory

Blaise DuPuy, formerly in the Micropropagation Unit,
    Living Collections Department

David DuPuy, formerly postgraduate student,
    Herbarium

Michael Fay, Supervisor, Micropropagation Unit,
    Living Collections Department

Tony Hall, Supervisor, Alpine Section, Living
    Collections Department

Jim Keesing, Quarantine Officer, Living Collections
    Department

Noel McGough, Conservation Section, Herbarium

Robert Mitchell, formerly Sainsbury Orchid
    Conservation Officer, Micropropagation Unit,
    Living Collections Department

Simon Owens, Anatomy Section, Jodrell Laboratory

Hugh Pritchard, Physiology Section, Wakehurst Place

Tony Schilling, formerly Curator, Wakehurst Place

Joyce Stewart, Sainsbury Orchid Fellow

John Woodhams, Assistant Curator (Tropical Section),
    Living Collections Department

Foreword

The orchid family is one of the major research subjects of the Royal Botanic Gardens, Kew. Even a garden of our size cannot carry out detailed studies of all the world's flora, so we have chosen to concentrate our research on a number of particularly important plant families. As the largest plant family in the world, and one that has long been of great interest to many people, the orchids are an obvious choice for our studies. This book, by past and present staff members at Kew, shows the multifaceted approach adopted towards a group of plants. The studies are possible because of the large collection of 20,000 orchid plants that we hold in the Living Orchid Collection, and because of the size of our Orchid Herbarium which has been built up over the last 150 years. With these collections as a basis, we are able to carry out research on the cultivation, classification, cytology, anatomy, pollination, physiology and conservation of orchids. This involves close collaboration by members of staff from our three main scientific departments: the Living Collections, the Herbarium and the Jodrell Laboratory. This teamwork approach, much of which is described in this book, enables us to learn more about orchids than would a scientist working in isolation.

No botanist can fail to be fascinated by the variety of form and function that has evolved in

the orchid family as it has radiated over the entire globe, throughout tropical and temperate zones and in both humid and dry climates. This book provides a glimpse of this remarkable family of plants, whether grown in the conservatories of Kew or the rain forests of Borneo. Today, orchids have gained increased importance as barometers of the conservation status of many natural areas. Their diversity and the way in which most species grow over restricted ranges and in specific habitats make them ideal organisms with which to monitor the status of a habitat.

The orchid studies reported in this volume would not be nearly as far advanced were it not for the long-term financial support of Sir Robert and Lady Sainsbury, culminating in the endowment of our orchid programme at Kew. I am extremely grateful for this support and for the Living Orchid Collection presented to us by Lady Sainsbury. It is highly appropriate that this book should be edited by our Sainsbury Orchid Fellow, Mrs Joyce Stewart, who has brought together a collection of papers that demonstrate both the diversity of the orchid family and the extent to which the Royal Botanic Gardens are involved in their study.

Ghillean T Prance
Director
Royal Botanic Gardens, Kew

Acknowledgements

The Editor wishes to thank Professor E A Bell, former Director, Royal Botanic Gardens, Kew, for the opportunity to compile this book, and the present Director, Professor G T Prance, for writing the Foreword. I also wish to thank all my colleagues who have so promptly and patiently assisted in its writing, editing and production.

I also wish to thank Peter Brandham, Cytology Section, Jodrell Laboratory, Tony Schilling, formerly Curator, Wakehurst Place, and John Woodhams, Assistant Curator, for reading parts of the text and for their comments. I am most grateful to Noel McGough for reading the entire manuscript and for his suggestions and to Valerie Walley, Head of Publications at Kew, for managing the project.

For the illustrations, thanks are due to Marilyn Ward for her guidance in the Library, as well as to friends not at Kew for the use of photographs which are acknowledged on the appropriate pages. I especially want to thank the staff of the Photography Section of Media Resources, Kew, for many of the photographs of plants and paintings reproduced in this book. Finally, I warmly thank Ruth Bowden, Anne Muffett, Dee Slater and Philip Glover at HMSO Books, Norwich.

Introduction

By Joyce Stewart, with contributions from
Sandra Bell, Tony Hall and Tony Schilling

THE ORCHIDACEAE IS THE LARGEST family of flowering plants, with perhaps 25,000 different wild species throughout the world. Every year, as new parts of the tropics and subtropics are explored, at least 100 new ones are discovered and described. In addition to the wild orchids, nearly 100,000 different crosses of artificial hybrids have been raised in cultivation since the 1850s.

Orchids can be found in every country. Fifty species are known to occur in Britain, and seven species have been recorded within the Arctic Circle. The majority occur in tropical areas, where the forests and grasslands on hills and valleys at widely differing altitudes provide the great variety of habitats which orchid plants enjoy. They grow in the ground – as terrestrials, on outcrops of rock – as lithophytes, and on the branches of trees and shrubs – as epiphytes. A few grow as vines, scrambling over cliffs or through the forest canopy. Most are small plants while a few are so large that the combined weight of several plants can bring their forest host crashing to the ground. A very small number have no green leaves and grow as saprophytes, obtaining their nutrients by way of a mycorrhizal fungus from dead or dying material in their immediate environment.

Most orchids are perennial plants with pronounced seasonal habits of growth, resting and flowering. Many produce their blooms after a period of little or no growth because of low temperatures or little light. Hence the spring months are the best time to see a wide variety of orchids in flower.

It is for their exotic flowers that most orchids are cultivated by enthusiasts, amateurs and commercial growers throughout the world. At the Royal Botanic Gardens, however, a collection that demonstrates the extraordinary diversity of the family has always been maintained. Large or small, striking or insignificant, beautiful or bizarre, scented or smelly, there are plants with flowers of every description present in the collection, all tended with equal care.

Every colour is represented in the flowers of this exciting family, while the diversity of shape, size, decoration and design is almost incredible. Yet in spite of their almost infinite variety, each flower is based on the same basic plan. Six colourful parts, three sepals, and three petals, one modified as a lip, surround a central column which bears the pollen and stigma.

The shape and colour of each flower is specifically designed to attract a pollinator, usually an insect, who, in seeking what it perceives as food, alcohol or a mate, will brush against the column of successive flowers and so effect cross-pollination. Thousands of seeds are produced in each orchid fruit or capsule and these are so small and light they are readily dispersed by the wind. For germination each must become established with a symbiotic fungus which helps to sustain growth during the seedling's early life.

Orchids have been grown at Kew since the early days of its history as a royal garden. According to a catalogue produced in 1768, 24 species of orchids were growing here when it was still Princess Augusta's private garden. Later, many plants were added after George III inherited the garden from his mother and on the advice and assistance of Sir Joseph Banks. The gardens changed from private to public ownership in 1840, as a result of recommendations made to the Treasury by John Lindley, whose great interest was botany, especially orchids. The first Director of the Royal Botanic Gardens, Sir William Hooker, had his own private collection of orchids and during the years of his directorship, and that of his son Joseph who succeeded him, the orchid collection at Kew was greatly increased.

Today, the orchid collection continues to expand. At any one time it contains about 20,000 plants and there is always a display of plants in flower for the public to enjoy. Kew attracts more than a million visitors every year who come to enjoy the trees, the green lawns, the Palm House, Pagoda and other historic buildings as well as the great diversity of plants in the 121 hectares. Many visitors also go to Wakehurst Place in Sussex, the garden which Kew has leased from the National Trust since 1965. It has a very different soil and climate and many plants grow there which would not survive in west London.

The policy at the Royal Botanic Gardens has always been to display plants of scientific and economic interest in a variety of pleasing ways, but the extensive gardens are, primarily, a scientific collection maintained for research in several fields of botany and a centre for the distribution of plant material, both decorative and economic. More than 85,000 different taxa in some 340 plant families are grown at Kew and Wakehurst Place, among which nearly 4,000 different species of wild orchids are represented, with plants from every continent and many different habitats. Man-made hybrids are present, too, in limited numbers, and with these the emphasis is on cultivars of important genera which are of historic importance in the breeding of modern hybrids.

The main objective in cultivating a wide range of orchid plants is to provide material for scientific research. Increasingly, the orchids provide a source of germplasm for species which have become endangered in the wild, or may become so. This book describes the orchid collections at Kew and Wakehurst Place and the work associated with them today, as well as providing a look at the way the collections, and various features associated with them, have grown and changed over a period of more than 250 years.

Overleaf: *Dendrobium densiflorum*. Joyce Stewart

1 Orchids at Kew and Wakehurst Place

MOST PEOPLE THINK OF ORCHIDS as greenhouse plants which require great heat and high humidity to grow and flower well. Others are more familiar with the wild orchids of Britain and Europe, which are mostly small plants with seasonal growth and short flowering seasons during the spring or summer. Both kinds are grown today at Kew and a few native species were already happily established at Wakehurst Place before it became a part of the Royal Botanic Gardens.

Late winter and spring are probably the best times to visit Kew in order to see the widest possible variety, but there are orchids on view throughout the year in the Princess of Wales Conservatory and usually in the Alpine House as well. A careful inspection of the Peat Garden, Rock Garden and adjacent woodland garden will often reveal a few species in leaf and flower. At Wakehurst Place, some naturally occurring orchids in the area known as the Slips have been added to by plants raised from seeds at Kew, and there are additional wild species in the woodlands and nearby Loder Valley Nature Reserve.

The Princess of Wales Conservatory

The main glasshouse displays of orchids at Kew are staged in the Princess of Wales Conservatory. This building, opened by the Princess of Wales in July 1987, replaced the groups of older style houses, mostly of wood and brick, known as the Ferneries and the T-range (orchids had been grown in the latter, both on benches and planted out in beds with other tropical plants, for many years).

The conservatory covers an area of 4490 sq m and brings under one roof the main tropical and subtropical herbaceous collections on public display. The design of

The Princess of Wales Conservatory was opened in 1987 and houses many tropical plants, including permanent and changing displays of tropical and temperate orchids. RBG, Kew

the building makes maximum use of the sun's power for heating, and enables rainwater to be collected and stored for watering, as well as making an architectural contribution to Kew's heritage of outstanding glasshouses.

The tropical plant collections require widely varying environments, so the glasshouse is divided by means of glass walls into 10 climatic zones. The temperature required in each zone is pre-set and controlled by a central computer which also monitors humidity levels and switches on overhead mist lines if the humidity in any zone falls below a predetermined figure. In the same way, shading in response to direct sunlight, and ventilation when temperatures rise, are controlled automatically. This automation means that there is a rapid response to changes in the house when the sun comes out, or if there is a sudden shower, which is not only good for the plants but also creates great savings in staff time.

Zones 6 and 7 are adjacent to each other on the western side of the glasshouse and are allocated to tropical and cooler-growing orchids respectively. In order for the orchids to grow in a natural way, it is essential to create the correct balance of temperature and humidity in their environment. In Zone 6 a minimum temperature of 18°C (64°F) is maintained at night and a relative humidity of about 95%. During the day the temperature rises gently to 23°C (73°F), causing a fall in relative humidity to around 85%. Misting the epiphytic orchids by hand early in the morning offsets this fall in humidity, and in high summer, when ventilators are wide open, an afternoon misting may also be necessary. During the rest of the year the humidity is allowed to fall to about 60% in the afternoon so that the plants are all quite dry before the

Large orchids such as *Coelogyne pandurata* are planted among rocks in the Princess of Wales Conservatory. RBG, Kew

temperature falls in the evening. A similar cycle is maintained in Zone 7, where the minimum night temperature is 11°C (52°F) rising to 18°C (64°F) during the day. Neither zone is allowed to become warmer than 30°C (86°F). Many of the plants grown in Zone 7 require a cool, dry resting period during the winter and the relative humidity is then reduced. Constant manipulation of the computer controls helps staff to maintain the prescribed conditions in the most efficient way.

Like the rest of the Princess of Wales Conservatory, Zones 6 and 7 are designed as landscapes in which most of the planting is permanent. This reduces the labour needed to maintain the plants and results in a more natural display for visitors, who may begin to appreciate how epiphytic and terrestrial orchids grow in the wild. Rockwork gives height and shape to the beds and provides suitable planting spaces for those species which normally grow on rocks. The compost mixture used in the beds is made up of two parts of coarse peat to one part each of coarse bark, medium bark, charcoal and hydroleca. It is moisture-retentive while being well drained and well aerated. Large tree ferns in each zone give a look of maturity to the planting by their size, as well as providing shade and a more humid microclimate.

Trees are needed to display epiphytic orchids effectively and can be provided in three ways. The first is to build artificial trees from pieces of cork oak bark fixed to a concrete or wire framework. Trees made in this way look rather artificial but are very long-lasting. The second method is to use real branches sawn to suitable shape and size and plunged in the beds. Early on in the planning of the orchid zones of the conservatory, it was decided to adopt the second method as it gives a more natural effect. However,

Spring display in the Princess of Wales Conservatory: *Paphiopedilum* species and hybrids are arranged with mosses and ferns in the tropical orchid section. RBG, Kew

Coelogyne dayana, an epiphyte from Borneo, bears its characteristic pendent inflorescences in the summer months. RBG, Kew

under the glasshouse conditions of high temperature and high humidity, wooden branches decay rapidly: *Robinia* is considered to last the longest, followed by oak, but neither can be expected to last for much longer than three years. For this reason, the advance assembly of 'epiphyte trees' in the nursery is needed to ensure a succession for coming years.

The third method is to grow orchids on living host trees, but this requires careful long-term planning. Suitable hosts need to be large enough to support the orchids, yet not so vigorous that they outgrow the glasshouse too quickly. Rough bark, which retains a little moisture to encourage orchid roots, is advantageous. In Zone 7 a graceful cycad, *Cycas siamensis*, supports two dendrobiums from Thailand – *D. aphyllum* and *D. primulinum*. These dendrobiums are deciduous and benefit from a dry rest in winter at a time when the cycad also requires a drier period. A Mexican palm, *Brahea calcarea*, has a rough hairy trunk and has been planted with *Laelia anceps* and *L. furfuracea*. Their roots quickly took advantage of the moisture held there and have penetrated the leaf bases of the palm. In Zone 6 *Cyathea crinita* from Sri Lanka supports the rapidly growing *Coelogyne mayeriana* whose roots are quick to probe the scaly trunk of the tree fern.

Many coelogynes will form large clumps of pseudobulbs in time, and some of these, such as *C. dayana* and *C. swaniana* from south-east Asia, have been established on oak branches in Zone 6. Their pendulous spikes of white or cream flowers with brown markings can be seen hanging below the branches. Their close relative *Pholidota imbricata* also makes a sizeable clump when grown on a branch. Its erect or arching spikes bear many small white flowers two or three times a year.

Masdevallia angulata, a robust species which is widespread in the forests of north-eastern Ecuador; the flowers have an unpleasant smell. AOS Award files

Coelogynes and pholidotas are planted together on branches as they all enjoy well-watered conditions throughout the year. Some tropical epiphytes which require a dry, dormant period in winter are planted in groups where this need can be met. One branch supports three *Dendrobium* species, all from various parts of Thailand. The two species at the top of the branch are *D. aphyllum* and *D. primulinum*. They are deciduous and flowers develop on the leafless, pendent canes before their new growth begins in spring. *D. aphyllum* has soft mauve flowers with a white lip, while *D. primulinum* has white flowers with a yellow lip. Below them, on the same branch, *D. cariniferum* has been planted. In the glasshouse this species needs to be kept drier in the winter than summer but not as dry as the preceding two. *D. cariniferum* is semi-deciduous and in the early spring produces cream flowers suffused with bright orange, with a brighter orange patch on the lip.

In Zone 7 epiphytes from Mexico such as *Lycaste aromatica* have been established by attaching them to branches with the base of the plant surrounded by sphagnum moss. This retains enough moisture in the summer to permit the full expansion of the large, fast-growing leaves. In the winter months, after shedding the leaves, the pseudobulbs are allowed to dry out and this ensures successful flowering the following spring.

Not all the epiphytes in Zone 7 require a dry winter. Many species originating from the cloud forests of central and southern America need to be kept damp and humid even in the cooler months. These have been planted on logs and stumps close to the ground where it is always cooler and more humid, and the curiously shaped flowers of *Restrepia guttata* and the blood-red colouring of *Masdevallia angulata* always surprise visitors who bend down to examine them.

Coelogyne asperata, a widespread species in south-east Asia and New Guinea, grows on trees near streams and on rocks. Beverley Lewis

Some epiphytic orchids have proved to be too large and heavy to be displayed on branches. Dendrobiums in the section *Spatulata*, the antelope dendrobiums, can form large clumps of canes when mature and have been planted in the ground behind retaining logs. Their roots will eventually grow out over the logs, and this will convey the impression of their epiphytic nature. When mature, the canes of *Dendrobium helix* easily reach a height of 2 m and bear many spikes of flowers in pastel pinks, greens and yellows, with characteristic, corkscrew-shaped petals. *Dendrobium gouldii* reaches the same proportions and has yellow-ochre coloured flowers with deep brown twisted petals.

Some epiphytic orchids are grown in hanging baskets rather than on branches. *Ansellia africana* is particularly suited to this method of cultivation, as, in addition to its silvery, cane-like pseudobulbs and fresh green leaves, it forms a fascinating cluster of tightly packed, spiky aerial roots around the basket, completely obscuring it from view. The pseudobulbs become weighed down by the heads of yellow flowers spotted with brown during the early spring and their fragrance perfumes the whole glasshouse when the temperature is warm.

Cultivation and display in hanging baskets is especially suited to species with pendulous flowers, for these can then be examined at eye level. *Dracula bella* from Colombia is grown in this way in Zone 7. Its flowers open out widely to form a triangle of yellow sepals which are nearly covered with blood-red spots. A long, red tail hangs from the tip of each sepal and the inflated white is lip hinged so that it wobbles in the breeze.

The Australian lithophytic dendrobiums are grown on rocks behind the pools in Zone 7. *Dendrobium speciosum* has stubby pseudobulbs and arching sprays of creamy flowers. *Dendrobium kingianum* has more slender pseudobulbs and leaves and bears dark pinky purple flowers in February. These two species form a hybrid, *Dendrobium × delicatum*, which is rare in the wild but responds well to cultivation and has pink or white flowers.

Orchids which would normally grow in the ground are planted in the beds where their terrestrial habit can

Some epiphytic orchids are grown in hanging baskets in the Princess of Wales Conservatory; several plants of *Ansellia africana* flourish in this way. RBG, Kew

best be appreciated. In Zone 6, *Spiranthes cernua* var. *odorata*, which comes from the swamps of Florida, flourishes underneath a tree fern which is given copious amounts of water. The orchid grows luxuriant tufts of shiny foliage and spikes of white flowers throughout the autumn. *Phaius tankervilleae* also originates from marshy habitats and one of its hybrids grows particularly strongly here. The flower spikes of red and pink flowers grow to a height of 1.5 m and their robust foliage is imposing at any time of the year. *Phaius australis* var. *bernaysii* is a slightly smaller species

with flower spikes up to 1.2 m tall. The flowers are yellow and white. Between them the three kinds of *Phaius* produce flowers for eight months of the year: The hybrid *Phaius* usually begins to flower in October and lasts until February; *P. tankervilleae* flowers from Christmas until April and *P. australis* var. *bernaysii* from March until May.

One of the jewel orchids, so-named for their beautiful leaves, is *Ludisia discolor* from Indonesia. The leaves of this species are a velvety-green tinged with bronze and marked with a delicate network of pink veins. It grows

Calanthe sylvatica, a terrestrial orchid that is widespread in shady forests in Africa, and is similar to related species in Asia.
Bob Campbell

close to the surface of the compost but produces spikes of white flowers about 30 cm high which have a beautiful perfume. The cultivar *L. discolor* 'Doris Stein' has longer flowers and more vigorous growth but is sadly lacking in scent.

The South American slipper orchids in the genus *Phragmipedium* give interest over a long period as they are rarely bare of flowers. *Phragmipedium longifolium* can be seen growing with some of the hybrids of which it is a parent, including *P.* Sedeni with deep crimson and pink flowers, *P.* Calurum with pale pink and white flowers veined with green, *P.* Lemoinerianum with cream flowers veined in red, and *P.* Ainsworthii with flowers of a soft pink colour veined with green.

Calanthe triplicata and *C. sylvatica* both have robust evergreen foliage and are planted permanently in the conservatory. *Calanthe triplicata* has white flowers while those of *C. sylvatica* are a rich purple. The deciduous calanthes, such as *C. vestita*, *C. rubens* and the hybrids *C.* Veitchii and *C.* Diana Broughton, are plunged in the beds when they flower but cultivated in the nursery for the rest of the year, since their need for a dry, dormant period would be difficult to cater for if they were planted permanently in the moist conservatory beds.

Whilst most of the tropical terrestrial orchids growing in Zone 6 have been found to grow well in a bark-based compost, a small area of loam-based mix seems to be more suitable for the eulophias, which are planted in the area linking the African and Asian orchids. *Eulophia andamanensis* is a species from Thailand which flowers in late spring and produces many spikes 60 cm tall. The delicate, elegant flowers are a muted green and cream. *Eulophia guineensis* inhabits the African side of the conservatory and has larger pink flowers with a pink and white lip. These two species are both deciduous and their leafless pseudobulbs contrast in winter with some of the evergreen species such as *E. petersii*. This succulent species is widespread in the dry parts of the Middle East and Africa and has thick leaves which conserve water. Its flower spikes may be as much as 1.5 m tall and bear many small pink and green flowers.

The genus *Cymbidium* is of outstanding horticultural importance for the large number of man-made hybrids produced from a few of its 44 species. The tropical species, such as *C. aloifolium* and *C. bicolor*, are grown in Zone 6 on a mesh pillar against which their hanging flowers can be properly viewed and appreciated. Those species originating from the cooler conditions of higher altitudes are grown in Zone 7. Several species, including *C. tracyanum* and *C. lowianum*, are planted at ground level among tree stumps and rocks to show their lithophytic habit. *Cymbidium tracyanum* flowers in the early winter and fills the area with the pervasive fragrance of its gingery-striped flowers. *Cymbidium*

lowianum flowers in spring and several colour forms are planted in the conservatory. The typical form is the best known with its long arching sprays of soft green flowers with a deep red marking on each lip. In some plants the red is lacking and plants with a yellow or greenish patch have been known in the past as var. *concolor*. These plants are now recognised as a distinct cultivar, *C. lowianum* 'Concolor'. The var. *iansonii* has a light brown patch on the lip. Genuinely terrestrial cymbidiums, such as *C. cyperifolium* from Nepal, have been planted closer to the front of the bed, where their relatively small and subtly coloured flowers can be seen. A group of interesting primary hybrids between *C. madidum* and *C. elegans* have been established epiphytically on branches. Cymbidiums have large root systems, so in order to get the seedlings established the roots are padded with mineral rock fibre and wrapped around with moss. This ensure that enough moisture is retained around the roots.

In addition to the permanent plantings of orchids there is a small area in both Zone 6 and 7 for more transient displays. These areas, behind glass security screens, are used to display plants in flower which are grown for most of the year in the Reserve Collection of orchids in the Lower Nursery (see chapters 4–8). Displays are changed frequently so that regular visitors can see colourful flowering orchids at any time of the year.

As in any other garden, the orchid display areas in the Princess of Wales Conservatory will change as plantings mature. It is hoped that every visitor will gain enjoyment from the range of form and colour which the orchids in flower demonstrate and will also appreciate something of the way orchids grow in their natural habitats.

The Alpine House and its Surrounds

The new Alpine House at Kew was opened in 1981 and is rather different from the more traditional houses of its kind. Square in outline, it somewhat resembles a pyramid raised on vertical walls above a surrounding moat. Ventilators are operated automatically making it possible for a very high proportion of the roof to be open. The atmosphere in the house is always cool and fresh.

A dominant feature is a large, refrigerated, rectangular bench which is specially managed for arctic and tropical montane plants with great success. The curious South American orchid *Altensteinia paleacea* can be seen in the tropical montane section of this 'fridge'. It bears a slender spike of papery bracts which partially hide the small and rather insignificant white flowers.

Around the 'fridge', the rest of the house has been landscaped with Sussex sandstone to provide a variety of niches for alpine and cool temperate plants from all over the world. In front of the sandstone are plunge areas where plants grown in pots in the nursery give a continuous procession of flowering material against the backcloth of the more permanent plantings. Display benches also provide space for the exhibition of some of the larger pot-grown plants and recent acquisitions. Much of the permanent planting requires conditions that are frost-free, and if it is cold, then dry cold is less damaging than a lot of rain. Thus plants in the Alpine House are kept somewhat dry in winter and, compared with the surrounding area outside, a little warmer in summer.

At the edge of a small pond the soil is permanently moist and one of the finest of the marsh orchids flourishes here. *Dactylorhiza foliosa* has increased in size tremendously since it was first planted. Its shiny leaves are conspicuous throughout most of the year and it regularly produces more than 20 flowering spikes which last for a month or more in perfection. In the wild, it is known only in Madeira and it is now rare in its native habitat, though single growth plants can still be found. Seedlings from the plant at Kew have been raised in the Micropropagation Unit and are regularly

in demand for distribution to other botanic gardens.

On the other side of the Alpine House, a small gully has been prepared for peat-loving plants which like a little more shade. A few temperate orchids from the Pacific region have become established here and flower well. In mid-summer the slender pink spikes of *Spiranthes sinensis* are conspicuous. In late winter the Japanese dendrobium, *Dendrobium moniliforme*, loses its leaves, and white or pale pink flowers appear on its upright canes. Nearer the front, a tiny Australian helmet orchid, *Corybas diemenicus*, has a tiny leaf almost flat on the ground and produces a small dark brown flower, usually in the spring. Other species planted here include one or two *Pterostylis* species from Australia, the so-called greenhoods, and some of the more tender Japanese calanthes.

Satyrium nepalense is maintained in a pan in the nursery and plunged amongst the rocks for display when the flowers appear. Most years this happens in spring and autumn, with a dry rest period after each flowering. The shell-pink flowers on tall spikes are a pretty contrast to the pale green leaves that clasp the base of the stem.

Many other temperate orchids are grown behind the scenes in the nursery and put on display in the Alpine House as they come into flower, either on a bench

Dactylorhiza foliosa is found only in Madeira, where it is a rare species; this plant in the Alpine House at Kew grows larger every year. Joyce Stewart

among other plants in pots, or plunged into the moist soil by the pond or the rocky slope by the doors depending on their individual needs. Pans of *Pleione* species and hybrids are always spectacular and, by careful timing in repotting and bringing into growth each spring, there is a long succession of blooms on view. Terrestrial orchids from Australia, including some of the *Diuris* species, can be seen regularly. Robust plants of some of the Mediterranean orchids which grow and flower during the winter and spring, are also displayed and then removed to dry off and rest under cover during the summer months. Splendid plants of the tongue orchid, *Serapias vomeracea*, are always an intriguing sight, while a number of the *Ophrys* species have fascinating bee-like flowers. Many species of *Cypripedium* from China, calanthes, *Ponerorchis graminifolia* and *Cymbidium goeringii* from Japan, as well as other cool-growing Asian orchids, may be seen on display in season.

The landscaping around the Alpine House permits the growth of additional species which require a hot sunny site or a cool shady one and as a result a number of shade-loving orchids are becoming established in sheltered places. Some of the spotted orchids (*Dactylorhiza* species) have done so well that seedlings have grown up which appear to be hybrids. *Epipactis gigantea* from North America grows well here and is also spreading, flowering every year in June. Some Japanese calanthes flower very well when the season is kind, but unfortunately their rather fleshy flower spikes are very susceptible to sudden, late frosts.

In 1980, a peat garden was built nearby in the shade cast by the Jodrell Laboratory. It was a splendid site for cypripediums and seven different species flourished here, but sadly they were all stolen one night. However, a number of orchids are still doing well. One of the spotted orchids, *Dactylorhiza iberica*, from the eastern Mediterranean, spreads by underground rhizomes and has become so prolific that it has to be weeded out where it invades other precious plants. Another spectacular plant in this bed is *Dactylorhiza* × *transiens*, a natural hybrid rescued, as a small plant, from a building site in Suffolk and sent to Kew in 1979. Good cultivation and hybrid vigour have resulted in the present specimen, which bore 45 spikes in 1990.

The Rock Garden

The Rock Garden at Kew extends over more than an acre between the Herbaceous Ground and the Princess of Wales Conservatory. Originally excavated from a level site more than a hundred years ago, it has been changed and improved in various ways. The banks of soil are now held in place by large rectangular pieces of

Sussex sandstone which resemble outcrops. Streams flow away from several waterfalls, and along their banks the soil is permanently moist. Several species of *Dactylorhiza*, the marsh and spotted orchids, have become established here, some as chance seedlings while others have been planted. The most conspicuous orchid, however, is a large planting of *Epipactis gigantea*, the large helleborine from North America. It flowers in June and there are usually a dozen or more gingery brown flowers on each upright leafy stem.

The Woodland Garden

At the southern end of the Rock Garden the alpine plants give way to a Woodland Garden where a selection of deciduous trees provides a canopy of shade over the shrubs and herbaceous plants. A number of orchids have flourished here at various times, though sadly many of them were stolen a few years ago. Plant theft has been a surprising problem over the last ten years and for this reason many orchids that could be planted out are now being grown in pots in greenhouses not open to the public, but occasionally some may be put on display.

Still flourishing, and providing quite a spectacle in July, is a group of the marsh helleborine, *Epipactis palustris*. Though growing in rather more shade than they usually tolerate in the wild, the plants of this British orchid grow luxuriantly here and flower well. The beige and pinkish brown flowers have a large white lip with a conspicuous yellow crest.

Wakehurst Place

Woods and fields occupy the major part of this property of more than 200 hectares, where a wide variety of native plants grow, including at least six different orchids.

The best known parts of the estate contain the exotic plants which do not grow well in Kew, especially rhododendrons and some of the southern hemisphere trees and shrubs. The climate is much more equable than that at Kew, although Wakehurst is less than 40 miles away. The rainfall is higher in amount and the temperatures less extreme. Combined with the moisture-retentive soils, these features provide excellent conditions for the growth of temperate plants from around the world. Plants from China and Japan, as well as other parts of the Himalayan region, are a speciality and include more than a dozen orchids.

Neither the wild nor the introduced orchids are a conspicuous feature at Wakehurst. They have to be searched for during the flowering season, or located

Orchis laxiflora in grassland at Wakehurst Place; the plants were raised from seeds at Kew as part of the work of the Sainsbury Orchid Conservation Project. Robert Mitchell

with even greater care in spring before they come into flower. The area known as the Slips and adjacent gardens near the stream are good places to look, followed by the woodlands of the Westwood Valley and, with permission, the Loder Valley Nature Reserve.

In April the grass between the magnolia trees at the top of the Slips is still short and a number of wild flowers appear there. Amongst them is the green winged orchid, *Orchis morio*, always one of the earliest of the British orchids to flower. Its short spikes are soon followed, in early May, by those of a much taller cousin. *O. laxiflora*. This species has never been recorded in mainland Britain though it is common in suitable damp spots in the Channel Islands. The plants at Wakehurst Place were raised from seeds at Kew under the auspices of the Sainsbury Orchid Conservation Project (see chapter 15). This was one of the first species raised in the laboratory and then transferred from the greenhouse to the open garden, Wakehurst being chosen for the experiment as it was thought to be more suitable than the lawns at Kew. An area where the progress of the plants could be monitored easily was chosen, and within a year of their transplanting, several of the plants flowered. More have matured every year, and other laboratory-raised plants have been added to the planting. They now make a welcome addition to the garden. Several plants of the spotted orchid, *Dactylorhiza fuchsii*, also grow in this area and flower a little later, though as the grass is longer by then they are less easily seen.

Two species of *Epipactis* grow wild in the woodlands of the Westwood Valley. These are the broad-leaved helleborine, *E. helleborine*, which has greenish purple flowers on a tall spike, and the more slender violet or clustered helleborine, *E. purpurata*, which has purplish flowers. Neither of these is very common. However, the

common twayblade, *Listera ovata*, is frequently seen in the woods and dappled shade near the path. With its spikes of yellowish-green flowers above a pair of basal leaves it is easily recognised. The spotted orchid is also often encountered along the path through Westwood Valley both above and below the Himalayan Glade.

Several Japanese orchids have been introduced to the shaded garden areas between the Slips and the top of Westwood Valley, particularly near the Primula Dell, but they are not yet well established. Calanthes and cypripediums should do well here, provided the winters are not too cold. *Gymnadenia conopsea*, *Dactylorhiza aristata* and *Epipactis thunbergii*, all Japanese relatives of familiar European orchids, are also being tried.

Another Asian species, *Bletilla striata*, has survived for many years in several parts of the gardens, and makes an attractive border plant. The magenta flowers are held above fresh green foliage in early summer. Later, the plant turns brown and the leaves are shed. The pseudobulbs are protected by the soil and mulch from winter frosts.

One of the less common British helleborines, *Epipactis purpurata*, can be found in the woodlands at Wakehurst Place in August. Hugh Pritchard

2 The History of Orchids at Kew

ORCHIDS HAVE BEEN CULTIVATED at Kew for more than two hundred years. The garden made by Frederick, Prince of Wales, in the estate he leased in 1730, and the scientific institute which began to develop on the same site in 1841, both included orchids. Not unexpectedly, over the years the ever-changing collection has experienced a remarkable series of vicissitudes. For most of the time the orchids have received special attention from dedicated professional gardeners. Special houses have been provided for the plants and the collection has been enhanced by bequests and donations. But these good times have alternated with a series of setbacks. Many plants have been lost by poor cultural conditions, indifferent housing, changing and often inexperienced staff, and a shortage of funds for the care and maintenance of plants that were sometimes regarded as curious luxuries. Orchids at Kew were a special target for destruction by a group of suffragettes in 1912. The great drought of 1921, when only half the usual amount of rain fell, resulted in unexpected losses inside some of the glasshouses (the cause was eventually traced to the water being used on the plants – it was seawater, taken from the tidal Thames!); after that, rainwater tanks were installed. More recently, a disastrous power failure on a cold night in the winter of 1976 caused many losses among the orchids. The severe storms of 1987 and 1990, though causing great damage to the trees at Kew, did not directly affect the orchid plants, but the Lower Nursery, where they are mostly housed, was badly damaged. Similar setbacks are experienced in any garden, however, and often result in improvements and renewed enthusiasm once normality has been restored.

Since its inception, the orchid collection at Kew has been derived from a variety of sources. Botanists on expeditions have always sent back plants, but many orchids have been presented by growers and enthusiasts from many different walks of life. Despite the fact that the collection has always been one predominantly of wild species, some of the earliest hybrids were made at Kew about a hundred years ago. The Kew botanist Robert Rolfe was instrumental in starting the records of orchid hybridising in a careful and scientific way which has continued to this day, while publications on the cultivation of orchids by curators and orchid growers alike have been widely acclaimed and are still useful references. A resurgence of interest in recent years in growing, propagation and research, has put the collection in the forefront again, as this book makes clear.

The First Records

The first gardens recorded in the village of Kew date from the seventeenth century. Sir Henry Capel's garden was visited several times by the diarist John Evelyn who was full of praise for 'the celebrated garden at Kew' and the unusual plants growing there.

The connection with the royal family began in the early years of the eighteenth century, when George II and Queen Caroline made their summer home at Ormonde Lodge, Richmond, whose estate ran alongside the river between Richmond and Kew. In 1730 their eldest son, Frederick, Prince of Wales, took a lease on the adjoining estate at Kew which had previously belonged to the Capel family. With the aid of William Kent, the noted landscape gardener, artist and sculptor, Frederick laid out a new garden and began to amass a collection of exotic plants. Princess Augusta, whom he married in 1736, not only shared his enthusiasm but also took a great personal interest in the gardens. They were advised by the Scottish botanist John Stuart, 3rd Earl of Bute, who became extremely influential after the death of the Prince of Wales in 1751. The gardens expanded in size and scope and were embellished with new buildings designed by William Chambers. A Scottish gardener, William Aiton, who had trained at the Chelsea Physic Garden under the celebrated Philip Miller, was employed in 1759 to take charge of a small physic garden which was dedicated to botany, and aimed 'to contain all the plants known upon earth'! Thus 1759 is often cited as the start of the collection as a 'botanic garden' as we understand it today.

The first record of orchids in the royal collection of plants appears in the *Hortus Kewensis*, compiled by John Hill, one of Lord Bute's protégés, in 1768. Twenty-four species were recorded in cultivation at that time, all but two of them from European sources and mostly British natives. The two exotic species were *Rhynchostylis retusa* (recorded as *Epidendrum retusum*) and a species of

Princess Augusta, who married Frederick, Prince of Wales in 1736, started the scientific collection of plants at Kew in 1759. RBG, Kew

Sir Joseph Banks, botanical adviser to George III, was the first unofficial director at Kew. RBG, Kew

Bletia (listed as *Limodorum tuberosum*).

When Princess Augusta died in 1772, George III amalgamated her estate with his own immediately adjacent garden, and asked the botanist Sir Joseph Banks for help in directing the gardens in a scientific manner. Banks had his own estate nearby at Spring Grove, Isleworth, where he gardened and grew orchids and other exotic plants in a series of glasshouses. Under his influence many improvements were made at Kew, and plants were added to the collections from many different parts of the world. It was Banks who persuaded the government of the day in 1772 to send Kew's first official collector, Francis Masson, to collect plants in the Cape of Good Hope.

With the help of Banks and his librarian, Jonas Dryander, William Aiton published his *Hortus Kewensis* in three volumes in 1789. Until then the records of plants coming into the gardens and surviving in cultivation were somewhat haphazard. The third volume contains a list of the orchids grown at that time, of which there were more than 40 species. The volume is illustrated by a life-size, fold-out, coloured drawing

by James Sowerby of *Phaius tankervilleae*, the first tropical orchid to flower in the glasshouses at Kew. It had been introduced from China by Dr John Fothergill in 1778. This plant is of particular interest because the flowers were dissected, in 1801 and 1802, by Francis Bauer who was resident draughtsman at the Royal Botanic Gardens for 50 years. Not only did Bauer make some of the first drawings of plant cells, magnified 200 times, from the stigmatic surface of this orchid, but he also discovered and illustrated the nucleus of the cell, the first description of which was published by Robert Brown in 1833.

Other plants from distant parts recorded by Aiton included *Satyrium carneum* and *S. bicorne* (both recorded under the generic name *Orchis*) and *Bartholina burmanniana* (recorded as *Arethusa ciliaris*), all sent home as dormant tubers from the Cape by Masson in 1787. Several species from the West Indies had also been introduced recently, including two species of *Encyclia* – *E. cochleata* and *E. fragrans* (as species of *Epidendrum*). In 1782, the latter was the first epiphyte to flower in cultivation at Kew. The earliest record of all appears to be *Bletia purpurea* (as *Limodorum altum*) which Aiton records as having been introduced before 1733. This was probably the same introduction as plants sent to Philip Miller at Chelsea by Dr. William Houston from Jamaica.

By the time the second edition of this *Hortus Kewensis* and a new catalogue were published in 1813–14, by Aiton's son and successor, William Townsend Aiton, the list of orchids cultivated at Kew had expanded to 48 genera and 115 species, of which 84 were exotics. Of particular interest were several species brought back by Bligh in 1793 in HMS *Providence*, including *Dendrobium linguiforme* from Australia, *Oncidium altissimum* from the West Indies and *O. triquetrum* from Jamaica. *Dendrobium speciosum*, from Australia, *Brassia maculata* from Jamaica and *Aerides odorata* from China were donated by Banks from his own collection. Several of the orchids, including the last mentioned, were recorded as not having flowered since their introduction, and it must be doubtful if some of them ever did so under the cultural conditions in use at that time.

One of the orchids sent back by Kew's first official collector, Francis Masson, was *Satyrium carneum*, from the Cape Province of South Africa. (Illustration from *Curtis's Botanical Magazine*, 1812.) RBG, Kew

Bletia purpurea was introduced from the West Indies early in the eighteenth century and flowered first at Kew and in the Chelsea Physic Garden. (Illustration from *Curtis's Botanical Magazine*, 1833.) RBG, Kew

Early Accessions

The only 'trade' collection in those early days was that of Messrs Loddiges of Hackney. They contributed plants from the nursery to the royal collections, sending *Cymbidium aloifolium* in 1789 and *Oncidium bifolium* in 1811 and no doubt many others which did not long survive. They produced a list in 1825 which offered 84 species in 31 genera.

Australian orchids were added to the collections from a variety of sources. Captain Flinders' expedition to survey the coast of New Holland was accompanied by the botanist Robert Brown and a young gardener, Peter Good, who acted as his assistant and seed collector. In 1803 about a hundred different species came into the collection when the ship returned to England.

A considerable number of orchids were collected by George Caley, Joseph Banks's collector, in the area around what is now Sydney and in the Blue Mountains. Several of his additions were listed in 1813 though most had not yet flowered. *Pterostylis obtusa* and *Caladenia alba* appear to have flowered regularly in July and August.

Allan Cunningham, also a Banks protégé, was another botanical collector who landed in Sydney in 1816 and spent 16 years in Australia, sending a number of plant collections to Kew during that period. In 1823 a number of Australian species of *Dendrobium* were received from him, and between 1823 and 1828 he sent about 40 species of tuberous-rooted terrestrials. His collection of *Pterostylis concinna*, a species first discovered and described by Robert Brown in the vicinity of Port Jackson (later Sydney) was introduced to Kew in 1828, and illustrated many years later by William Hooker.

Most of the epiphytic orchids that came to Kew in the early days came from the West Indies. They were all listed as *Epidendrum* at first but a number of other genera, including *Oncidium*, *Cyrtopodium*, *Lycaste* and *Brassavola* were soon recognised. At first these epiphytes thrived, cultivated at high temperatures in the Great Stove, and propagated by division of the plants. But many of the species languished after producing their first flowers and one or two season's growth, and eventually died.

In the first decade of the 19th century, terrestrial and epiphytic orchids were sent to Kew from India by Dr William Roxburgh, Superintendent of the Calcutta Botanic Garden. Several of these survived for many years. John Smith, who was appointed as W T Aiton's assistant in 1822, described how he discovered *Cymbidium aloifolium*, *Acampe praemorsa*, *Aerides odorata* and others, together with *Phaius tankervilleae* and *Bletilla striata (hyacinthina)* from China, growing on a shelf above a flue against the back wall of the propagating house. The *Aerides* was growing and flowering freely, its roots clinging to the back wall. There were also flowering plants of *Dendrobium aphyllum (D. pierardii)* and *D. cucullatum*, which had been brought home by Francis Pierard, an Indian civil servant who retired to Kew.

In 1815, James Bowie and Allan Cunningham, again at Banks's behest, were sent to Brazil as botanical collectors for Kew and worked there for two years, dispatching collections of a variety of plants including epiphytic orchids. But when John Smith surveyed the collections in 1822 he found they were in a deplorable state, 'potted in common soil, the pots plunged to the rim in a tan bed, within a few feet of the glass roof, without being shaded from the summer sun, the hothouse being heated by a common flue producing dry heat not conducive to epiphytal plants.'

Between 1823 and 1825 a considerable number of species were received from Trinidad, sent by David Lockhart, who had become Superintendent of the Botanic Gardens there in 1818. Among these were the first plants seen in England of *Stanhopea insignis*, *Psychopsis papilio* (as *Oncidium*), *Catasetum tridentatum*, *Lockhartia elegans*, and others. Many were sent still attached to the branches of trees on which they grew naturally and were accompanied by suggestions from Lockhart as to how they should be treated in the glasshouse. These suggestions provided the information that was needed, and at last epiphytic orchids began to be grown successfully.

Building up the Collection

Up until about 1830, orchids were looked upon merely as curiosities, suitable for cultivation in botanic gardens and by a few amateur plant lovers. But at about this time a number of very showy orchids were imported and flowered for the first time in cultivation. The Royal Horticultural Society had a glasshouse set apart especially for their cultivation in their garden at Chiswick not far from Kew, and at this point orchids rapidly became favourites at horticultural shows, with large 'specimen' plants being prepared for competition. The splendid cattleyas, in particular, had brought epiphytic orchids into special favour with several growers. One of these was William Hooker, who maintained a small collection of orchids at his home in Suffolk before he became Professor of Botany in Glasgow in 1820. Indeed, it seems likely that the type species, *Cattleya labiata*, flowered first in this country in his collection in 1818.

Soon after his appointment as the first Director of Kew in 1841, William Hooker decided that the orchid collection should be greatly increased. Though the

Sir William Jackson Hooker, who grew orchids at his home in Suffolk before moving to the University of Glasgow, became Kew's first Director in 1841. RBG, Kew

In 1849 Lyons contributed notes on cultivation to Hooker's *A Century of Orchidaceous Plants*. This was a compilation of plates which had already been published in *Curtis's Botanical Magazine*, and many of the plants illustrated had come to Kew from Mexico and Brazil via the Duke of Bedford's collection at Woburn. A Mexican species which came direct to Kew from Oaxaca, where it was collected by Robert Smith, was *Encyclia (Epidendrum) vitellina*, which flowered first in 1843. The remarkable South African species *Bonatea speciosa* also figured in this publication with the comment that it was 'more easily cultivated than most terrestrial Orchidaceae. It flourished at Kew for many years in a small tub of peat mould, kept moist and in the greenhouse, and produces its blossoms annually in spring'.

Encyclia vitellina was collected in Mexico and first flowered at Kew in 1843. (Illustration from *Curtis's Botanical Magazine*, 1844.) RBG, Kew

showy species were welcome, he was particularly concerned that other less showy members of the family should be represented. Accordingly, Messrs Loddiges agreed to supply 200 of the least showy and low-priced orchids in their list for a total of £50.

The new Director also encouraged exchanges of plants with amateurs and other gardens and accepted presentations from wealthy growers who wished to dispose of their collections. The 6th Duke of Bedford gave his entire collection to Queen Victoria, who presented it to the Royal Botanic Gardens in 1844, and in 1846 Kew received its first bequest – the orchid collection of the late Reverend John Clowes of Manchester was so extensive that a new house had to be built at Kew to accommodate it.

One of Hooker's correspondents was J C Lyons, who was remarkably successful in growing orchids at his home at Ladiston in Ireland. His *Remarks on the Management of Orchidaceous Plants*, printed and published by himself in 1843, was the first manual on orchid cultivation. His comments on temperature, humidity, fresh air and misting newly acquired plants in the glasshouse also made a great difference to the way orchids were cultivated at Kew and elsewhere.

Bonatea speciosa, a terrestrial orchid from South Africa, has been cultivated without difficulty for many years. Joyce Stewart

Sir Joseph Dalton Hooker was also an orchid enthusiast and succeeded his father as Director of the Royal Botanic Gardens, Kew in 1865. RBG, Kew

John Smith, who came to Kew in 1822 and was made Aiton's chief assistant in 1826, became Curator under Sir William Hooker and continued until 1864. Although his main interest was in ferns, he had a wide knowledge of plants and their cultivation. In 1848 the orchids recorded numbered 755 species, but soon after there were a number of setbacks. New housing proved unsatisfactory, and several inexperienced growers and poor facilities wreaked havoc among the surviving plants. However, in the early 1860s, cattleyas, dendrobiums and oncidiums again became good specimens and many of the prettier examples of the smaller kinds of orchids were replaced with fresh collections.

Orchids were very much encouraged by Joseph Dalton Hooker, who succeeded his father as Director in 1865. They were among his favourite plants and, as editor of *Curtis's Botanical Magazine* for nearly 40 years, he was responsible for publishing many new descriptions. He began to delegate the authorship of the texts, however, and James Bateman, who is better known for his colour plate work *A Monograph of Odontoglossum* and the elephant folio, *The Orchidaceae of Mexico and Guatemala*, wrote the texts accompanying

the plates of new orchids from 1864–6. During this period, additions continued to be made in the gardens, and in 1872 there is a record of some 851 species belonging to 138 genera.

In 1885, at the first Orchid Conference organised in Westminster by the Royal Horticultural Society, Sir Joseph Hooker greatly admired the many exotic plants on show and was able to contribute a number of species from the Kew collections. One of these was *Anguloa clowesii*, a plant which commemorated the late Reverend John Clowes. There were fine and well cultivated specimens of the white form of *Cattleya skinneri* and of *Caularthron bicornutum* with its white and purple-spotted flowers. *Bulbophyllum fimbriatum* (as *Cirrhopetalum*) had several whorls of purplish flowers and there was a splendidly grown plant of *Phalaenopsis parishii*. Among the plants of chiefly botanical interest were *Stelis muscifera* with small dark red flowers, *Physosiphon tubatus* with long spikes of pale orange flowers, *Panisea uniflora*, described as 'a humble, inconspicuous species with solitary dull ochreous flowers', and *Eria excavata* – 'not a conspicuous' member of the genus. Other Kew plants which attracted notice were the yellow-flowered

Anguloa clowesii, the tulip orchid from Colombia and Venezuela, was named in honour of the Reverend John Clowes, who later donated his orchid collection to Kew. RBG, Kew

Polystachya pubescens from South Africa, and two terrestrial species, *Serapias parviflora* from Italy and *Ponthieva maculata* from Mexico.

In his opening speech, however, the President, Sir Trevor Lawrence regretted that, 'mainly owing to the excessive economy with which money is given to that very valuable institution, there is no sufficiently representative collection of orchids there at present.' He made a plea for wealthy bachelors, and others, to leave their plants to Kew 'in order to enhance this public collection'.

Spurred on by this criticism, the collection and its cultivation continued to improve. Several establishments and individuals were particularly generous, especially the Royal Botanic Garden at Glasnevin, the orchid firm of Frederick Sander, and Sir Trevor Lawrence himself. By 1891 a list published in the *Kew Bulletin* recorded 766 different orchids that had

flowered at Kew the previous year, and some 1,800 species in 200 genera were listed in the first *Handlist of Orchids cultivated in the Royal Botanic Gardens* in 1896.

Orchid Houses at Kew

The earliest tropical orchids were grown at Kew in the Great Stove which was, in its day, the largest hot-house in Britain. It was a lean-to glasshouse, 34.7 m long, designed by William Chambers for Princess Augusta and erected in 1761. A wide variety of tropical plants was housed in it and several smaller houses were gradually added nearby for specialised collections. In 1836 a glasshouse was set aside for tropical orchids for the first time. A few years later another house was added which in 1846 Sir William Hooker described as 'occupied with a rich and inestimable collection of

Orchid houses formed part of the T-range until 1970 and many different kinds grew and flowered there. RBG, Kew

orchideous plants . . . the centre is filled with a handsome slate staging, so large as to admit of a raised walk through the centre, thus enabling the visitor to look down upon each side of the house, while, over his head and from the rafters on either hand, are suspended wire baskets filled with beautiful tropical epiphytes . . . As the house in question opens on to another and cooler stove, we are enabled to remove the splendid epiphytes, when in blossom, to a less heated atmosphere, and thus preserve them in beauty for a much longer time.'

Many of the orchids, however, did not thrive in this large house, especially the smaller ones, and they were moved to several smaller houses known as the orchid pits.

A group of houses called the New Range, and known later as the T-range, was built in 1868–9 on the site of some of these small houses. There were eventually several display houses for orchids and other growing and propagating houses within this group. Timber-framed glasshouses need considerable renovation at intervals of 30 to 40 years and this took place regularly. Sir Joseph Hooker's successor, William Thiselton-Dyer, was able to write in 1904 that 'the Kew collection has much improved in health since the reconstruction in 1898 of the houses accessible to the public. These were originally erected in 1868 and were 13 feet high. They have now been reduced to 9 feet. This has the double advantage of bringing the plants more closely to the light as well as to the eyes of visitors. The conditions have also been divided into four compartments, the conditions of which vary in regard to temperature and atmospheric moisture. In 1901 a small pit was adapted for the cultivation of Dendrobiums.'

In the 1970s the orchids were moved to the Lower Nursery, where the large collection is now housed, and

Timber-framed orchid houses need frequent maintenance; at Kew they were usually treated to an annual clean-up by students of horticulture. RBG, Kew

only a small display was maintained in the T-range. In 1983 this was partly demolished to make space for the construction of the new Princess of Wales Conservatory for tropical herbaceous plants. Finally the remainder of the T-range, adjacent ferneries and other old buildings in the tropical complex were demolished. The new Conservatory, opened in 1987, contains orchids in two display areas with different temperature regimes, and these have been described in chapter 1.

Specialist growers

It was during the directorship of Joseph Hooker that orchid growing became popular and prolific throughout Europe and at Kew. A series of specialist orchid growers greatly improved the cultivation of the plants and wrote about their experiences to help other growers.

One of the first of the gardening staff to become particularly knowledgeable about orchid growing was F W T Burbidge, who later became famous for his plant collecting in Borneo and his illustrations of plants. Employed at Kew until 1870, he produced *Cool Orchids*

William Watson was a gardener and orchid grower at Kew for much of his life and became Curator in 1901. RBG, Kew

and how to Grow Them in 1874, and in 1885 wrote a detailed report on the plants exhibited at the first Orchid Conference held by the Royal Horticultural Society.

Robert Allen Rolfe, who founded *The Orchid Review* in 1893, started work in the gardens in 1879, but transferred to the Herbarium the following year. It was not long before Sir Joseph Hooker advised him to make orchids his speciality, and he was employed as Kew's first orchid taxonomist for forty years (see chapter 12).

William Watson also came to Kew as a gardener in 1879, but was concerned with living plants for much longer, becoming Assistant Curator in 1886 and Curator from 1901–22. Watson was instrumental in the revival of Kew as a horticultural, as distinct from a botanical, establishment. He was joined, in 1883, by William Jackson Bean, who became Assistant Curator in 1900 and eventually succeeded Watson as Curator in 1922. Together they produced a major publication on orchid growing, *Orchids: Their Culture and Management* in 1890.

Charles Henry Curtis is another famous name associated with orchids. He joined Kew in 1889, moving to the Royal Horticultural Society's garden at Chiswick in 1890. Throughout his long career as a horticulturist and journalist he had a special interest in orchids, writing several books, including *Orchids for Everyone* in 1910, and *Orchids, Their Distribution and Cultivation* in 1950. He took over the editorship of *The Orchid Review* from 1933 to 1958.

Early Research

The living collection of orchids at Kew and the specimens preserved in the herbarium have always been made available to botanists for research. Some of the earliest and most famous of studies which utilised the collections were those of Charles Darwin. His interest had been captured by orchids growing near his home in 1838 or 1839, and his studies of the flower structure and pollination mechanisms of orchids began with the species which grew along the Orchis Bank in the Cudham valley, in Kent.

Having studied 15 genera of native orchids, he set out to compare them with some of the tropical genera which were coming into flower in various collections at that time, notably at Kew. He borrowed plants and kept them in a small glass lean-to behind the kitchen of his home, Down House, until the flowers opened, becoming particularly fascinated by the genus *Catasetum* because of its unusual mechanism for releasing the pollinia. Watching and describing the catapult action that several of the species displayed gave him great pleasure. At one point he wrote to

The famous biologist Charles Darwin borrowed orchid plants and flowers from his friend Joseph Hooker at Kew for pollination studies. RBG, Kew

Hooker: 'If you can really spare another *Catasetum*, when nearly ready, I shall be most grateful. Had I not better send for it? . . . A cursed insect or something let my last flower off last night.' In another letter he wrote: 'I carefully described to Huxley the shooting out of the pollinia in *Catasetum*, and received for an answer "Do you really think I can believe all that?" '

Other features of *Catasetum* and its allies were also of great interest, in particular because of their peculiar flower structure and the fact that some plants never set fruit while others did so prolifically. Then Sir Robert Schomburgk described how he had found the flowers of three different genera on the same plant! Darwin's patient studies and dissections of fresh and preserved flowers revealed that the *Catasetum* flowers were male, while plants known as *Monacanthus* were the female form of the same species, and the similar *Myanthus* were hermaphrodite but sterile. Thus pollination studies came to the aid of taxonomy, and two genera were sunk into synonymy.

These and other studies of some 50 genera of tropical orchids provided the basis for Darwin's book *The Various Contrivances by which British and Foreign Orchids are Fertilised by Insects*, first published in 1862. It has been a source of reference for pollination studies ever since.

In 1880 Ernst Pfitzer came to Kew from the University of Heidelberg to study the collection of orchids. Material was made available to him over a period of several years and resulted in various important publications on orchid morphology and classification which are still consulted. He was one of the first in a long line of distinguished botanists from other countries who made use of the plants at Kew, especially their flowers.

Hybridising

Robert Rolfe wrote a fascinating series of articles in the first volume of *The Orchid Review* in order to record the early days of orchid hybridising, a subject that was of great interest to his readers in 1893. Even at that time, he wrote, 'hybrid orchids occupy a very important place in modern collections'. This statement is even more relevant and true today – except at Kew, where the emphasis has always been on species, formerly of known wild origin, now increasingly raised from seeds in the laboratory, though some hybrids of natural origin, or historic interest, or raised for experimental reasons, are still maintained.

At the time interest in hybridisation first began, however, everyone – even the growers at Kew – was trying out the possibilities with a wide range of orchids. In 1909 Rolfe and C H Hurst published *The Orchid Stud-book*, a companion volume to *The Orchid Review*, in which they recorded details of all the hybrids they could trace up to 1907 together with a great deal of supplementary information.

It was in about 1852 that John Dominy, a grower at the Veitch nursery in Exeter, first began to make experiments, acting on the suggestion of a local surgeon, John Harris. Although his first experiments were with the genus *Cattleya*, it was actually a *Calanthe* hybrid which flowered first, in 1856, and was described by John Lindley in *The Gardeners' Chronicle* in 1858. There seems to have been an unusually long delay between its first appearance and its description, perhaps related to the realisation by Lindley of the enormous possibilities for the future that this hybrid heralded. His first reaction, when Veitch showed him the plant, was to remark, 'Why, you will drive the botanists mad!'

Many different genera were experimented with, and new hybrids followed at a dramatic rate, with each one being carefully recorded and described. The first *Cattleya* hybrid was exhibited in 1859, the first *Laelia* in 1864, and the first *Paphiopedilum (Cypripedium)* in 1869. Dominy's list of named hybrids eventually grew to 25, the last one flowering in 1878. In the meantime, however, several other hybridisers had entered the

Catasetum saccatum was one of the tropical orchids at Kew whose pollination mechanism was studied by Charles Darwin. (Coloured drawing by Miss Drake for John Lindley's *Sertum Orchidaceum*.) RBG, Kew

field and a wide range of orchid genera and species were providing the basis for their experiments, provoking the botanist H G Reichenbach to comment that every orchid grower in Britain was 'engaged in the production of mules'.

The first new artificial hybrid produced at Kew appears to have been *Disa* Kewensis (*D. uniflora* × *D. tripetaloides*) which flowered first in May 1893, which set a new record for speed of development of seedling and flowering after hand pollination. The seed was sown in November 1891, and the plants thus reached maturity in 18 months. This was only the second *Disa* hybrid known at the time, *D. Veitchii* (*D. uniflora* × *D. racemosa*) having flowered in Veitch's nursery at Chelsea in 1891, a new genus to be added to the expanding list of hybrids. Two other *Disa* crosses were made and their seeds sown at the same time as the *D.* Kewensis. The seedlings grew strongly and flowered

This new colour form of *Disa* Kewensis resulted from an artificial cross made recently in Cape Town; the first *D.* Kewensis was pink, made at Kew and flowered in 1893. Joyce Stewart

later, *D.* Langleyensis (*D. racemosa* × *D. tripetaloides*) in 1894, and *D.* Premier (*D. tripetaloides* × *D.* Veitchii) in October 1893. The latter was duly awarded a First Class Certificate from the Royal Horticultural Society at its October show and is of particular interest because one of its parents was itself a hybrid. Another second generation hybrid flowered in 1900, and the name *D.* Watsoni was suggested for the cross (*D.* Kewensis × *D. uniflora*) by Rolfe in honour of the Assistant Curator responsible for the orchids at Kew, William Watson.

Rolfe recorded the flowering at Kew of artificial hybrids in two other genera of terrestrial orchids in *The Orchid Review* of 1903. *Spathoglottis* Kewensis (*S. plicata* × *S. vieillardii*) and *Cynorkis* Kewensis (*C. lowiana* × *C. purpurata*) were noted for their hybrid vigour and were intermediate in character between the parents in size and form of the plants and flowers. In both hybrids the seeds matured quickly and the seedlings flowered in about two years from the date the cross was made.

It was in January of the same year that Rolfe recorded *Epidendrum* Kewense (*E. xanthinum* × *E. evectum*, now known as *E. elongatum*) flowering in the glasshouses at Kew. The parents have bright yellow and purple flowers respectively, and in the hybrids all the flowers were buff or salmon mottled with purple. The hybrid was self-pollinated in 1902 in the hope that, if fertile, some progeny similar to the parents might result, thus testing the validity of Mendel's theory with respect to orchids. This cross failed, but Rolfe was successful in back-crossing *E.* Kewense with each of its parents and in predicting the flower colour in the progeny of these crosses. Later, when the plant was stronger, he was successful in self-pollinating *E.* Kewense, and several seedlings were watched with great interest as their flower colour became visible, some intermediate, and others more nearly resembling one or other of the parents. The considerable excitement that the developing flowers of the different plants evoked is apparent from the monthly updates in *The Orchid Review* throughout 1909.

The Present Day

When the most recent *Handlist* of orchids at Kew was published, in 1961, it recorded 262 genera and over 1,800 taxa in the collection. Since then the number of species has more than doubled and they are listed in a new catalogue, published in 1990. Records are now computerised and as much information as possible is recorded for each accession.

Orchid growers are often criticised by conservationists for the length (or brevity) of the life of orchid plants in cultivation. The detailed information held in the computer indicates that there is little basis for this criticism. Despite the hazards of suffragettes, seawater, power failure, and the problems imposed by two World Wars, there are 24 accessions remaining and flourishing since the first decade of the present century. The same individual plants of more than 130 species have been cultivated at Kew for more than 50 years and a further 500 have been in cultivation for at least 20 years. Divisions of many of these have been shared with other establishments during this time.

Herbarium and laboratory studies by staff and visitors have greatly increased, and the plants are called upon more and more for research as well as for display to the public. There are also increasing numbers of requests for seeds from specialists who want to propagate some of the rarer species not available elsewhere. Whenever possible these demands are met, though sometimes there is a long delay before the plants flower and can be artificially pollinated.

Genera of horticultural interest, including *Pleione, Paphiopedilum, Cymbidium, Cypripedium* and

several sections of *Dendrobium*, have been studied monographically. These studies have been accompanied by new acquisitions from many sources of a great variety of these attractively flowered plants. Once the research has been completed, they are used increasingly for decoration, both as plants and as cut flowers.

One of the most esoteric uses of the collection, and one of the most delightful, is the painting or photographing of plants and flowers for books and journals. The majority of the orchids illustrated in *Curtis's Botanical Magazine* and its successor, since 1984, *The Kew Magazine*, are from the Kew collection, while *The Orchid Review* continues to portray Kew orchids on a regular basis. In addition, postage stamps, postcards, greeting cards and calendars have all been illustrated with pictures of plants kept at Kew.

Growing the orchids at Kew today is more demanding than it has ever been. Full details of the houses, techniques and plants are given in the chapters that follow.

Encyclia fragrans, one of the cockleshell orchids from Central America; in 1782 a specimen of this plant was the first epiphyte to flower in cultivation at Kew. RBG, Kew

The Living Collection

By Sandra Bell, with contributions from
Blaise DuPuy, Michael Fay, Jim Keesing, Joyce Stewart
and John Woodhams

IN THE LAST DECADE OF THE 20th century, the orchid collection at Kew contains over 20,000 flowering-size plants and about half as many seedlings. This total is made up of more than 3,750 orchid taxa, different species of wild origin and cultivars of man-made hybrids.

As has been mentioned, orchids are incorporated into the collection at Kew from a wide variety of sources. Bequests and donations of interesting plants have been welcomed from private growers and specialist nurseries in Britain and these enhance the diversity of plants of horticultural merit, particularly hybrids. From time to time new and rare species are also added to the collection in this way.

Plants from overseas are also added to the collection provided they are accompanied by the correct documentation in terms of plant health and the Convention on International Trade in Endangered Species (CITES), and only those which comply to the fullest extent with the current regulations can be accepted. Plants collected discriminatingly from the wild, with permission from the relevant authorities and accompanied by detailed notes describing their habitats, form the largest and most useful part of the new accessions. The collector may be a member of staff sent on an expedition from Kew to an area of particular interest, or one of dozens of regular correspondents living overseas. In the last decade the trend towards the collection of seeds, rather than plants, has been encouraged in order not to deplete wild populations. The propagation of orchids from seeds is a routine procedure, more complicated but no more difficult than raising other plants. It is carried out frequently in the Micropropagation Unit at Kew and the methods used are described in chapters 9 and 15. As a result of this work Kew often has more young plants than are needed, and so surplus plants and seedlings are distributed to botanic gardens and other orchid growers all over the world, many of whom send interesting plants to Kew in exchange.

In addition, Kew has the responsibility of holding plants on behalf of HM Customs and Excise. Orchids which are imported, by airmail or through a port or airport without the appropriate documents required by CITES and the relevant European Community regulations are very often seized or detained. If and when the plants become forfeit, they may be handed over to Kew for use in the best interests of conservation. Further details of Kew's role with regard to CITES are noted in chapter 16.

This section looks at the ways in which the essential needs in maintaining a large collection are met, and then reviews the plants themselves, presented continent by continent (chapters 4–8). A more detailed catalogue of all the species was prepared in 1990.

Cattleya percivaliana. G C K Dunsterville

Overleaf: *Cymbidium lowianum.* David DuPuy

3 Growing Orchids

IT IS THE AIM AT KEW to maintain a selection of orchids that is as large and diverse as possible. The plants are in constant use for display and research of various kinds and their role in conservation and in the propagation and reintroduction of rarities is becoming increasingly important. In this chapter some features of the greenhouses, processing introductions and composts relating to the orchids at Kew are recorded.

Glasshouses

The Reserve Collection of orchids presently occupies 862 square metres of glasshouse space in the Lower Nursery, a complex of greenhouses that is not open to the public. It is used for holding and propagating the tropical plant collections, and within it the orchids fill five large glasshouses and a separate seedling house. Some of these houses are partitioned, so there is a total of eight different growing environments. They have been controlled, since 1985, by a Van Vliet CR90 Environmental Computer System which was installed at the suggestion of Sir Robert and Lady Sainsbury. This generous donation provided Kew with one of the first computerised systems in use for orchid growing. It allows for very precise control of temperature, relative humidity, ventilation and air movement throughout the day. A sensor in each glasshouse constantly monitors the temperature and relative humidity and, if these vary from the values required, the computer brings into play the equipment needed to change them. Back-up, in case of a breakdown of any of the equipment, is provided by a system of alarms which ring if the temperature in any glasshouse drops below the acceptable minimum.

Heat is provided by piped hot water from natural gas-fired boilers. There is a separate, oil-fired system for use in emergency or if the gas supply should fail. All the glasshouses are shaded in summer, either with slatted exterior or interior blinds or shade cloth as well as with 'Summer Cloud' painted on the glass. Additional cooling is effected by the use of ventilators. Under-bench mist lines and overhead humidifiers are used to keep the relative humidity high. They need to be used more often when the temperature rises, especially if the ventilators are open, as humidity would otherwise drop rapidly. Air movement in each house is maintained by fans and ventilators. The speed of the fans is linked to the temperature and they are programmed to switch off when the vents are wide open.

Computer control of these variable factors in the glasshouse environment saves growers' time and, by enabling more precise control of the growing climates, effects a saving in energy consumption even when the nursery is not manned. Regular printouts and graphs of the features of each glasshouse climate enable fine adjustments to be programmed into the system to achieve exactly the climate that seems to suit each group of plants.

A summary of the different glasshouse environments at Kew is presented below. The minimum temperatures given refer to winter nights; a day lift of 5°C (8–10°F) is always given.

1 Warm (House 31, warm, built 1964, wood and glass). 18°C (64°F) minimum, 32°C (90°F) day maximum, ventilated at 26°C (79°F). Very light.
For low altitude monopodial genera, *Vanda*, *Angraecum* and others, also low altitude *Dendrobium* species in sections *Ceratobium* and *Phalaenopsis* and the warm-growing *Cymbidium* species.

2 Warm (House 39, built 1978, aluminum and glass). 17–18°C (64°F) minimum, 28–30°C (82–86°F) day maximum, ventilated at 25°C (77°F). Shady and humid.
Used for *Paphiopedilum* (warmer growing species), *Phalaenopsis*, tropical terrestrials and some African epiphytes.

3 Warm-intermediate (House 36, warm, built 1964, wood and glass).
15–16°C (59–61°F) minimum, 27–30°C (81–86°F) day maximum, ventilated at 21–23°C (70–73°F).
For most low and intermediate altitude tropical epiphytes, such as *Coelogyne*, *Maxillaria*, *Bulbophyllum* and many others.

4 Cool-intermediate, warm day (House 35, built 1971, aluminium and glass).
15°C (59°F) minimum, 32°C (90°F) day maximum in summer, ventilated at 25°C (77°F). Very light and airy.

A mixture of *Disa* species and hybrids flowers well in the Lower Nursery in mid-summer. Joyce Stewart

For *Cattleya, Laelia* and allied genera, soft cane dendrobiums and a wide variety of African epiphytes and terrestrials.

5 Cool-intermediate, cool day (House 36, cool, built 1964, wood and glass).
14°C (57°F) minimum, 25°C (77°F) day maximum, ventilated at 18°C (64°F).
For montane species, high altitude terrestrials and epiphytes from the tropics particularly Central and South America, including *Odontoglossum, Lycaste, Coelogyne* and pleurothallids.

6 Cool (House 31, cool, built 1964, wood and glass).
11°C (52°F) minimum, ventilated at 16°C (61°F).
For *Cymbidium* hybrids and zygopetalums.

7 Cool (House 42, cool, built 1984, aluminium, glass and melanex).
13°C (55°F) minimum, ventilated at 19°C (66°F). 40% shade in summer.
For epiphytes and terrestrials of cooler latitudes including some *Cymbidium* species, cool-growing paphiopedilums, winter-growing Australian and South African terrestrials including *Disa* species and hybrids.

8 Cold (House 42, cold, built 1984, aluminium, glass and melanex).
5°C (41°F) minimum, ventilated at 12°C (54°F).
Most of the terrestrial species from southern Europe are grown in this house which has less shading (40% in summer) and more ventilation than the others. It is also used for cool-growing orchids from Asia, including *Pleione, Calanthe* and *Cypripedium*.

Many of the orchids will grow and flower well in more than one of these environments, but others have been found, by trial and error, to be quite specific in their requirements.

The orchids are cared for by the Supervisor of the Orchid Unit, who has a staff of three to maintain the collection and at least one student of horticulture. The student receives three months of training in orchid culture as part of a three-year diploma course at Kew and is an invaluable addition to the team.

Introductions and Accessions

On average about 1,000 orchid plants arrive at Kew each year, some from nurseries or other collections within Britain but most from overseas. First, the documentation is checked. Sometimes the necessary papers become separated from parcels in transit and strenuous efforts are made to ensure the relevant permits or certificates are available or can be traced. No accessions are made until the required documents are available when details are entered in the computer records for each item.

Unpacking boxes of new plants is done with eager anticipation. First the plants are inspected carefully by the specialist Quarantine Officer at Kew, who looks for any signs of pests, such as scale insects, or disease damage, such as the mottling caused by Cymbidium Mosaic Virus. This is a necessary precaution to avoid the introduction of pests and diseases, possibly new to Britain, into the collections at Kew. If any insects are found they are removed and sent to laboratories of the Ministry of Agriculture, Fisheries and Food for identification and advice. (A significant number of invertebrates are forwarded by MAFF to the Natural History Museum for inclusion in its collections. Just like the plants, the associated creatures are of scientific value, and several come into Kew each year which prove to be undescribed or little-known species.) Diseased leaves or roots are removed and may also be sent to MAFF laboratories for identification of the pathogen. Subsequently, plants are treated effectively or destroyed. The majority of orchids sent to Kew are clean, healthy and in good condition, but if they are desiccated or damaged when they are received this is noted before they go any further. It may be useful information if the plants do not establish well.

Detailed provenance data is always requested for incoming plants and consulting field notes enables the horticulturist to establish and maintain the plants in the most suitable way. The notes are often vital to scientists who study the orchid collection and need to know the origin of a particular plant.

After inspection and any necessary period of isolation or treatment, the orchids are passed to the staff in the Orchid Unit. Here it is decided how best to treat them, whether they should be grown mounted on cork oak bark or, if potted, which kind of compost to use. The staff also decide which of the different glasshouse environments would best suit the new plants, depending upon their country of origin and the altitude and conditions from which they were collected. The new orchids are potted up, labelled, placed in the environment that is anticipated will be most suitable and looked after carefully. Within a short time, signs of growth are apparent, usually new roots, but if the plants do not respond well to one set of glasshouse conditions they are moved to another in which they may grow better.

Careful record-keeping is very important at Kew. All the information about each plant is stored and must be accessible to all who may need to use it. Each new plant introduced is given a number (its accession number), and entered, first into a book recording all new plants for each year and then on to the computer database.

Along with the accession number and the name of the plant, additional information such as the field notes, flowering season and whether herbarium specimens were collected at the same time is recorded. More details can be added at any time in the future, as information about the plant is acquired. Access to the computer database is quick and easy for anyone who needs it in the course of their work.

Every orchid at Kew has a plastic label on which essential and clearly summarised information is recorded. It is inserted in the pot or attached to the medium or mount. Across the top of the label is a three-part accession number. The first part, a three figure number, is the batch number and is common to all the plants collected by the same collector and sent to Kew at the same time. The second, two figure number records the year in which the plant was received at Kew. The third, with five figures, is called the sequence number and is unique to each individual plant within the batch and to any plants which may be propagated

from it. Underneath the accession number is the collector's name and number, or the name of the person who donated the plant to the Kew collection.

In due course another line of information is added below the collector's number, the letter 'V' followed by a date. This refers to the date when the plant, in flower, was taken to the Herbarium for a botanist to identify it or to check its name – a process known as verification, hence the abbreviation. When a plant has been identified or verified, the computer record is updated and information supplied by the botanist, such as the known geographical range of the species and whether it is endangered in the wild, can be incorporated.

The full name of the plant is written on the label as well as the country from which it comes and possibly the altitude at which it was growing.

The back of the label may be used by each grower to record facts and observations which they find useful, such as when the plant was last repotted or whether the flower is a particularly fine form.

A box of orchids from Thailand confiscated by HM Customs and Excise and delivered to Kew for care and cultivation pending prosecution of the importer. RBG, Kew

Composts

Composts for growing orchids are a subject of great interest, and individual growers enjoy experimenting with slightly varying mixes to find the ones that work best under their particular glasshouse conditions. The style of growing will determine composts to some extent; a very coarse mix is suitable for those who like to water frequently, while a finer mix holds moisture much longer. At Kew the compost mixture is prepared or chosen to suit the size and habit of each plant.

Temperate terrestrials, such as the winter-flowering Australian and South African terrestrials, are grown in a mixture of: 3 parts grit, 2 parts fine bark, 1 part leaf mould and 1 part unsterilised loam.

For the European terrestrials this is modified by adding an extra part each of unsterilised loam and leaf mould to make the proportions: 3 parts grit, 2 parts fine bark, 2 parts leaf mould and 2 parts unsterilised loam.

Rather more leaf mould is added to the mixture for growing plants originating from woodlands, such as *Cypripedium calceolus*, the lady's slipper orchid, and *Goodyera repens*, the creeping lady's tresses. A high content of organic matter is vital for orchids which grow symbiotically with fungi throughout their life, and these include many of the terrestrial species. The fungi live by breaking down organic matter in the soil, and if this is exhausted, or the compost becomes too dry, the fungus will not grow and the orchid cannot thrive.

One group of South African terrestrials, species and hybrids of the genus *Disa*, is grown in a simple mixture consisting of: 1 part peat and 1 part perlite. Disas grow in or close to running water and this compost not only allows good water-retention but also good drainage. Disas are repotted at least twice every year, as this very peaty compost would otherwise become rather stagnant.

For tropical terrestrials, the grit and loam content of the compost is lower than that used for the temperate terrestrial orchids and the leaf mould and peat content is higher. Many forest and woodland orchids in the tropics have a shallow rooting system, which is limited to the layer of litter overlying the soil. Good drainage is essential.

The genus *Paphiopedilum* is an important feature of the orchid collection at Kew. For all the species and hybrids the mix contains: 5 parts medium grade bark, 2 parts perlag, 1 part charcoal and 1 part peat. This mixture is modified by the addition of crushed dolomite chippings for paphiopedilums which grow on limestone in their natural habitats, and by the addition of chopped sphagnum moss for those which are known to enjoy moist conditions.

The *Cymbidium* compost is rather similar and consists

Containers are chosen to suit individual orchid species; *Paphiopedilum niveum* grows on rocks in the wild and does well at Kew in a clay pot. RBG, Kew

of: 3 parts bark, 3 parts coarse sphagnum peat, 1 part perlag, 1 part perlite, 1 part charcoal, plus a dressing of hoof and horn meal or 5 oz per bushel of Vitax Q4, a balanced general plant food.

Epiphytic orchids are grown either mounted on bark or in one of a variety of pots. Smaller epiphytes are often grown by tying them on to a block of rough cork oak bark with transparent nylon thread. The piece of bark can then be suspended from a wire mesh framework against the wall or from a rafter in the glasshouse and, if misted daily, the orchid will soon put out new roots over the surface of the bark. Firm tying is essential; if the plants are not held tightly against the bark, new roots do not easily adhere to it.

Many epiphytes grow well in pots filled with a standard epiphyte compost made up of: 5 parts bark, 1 part perlag and 1 part charcoal.

Three epiphyte mixes are used, all having the same ingredients, but in different degrees of coarseness. For small plants a mixture of fine bark, fine perlag and fine charcoal is used. For a very large plant a rather coarse mixture is more suitable. Medium-sized plants are potted using a medium grade compost. The epiphyte compost is the subject of endless variation as growers like to experiment with a standard compost to make it more suitable for each individual plant. Peat or chopped sphagnum moss may be added to make the mixture more moisture-retentive, while the use of coconut husk fibre makes the mixture more open and fast-draining.

Seedlings which are being weaned from sterile culture need a fine compost which will give their roots good anchorage quickly and also hold just a little more moisture than a standard compost until the young root system grows larger. The ingredients for the typical seedling mix are: 3 parts fine bark, 1 part perlag, 1 part peat and ½ part fine charcoal.

This range of orchid composts is subject to change as new products become available. For example, rockwool, a synthetic product used as an insulating material, has been tried for a number of different genera. Many different pots, baskets, wire containers and mounting surfaces are also tried. Ultimately, it is the combination of container, compost and environmental conditions which ensures success or failure with orchids in cultivation. At Kew, as in other collections of these

Orchids mounted on bark and slabs of tree fern fibre are hung on wire frames which accommodate many plants in a small space. RBG, Kew

specialised plants, there are always some failures, but continuous observation of new accessions and plants which are becoming established, ensures that most of them survive to become permanent additions to the collection.

Paphiopedilum glanduliferum, a lithophytic slipper orchid from western New Guinea, grows well at Kew in a shady position in a warm glasshouse. RBG, Kew

4 Europe

THE ORCHIDS NATIVE TO EUROPE, north Africa and the Middle East are all terrestrial, but they grow in a wide range of habitats including woodland, marsh, well-drained grassland on various types of soil and dry roadside verges. A few are evergreen, such as the British native, creeping lady's tresses, *Goodyera repens*, which threads its way through the mossy floor of pine woodland, but most are deciduous.

A few British and European orchids have been grown at Kew for many years, planted out in the Rock Garden and woodland areas or as pot plants in the Alpine section. More recently, a wider selection has been acquired and maintained in the Lower Nursery, and these are used for research in the Sainsbury Orchid Conservation Project (see chapter 15) and sometimes for display. From February to May, when most of them flower, the greenhouse where they are kept is a stunning sight. For ease of cultivation these genera and species are divided into two groups which are related to their natural habitats, in the open or in more shaded situations.

Both groups of orchids are easily accommodated in the same greenhouse which is kept frost-free with a winter minimum temperature of 5°C (41°F). It is ventilated as much as possible to keep the atmosphere buoyant and fans give good air movement. The house is covered with a 50% shade cloth from April to October. The woodland orchids are provided with extra shading. All the plants are potted and stand on slatted wooden staging over a moist gritted bench which can be flooded to raise the humidity while the plants themselves remain dry. Standing the pots on slatted staging also prevents them from rooting into the benches with the consequent possibility of the spread of disease.

Open Habitat Orchids

Orchids which store food reserves in underground tubers include the genera *Ophrys*, *Orchis*, *Serapias*, *Aceras* and *Gymnadenia*. A new shoot grows from each tuber during the autumn to form a rosette of leaves in winter or early spring. The plants flower in spring or early summer, then die down and remain dormant for several months. This cycle is well adapted to a climate which is hot and dry in summer, cooler and damper in

autumn and winter. Plants in this group originate mainly from the Mediterranean region, although some range as far north-west as Britain, such as the bee orchid, *Ophrys apifera*, man orchid, *Aceras anthropophorum*, and the stately lizard orchid, *Himantoglossum hircinum*.

In cultivation the dormant tubers are repotted about 4 cm deep during the late summer. They are watered immediately after repotting and then perhaps once more before the new shoots appear a few weeks later. Leaf growth is rapid, and by December these orchids have formed a rosette of leaves. Watering through the winter is tricky; as the plants are growing they need a

Ophrys apifera, the bee orchid, has been raised from seeds at Kew; plants flower well both in the greenhouse and planted out in the conservation area. D M Turner Ettlinger

33

Aceras anthropophorum, the man orchid, is one of Britain's rarities today. David Chesterman

Epipactis palustris, the marsh helleborine, flowers well in the woodland garden at Kew. David Chesterman

little water but not too much. If it is left on the leaves, water seems to precipitate the development of fungal problems, which can be fatal. Pouring water around the edge of the pot early in the day, so that water does not lie on the leaves overnight, is usually safe. Watering is reduced as soon as the plants come into flower.

Glasshouse culture brings these orchids into flower earlier than if they were growing in the wild. *Ophrys fusca*, one of the common bee orchids of the Mediterranean region, normally flowers from February to April but starts flowering in early December under glass. Many flowers in the collection are pollinated so that the resulting seeds can be used in research on the propagation of European orchids.

After flowering the plants die down and are kept drier so that by mid-summer a little water may be given only once in four weeks or so. This is needed to keep alive the fungus without which the orchid will not thrive.

Repotting is done annually using the compost described in chapter 3. Plastic half-pots, 12 cm in diameter, have proved very satisfactory for the majority of European orchids, but some of the larger species grow more robustly in a larger and deeper pot of conventional shape. Each pot is filled one-third full with fresh compost and the next third is filled with old compost from around the tuber. In each pot two or three tubers are bedded into the old compost and then covered with the new mix. The incorporation of some of the old compost is important as it ensures that some of the associated fungus goes with the tuber into the new pot. A certain amount of the fungus mycelium can

sometimes be seen on the surface of the tuber but experience at Kew has shown that plants grow more vigorously after repotting if additional fungus is introduced by including some of the old compost too. The new compost provides a good supply of leaf mould and bark for the fungus to feed on for the coming year.

Woodland Orchids

Orchids from the woodlands in the more northerly parts of Europe include the genera *Epipactis*, *Cephalanthera*, *Listera* and *Cypripedium calceolus*, the lady's slipper orchid. Their annual growth cycle starts in the early spring, when a new shoot grows from each over-wintering bud. Plants flower in the summer and die down in autumn when their seeds disperse. They do not form tubers, but overwinter from an underground stem, or rhizome.

These orchids grow best when they are repotted infrequently, grown in larger pots and top-dressed annually to refresh the compost. This minimises the disturbance to their rhizome and roots. A compost mixture with extra leaf mould is used to simulate a woodland soil and provide a substratum for the fungus. Watering is done rather more frequently than for the tuberous orchids. The pots are kept just moist through the winter and watered more liberally in spring when the buds burst into active growth. They are watered well during the summer and slightly less in autumn when the shoots die off.

5 Africa and Madagascar

THE COLLECTION OF AFRICAN ORCHIDS in cultivation at Kew is probably the best in the world from that continent. At least 400 species are grown, with representatives from 60 of the 100 genera that have been recorded. Orchids are grown from most African countries, but the collection is most rich in species from Malawi, Kenya, Tanzania, South Africa and Gabon, partly because Kew has had very generous contacts in these countries and partly because plants from these countries have been more intensively researched in recent years. They provided much useful material for the account of the Orchidaceae for the *Flora of Tropical East Africa*, which was completed in 1989.

As in other parts of the world, terrestrial species are more frequent in the temperate climatic areas and epiphytes more common in the equatorial zones. Thus in South Africa, about one-tenth of the orchids are epiphytes whereas in Kenya and Zaire half of the orchid species are epiphytic.

African Terrestrials

Most of the African terrestrial orchids in the Kew collection come from South Africa. The genus *Disa*, the most well known, has been in cultivation at Kew intermittently since early in the 19th century; *D. cornuta* was recorded in the second edition of Aiton's *Hortus Kewensis*. By the end of the century several other species were grown and an artificial hybrid bred at Kew, *D. Kewensis* (*D. uniflora* × *D. tripetaloides*) was registered in 1893. Disas have great potential for display as they flower during the summer months when many other orchids are in vegetative growth. They produce tall racemes of many brightly coloured flowers, each rather distinctive and eye catching with its enlarged dorsal sepal and two wide lateral sepals.

In their natural habitats many of the 200 or so *Disa* species grow near streams or in damp grasslands, though they have a wide altitudinal range from sea level to at least 3000 m. Many growers in England have found that disas are difficult to keep in cultivation, but at Kew it has been shown that frequent repotting is the vital key for success. The plants are grown in a mixture of equal parts of fibrous peat and perlite, repotted after flowering and kept comparatively dry for several weeks so that they get a short rest. During the winter they grow actively and, with a minimum night temperature of 11°C (52°F), need watering at least twice each week. In the spring, water can be given daily to maintain the fat clumps of fresh green foliage. Foliar feeding ensures the development of good flower spikes. It seems to be important, however, that the plants do not stand in still water and that the compost does not become stagnant; frequent repotting prevents this.

Disa uniflora has flower spikes up to 50 cm tall and may bear four or five spikes in each 5-inch pot. The flowers are up to 10 cm across and very colourful, with scarlet lateral sepals and the dorsal sepal, which forms a hood, pink veined with scarlet. *Disa racemosa* has taller inflorescences with smaller flowers, about 6 cm across, pink with deeper pink veining on the dorsal sepal. *Disa tripetaloides* is a more delicate plant with pale pink or white spotted with pink flowers borne on stems up to 30 cm high. Several hybrids involving these three species are grown, in particular *D. Kewensis* (*D. uniflora* × *D. tripetaloides*), *D. Veitchii* (*D. racemosa* × *D. uniflora*), and *D. Diores* (*D. uniflora* × *D. Veitchii*).

Disa cardinalis has smaller, intense scarlet flowers on flower spikes up to 40 cm tall and is much less common in the wild than the other species in the collection. Several plants of its robust progeny, *D. Kirstenbosch Pride* (*D. uniflora* × *D. cardinalis*) are also grown. These were raised from a flask of seedlings sent by Kirstenbosch Botanic Garden. A pot full of spikes, each 100 cm or more high with many scarlet flowers, is a stunning sight.

In the wild, several species of *Disa* flower after fires have burned away all the vegetation surrounding them. It is thought that this enables their seedlings to grow without overwhelming competition from other plants and may account for the fact that disas can be difficult to flower in cultivation. At Kew the only species that does not seem to flower prodigiously is *D. racemosa*, so burning it has not been tried!

The genus *Stenoglottis* is also native to South Africa, with one of the four species, *S. zambesiaca*, extending its range north to Malawi and Tanzania.

Stenoglottis fimbriata grows terrestrially or on mossy rocks or even low down on tree trunks close to streams and waterfalls where its leaves are sometimes bathed in spray and mist. The basal rosette of spotted leaves makes it an attractive plant even when not in flower. Each rosette produces a flower spike which may be up to 45 cm tall and bears up to 70 tiny flowers. The flowers are pink with purple spots and last for about six weeks in the late summer. After flowering the leaves die down for a brief dormant period. The tubers are repotted then, before the fresh new rosettes appear.

Stenoglottis longifolia is more vigorous than *S. fimbriata* and produces a tuft of fresh green, strap-shaped leaves. Its flowers are white or lilac with pink spots, the longest flower spikes growing to 70 cm tall. There are usually more than 100 flowers on each spike and these remain fresh from early autumn to the end of the year. *Stenoglottis woodii* comes into flower in the early summer and is smaller. The plants have white or pink flowers in short spikes.

The genus *Eulophia* contains about 300 species which are spread throughout the tropical and subtropical areas of the world, the greatest concentration being in Central Africa. Most of the members of this genus are

Vanilla imperialis, a vine-like orchid whose stems grow to enormous length among the canopy of rain forest trees.
Bob Campbell

terrestrial but a great variety of habitats is utilised, ranging from dry grassland to swamps. *Eulophia petersii* grows among rocky granite outcrops in the Arabian peninsula, throughout tropical East Africa, and southwestwards as far as Namibia; with its hard fleshy leaves it can be said to be one of the very few really succulent orchids. It thrives well in its semi-arid environment and forms large clumps. The flowers are loosely spaced along a spike which can be over 3 m tall. The lip is white, veined with pink, while the sepals and petals are olive-green and curve backwards at their tips.

Probably the most sought-after species is *Eulophia guineensis*, a species from the equatorial regions of Africa, which can be found from Liberia eastwards to Ethiopia and Arabia and southwards as far as Tanzania. It grows in shady places, in the wild, in forests and in relict patches of scrub near rock outcrops or termite mounds. The plants are dormant for at least half the year, but the tall spike emerges with, or just before, the luxuriant leaves. The flowers are large and graceful, each with a large pale pink lip.

Eulophia streptopetala comes from the grasslands and woodland margins of Africa, from South Africa north to the Yemen. The pseudobulbs grow just above the ground surface and give rise to the soft broad leaves and tall flower spike. The individual flowers are bright yellow, with brown-spotted greenish sepals, and are very eye-catching.

African Epiphytes

One very distinctive feature of the African epiphytic orchids is that the majority of those in cultivation seem to have white flowers. This feature serves to make those plants with flowers of other colours all the more interesting. Two such genera are *Bulbophyllum* and *Polystachya*.

There are about 60 species of *Bulbophyllum* in Africa, all of which show great similarity in that they produce a procession of green pseudobulbs linked by short wiry rhizomes with a leaf or two on each young pseudobulb, the older ones being leafless. Their flowers and inflorescences are, however, varied. *Bulbophyllum purpureorachis* comes from tropical west Africa and Zaire and is huge by comparison with many other bulbophyllums. Its pseudobulbs stand about 6 cm tall and its rigid, leathery leaves are about 20 cm long. The flower spike takes the form of a large, dark purple knife blade that is spirally twisted and rises majestically above the plant. When this rachis is mature, the small purple flowers open in succession along both sides of its length over an extended period. By contrast *B. falcatum*, from Sierra Leone, has a flattened yellow-

Disa tripetaloides (above) flowering in the wild in the south of Natal and *Disa uniflora* (below), a selected clone flowering at Kew; these species are the parents of the well-known *Disa Kewensis*. Joyce Stewart and RBG, Kew

green rachis with two rows of tiny red and yellow flowers along its midrib.

Bulbophyllum buntingii from Nigeria and Uganda has flower spikes about 12 cm tall with feathery, cream-coloured flowers which are fragrant. *Bulbophyllum barbigerum* is different again. In this species the lip of each flower is covered with red hairs of varying lengths rather like a woolly mat. These wave and bounce in passing air currents in a very bizarre fashion.

All the tropical African bulbophyllums seem to thrive under similar cultural conditions. They are grown mounted on cork bark in a humid, semi-shaded environment where the temperature range is 15°C (60°F) to 27°C (81°F). They are misted over each morning.

Polystachyas are unusual in having non-resupinate flowers, that is, they look as if they are upside down with the lip peeping out between the paired lateral sepals on the upper side of the flower. There are about 130 species of *Polystachya*, most of which come from tropical Africa.

Polystachya virginea, from the Ruwenzori Mountains in Uganda, Rwanda and Zaire, is a small plant about 20 cm tall bearing a cluster of helmet-shaped white flowers. The lip callus and the tips of the petals are yellow. *Polystachya lawrenceana*, a rare endemic from southern Malawi, forms a small hummock of fresh green, strap-shaped leaves over which hang the greyish green and pink flowers. *Polystachya melliodora*, named for its honey-like scent, comes from Mufindi District in Tanzania and the plant at Kew is part of the type collection. This interesting novelty was found in 1979 by Phillip Cribb and colleagues on a fallen branch in the montane rain forest of the Southern Highlands but has not been collected since. Each sparkling pure white flower has a cherry-red lip and petal margin, a striking colour combination. The Kenya species *P. bella* has erect stems holding up to 20 gold or orange nodding flowers.

Tropical polystachyas are either mounted on cork oak bark or established in small pots of tightly packed epiphyte compost. An intermediate glasshouse with a winter night minimum temperature of 15°C (60°F) is used for them.

Ansellia africana is another African epiphyte or lithophyte with colourful flowers which, on a mature plant, are borne in great profusion. The scent of the

Stenoglottis woodii 'Kew Delight', a terrestrial orchid from Natal which flowers regularly at Kew during the summer months. RBG, Kew

Eulophia streptopetala, a terrestrial orchid which is widespread in Africa and easy to maintain in cultivation. Joyce Stewart

Polystachya melliodora, an epiphyte from Tanzania which was recently named and described at Kew; its apt name refers to the honey-like scent. RBG, Kew

flowers is somewhat overpowering, and one plant can easily perfume a whole greenhouse. The plant forms thick cane-like pseudobulbs up to 1 m long. The younger canes bear fresh green leaves while old canes eventually become leafless. The panicles of flowers arch out from the apex of mature canes and sometimes from the lower nodes of leafless ones. Each yellow flower is more or less heavily spotted or blotched with reddish brown. One dramatic feature of this species is the thick cluster of short spiky aerial roots which forms when the plant is grown in a hanging basket. *Ansellia africana* is grown at Kew in a light position in a glasshouse with a minimum night temperature of 18°C (64°F).

The white, pale yellowish or greenish-flowered African epiphytes are numerous and include the genera *Microcoelia, Aerangis, Angraecum, Diaphananthe, Cyrtorchis, Bolusiella, Ancistrorhynchus, Mystacidium, Rangaeris* and *Tridactyle*. A very large number of plants and species has been assembled at Kew in the last 40

years to facilitate the compilation of the accounts of the Orchidaceae for the *Flora of West Tropical Africa*, published in 1968, and for the *Flora of Tropical East Africa*, which was finally completed in 1989.

Microcoelia is one of a few genera in the Orchidaceae in which the plants have tiny brown scales instead of green leaves and the process of photosynthesis, by which the plant harnesses energy, is carried out in the roots. This curious adaptation is also found in the genera *Taeniophyllum*, from New Guinea, and *Polyrrhiza* from the Caribbean area. There are about 26 species of *Microcoelia* in Africa and Madagascar, eight of which are grown at Kew. They are cultivated on slabs of cork oak bark where they form tangled clumps of silvery roots and, in season, many arching racemes of tiny white flowers. They are grown in a light position in the glasshouse with a winter night minimum temperature of 15°C (60°F), with constant air movement and a high relative humidity.

Ansellia africana, an epiphyte which is widespread in Africa, often growing on bare trunks and the branches of large trees.
RBG, Kew

Few species of the genus *Aerangis* are common in cultivation in Britain as yet, but they are sure to become more widely grown in future. Most of those at Kew are grown mounted on slabs of cork oak bark although a few are grown in pots of epiphyte compost. The graceful, arching inflorescences and starry, white flowers can be best appreciated when the plants are grown on bark and suspended from a suitable structure in the glasshouse. All the species are scented, especially in the evenings as darkness falls.

Aerangis verdickii occurs sporadically throughout East and Central Africa and is a vigorous plant with up to six greyish green leaves and strong, thick roots which grip the bark. Up to a dozen flowers are borne on each raceme and the long, sinuously curving spurs are tinged with green or pink. In *A. mystacidii* the spur is shorter and suffused with pink or orange. The dark green leaves indicate the need for a shadier position in the greenhouse for this species. *Aerangis luteo-alba* var. *rhodosticta* is very spectacular as its closely spaced, pale cream flowers are adorned with a bright vermilion column. It grows most luxuriantly in the shadiest position in a cool greenhouse. In brighter light the leaves are shorter and more succulent.

Two glasshouses with winter minima of 13°C (55°F) and 15°F (60°F) are used for growing *Aerangis* and all the dark-green-leaved species prefer a heavily shaded position. As with most orchids grown on bark, daily misting over seems to be beneficial for *Aerangis*.

The genus *Angraecum* comprises some 200 species and encompasses an enormous variation in the form of the plants and size of the flowers. The large-flowered African angraecums, *A. infundibulare*, *A. birrimense* and *A. eichlerianum* are mounted and suspended on a wire frame so that their slender stems can assume a natural position, partly upright and partly pendent. They are very different in growth habit from the glossy-leaved *A. distichum* and the slender but usually upright *A. erectum*. Some of the smaller species are grown in pots of appropriate size in a compost of coarse components while others are mounted on cork bark. A fairly light position in one of the warmer glasshouses seems to suit them best with high relative humidity. Daily misting is beneficial.

Madagascar

The island of Madagascar lies in the Indian Ocean off the east coast of Africa and occupies some 228,000 square miles. Its thick forests and remote mountains are the home of many fascinating animals and plants found nowhere else in the world. Some are related to the genera and species of the neighbouring continent which is only 300–500 miles away; others are completely different. Some of Madagascar's most exciting endemic orchids are grown at Kew, a selection of which are mentioned below.

Probably the best known orchid from Madagascar is the comet orchid, *Angraecum sesquipedale*. The eminent biologist Charles Darwin first investigated the pollination mechanism of this species by experimenting with live flowers sent to him by a well known orchid grower and author, James Bateman. The spur of the lip can grow to over 30 cm long, and Darwin surmised that in Madagascar there must be a moth with a proboscis long enough to reach the nectar at the end of the spur. In doing this, the moth would inadvertently pick up the pollinia from a flower from which it fed and leave them on the stigma of the next flower it visited, thus cross-pollinating it. Years later a moth with a very elongated proboscis was found, and Darwin's prediction is commemorated in its Latin name, *Xanthopan morgani praedicta*. The flowers of *A. sesquipedale* are not always quite so large in cultivation but they are always very striking. The leaves are leathery and have a silvery bloom over their surface, making them quite distinctive.

Angraecum eburneum comes from the island of Réunion, further east in the Indian Ocean, but its larger relative, *A. eburneum* ssp. *superbum* is common along the north and east coasts of Madagascar and in the islands of the Comores group. It can grow up to 2 m tall and forms a thick clump of long, dark green, strap-shaped leaves. The stiff flower spikes grow up to 1 m long and carry up to 20 flowers, which have pale green sepals and petals and a pure white lip.

Two hybrids in the genus are grown at Kew. *Angraecum* × Veitchii, registered in 1899, is a cross between *A. eburneum* and *A. sesquipedale*. It has the vigour and size of *A. eburneum* and the enlarged flower similar to that of *A. sesquipedale*. *Angraecum* Alabaster is a back cross of *A.* Veitchii with *A. eburneum* and has more but rather smaller flowers than *A.* Veitchii.

The large angraecums are grown in pots of appropriate size in a compost of coarse components while the smaller ones can be grown on cork oak bark. A fairly light position in one of the warmer glasshouses seems to suit them best with high relative humidity. Daily misting is beneficial.

Angraecum compactum is endemic to the high altitude forests of Madagascar and, at first sight, looks very different from the angraecums just described. It has fat fleshy leaves and grows to about 30 cm long at the most. The flowers, though, are instantly recognisable and are star-shaped, sparkling white and have a graceful curved spur.

Eulophiella roempleriana is a large plant which grows exuberantly in the Princess of Wales Conservatory. Its

Angraecum sesquipedale, the comet orchid from Madagascar; Charles Darwin correctly predicted the existence of a long-tongued moth as the pollinator of this epiphytic species. Joyce Stewart

fat rhizomes branch and spread rapidly in several directions, producing vigorous clumps of large pleated leaves which grow up to 1 m long and are a fresh green colour when young, darkening as they age. In nature this plant is endemic to the forests on the east coast of Madagascar where it grows as an epiphyte in the crowns of *Pandanus* trees. Its spectacular racemes grow up to 2 m high and each bears up to 25 pink and red flowers.

Cymbidiella flabellata is rather similar in growth habit but much smaller and daintier. It is normally found in marshy places in the shade of other plants, its rather grassy foliage ensheathing narrow pseudobulbs which are well spaced on fine wiry rhizomes. The flowers are yellowish green with purplish black spots, except for the lip which is a bright rosy red.

Plants in the genus *Aeranthes* are grown in a shady humid glasshouse with a winter night minimum temperature of 16°C (60°F). They are suspended in hanging baskets from a suitable support above head height so that their pendulous flowers can be best appreciated. *Aeranthes caudata* has pale green flowers with long graceful petals and sepals while *A. grandiflora* has large flowers, up to 10 cm across, which are a translucent white with pale green tips to the petals and spur. *Aeranthes ramosa* has pale green flowers which dangle some 45 cm below the plant on stems as fine as threads.

6 Australia

AUSTRALIA, THE WORLD'S LARGEST ISLAND, has a land area of just over 2.9 million square miles, two-fifths of which lies north of the Tropic of Capricorn. It has been isolated for at least 50 million years and 85% of its unique flora is endemic. Although perhaps best known for its deserts, Australia has a wide diversity of climate and landscape which gives rise to a broad range of vegetation types, particularly in the coastal areas. In the north and north-east the coastal areas have a tropical climate with distinct wet and dry seasons, the summer (November to March) being the wettest time of the year. These coastal areas support rain forest and mangrove swamps with woodland and savannah inland. The south-west and south-eastern areas of Australia have a temperate to subtropical climate with rainfall throughout the year. Their natural vegetation is mixed woodland and *Eucalyptus* scrub known as 'mallee'. An alpine flora grows at higher altitudes in the mountains in the south-east. Much of the vast area of central Australia is dry throughout the year, and rather few plants grow there in the stunted *Acacia* scrub.

There are estimated to be about 110 genera and over 700 species of orchids native to Australia. Forty per cent of the species are epiphytic or lithophytic and grow in the tropical northern and north-eastern regions. Only five epiphytic species occur as far south as Victoria. The 60% of Australian orchids which grow terrestrially are found mainly in the south-west and south-east of the country and are nearly all endemic. The Kew orchid collection has many representatives both of terrestrial and epiphytic orchids from Australia.

Temperate Terrestrials

The Australian temperate terrestrials deserve to be much better known and more widely cultivated in Britain. Like the European terrestrials they grow in a symbiotic relationship with a mycorrhizal fungus which obtains organic matter from the compost and provides the orchid with nutrients.

The annual growth cycle at Kew starts at the end of October, when the first green shoots of *Pterostylis* plants appear. The early flowering species such as *P. angusta* and *P. nutans* quickly put up flower spikes. Gradually the leaves of *Diuris* species start to show

through, *D. palustris* being the first to flower, at the end of January. By this time the first *Caladenia* leaves are growing. After flowering, by about mid-May, the plants die down and the tubers remain dormant through the summer when repotting is done.

Dormant tubers are removed from the old pots, but a third of the old compost is retained and incorporated in the new compost. This ensures an adequate supply of mycorrhizal fungus for the orchid to make vigorous

Pterostylis × ingens, a natural hybrid that appears wherever *P. nutans* and *P. furcata* grow together; this pan of plants earned growers at Kew a Certificate of Cultural Commendation from the RHS. David Menzies

Glossodia major, the wax lip orchid, is widespread in Australia and still quite common; its fragrant flowers are particularly bright after forest fires. Joyce Stewart

growth. Some species increase readily in cultivation by forming up to five new tubers on stolons which can be divided when repotting. Many of the *Pterostylis* species can be propagated in this way, whereas most of the caladenias produce just one new tuber to replace the old one and so can only be increased from seeds. Tubers are repotted 3 cm below the surface of the compost with about 2 cm space between each one and then watered in. Normally another watering is not needed until the first shoots are growing. Watering is controlled according to the known habitat of the orchid in the wild. *Diuris palustris*, for example, grows in marshy areas and so is watered freely, while *Thelymitra antennifera*, which grows in dry areas, is kept just moist but watered infrequently.

The genus *Pterostylis* contains about 100 species, of which 15 are currently grown at Kew. The greenhoods, as they are commonly known, are among the easiest of the Australian temperate terrestrials to maintain in cultivation. The genus is characterised by the hood which is formed by the fusion of the dorsal sepal and lateral petals of the flower. The hood is usually green, streaked with white, red or brown in different species. Like many orchids, *Pterostylis* flowers have evolved a complex method of achieving pollination. The lip of the flower is hinged, and when an insect, normally a small gnat, lands upon it, the lip springs backwards against the column trapping the insect inside the flower. The insect climbs up the column, gripping the conveniently placed hairs and squeezes out of the gap at the top. In doing so it brushes against the pollinia, which adhere to the insect as it takes flight. Landing on the lip of another flower, the insect is again trapped when the lip springs back. The pollinia which it has carried from the previous flower stick to the stigmatic surface as the insect climbs the column. As it gains its freedom again, it flies off with a fresh set of pollinia from that flower.

The readiness of the spring in the lip of a *Pterostylis* flower can easily be tested by touching it with a pencil. Usually the lip flies back straight away.

The largest species of *Pterostylis* is *P. baptistii*, the king greenhood, which grows up to 40 cm tall with a hood up to 6 cm long. In Australia it grows in large colonies in the dense scrub surrounding streams and marshes. It has a translucent flower with green veins and brown markings at the tip of the hood. The hood is held erect. In *P. nutans*, the nodding greenhood, the flower is bent over facing the ground. Most *Pterostylis* species bear a single flower at the top of the flowering shoot, but a few are multiflowered. *Pterostylis vittata* is one of this group and has up to eight green-veined flowers on each stem. It grows naturally in the light scrub close to the southern coast of the country.

The genus *Diuris*, commonly called donkey orchids or double tails, is almost completely confined to Australia, with just one species found elsewhere – *Diuris fryana* is endemic to Timor. *Diuris carinata*, *D. palustris* and *D. emarginata* all grow in damp areas while most other species occur in grassland or open woodland. It is

Calochilus paludosus, the red beard orchid, is widespread in Australia, including Tasmania, and grows in seasonally swampy or well drained sites. David Lang

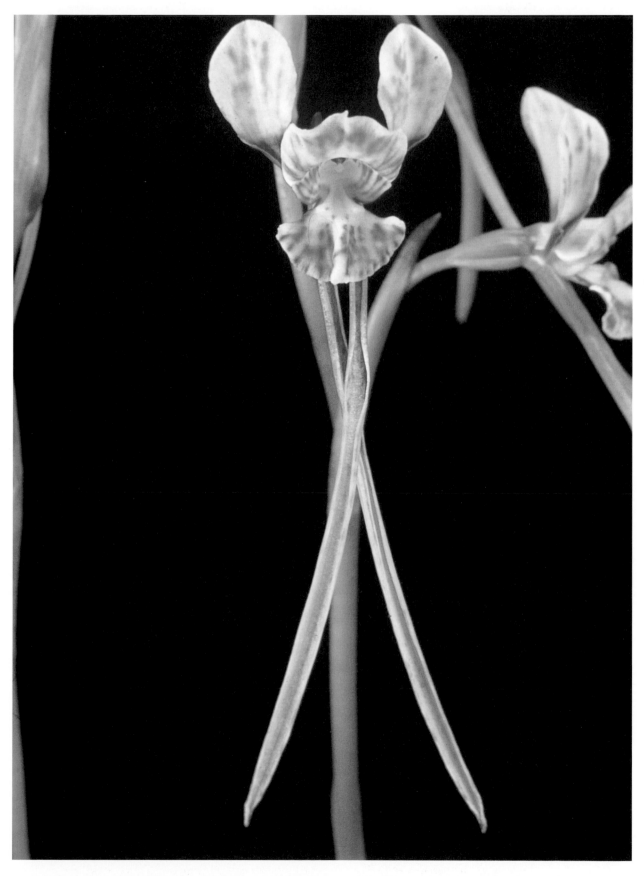

Diuris fragrantissima, a rare orchid which has been raised from seeds by the symbiotic method and reintroduced successfully to its threatened habitat in Victoria. RBG, Kew

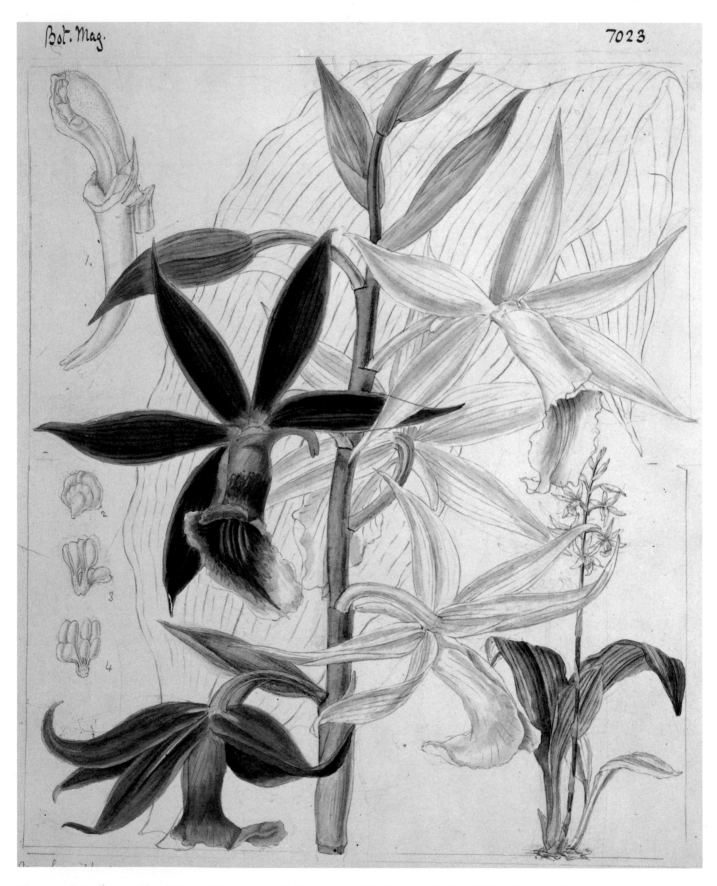

Phaius tankervilleae, a robust terrestrial species which was one of the first tropical orchids to flower at Kew more than 200 years ago. (Illustration from *Curtis's Botanical Magazine*, 1888.) RBG, Kew

thought that some *Diuris* species have evolved flower shapes and colours which mimic those of leguminous shrubs in order to attract insects to pollinate them.

There are about 50 species of *Corybas*, worldwide, ranging from the Himalayan foothills, through Malaysia to New Zealand, and 20 species are found in Australia. *Corybas* species grow in damp sheltered mossy areas under low bushes or ferns. They have a reputation for not flowering well in cultivation; and the partly formed flowers will abort if they are in a cold draught. To prevent this happening, *Corybas* plants are always grown in a sheltered spot in the greenhouse, under the shade of leaves of other plants. If kept in too much light their leaves become yellowish, and if in too much shade they stand rather unnaturally high above the surface of the compost. About 75% shade is most suitable. When conditions are right their fascinating flowers are ample reward for the extra trouble needed to cultivate them.

Tropical Terrestrials

Several terrestrial orchid genera originate from the northern tropical areas of Australia. The plants grow rapidly through the hot, wet summer and rest during the slightly cooler winter. The largest species in the Kew collection is *Phaius tankervilleae*. Copious watering and foliar feeding at fortnightly intervals result in its majestic leaves growing up to 100 cm. This species grows naturally along the margins of swamps, with its roots in the water for part of the year, and has flower spikes up to 2 m tall. The flowers are white on the outside and gingery brown within except for the lip which is usually pale on the outside and rose-pink within. This species flowered first in England in Yorkshire in 1778, and was introduced to Kew in the same year by Sir Joseph Banks, the President of the Royal Society at the time. *Phaius australis* var. *bernaysii*, which has yellow and white flowers, is also grown at Kew.

The related genus *Calanthe* has 120 species worldwide, but only the widespread *Calanthe triplicata* is found in Australia. This species forms fine clumps of deep green, ribbed leaves about 60 cm tall through which the spikes of delicate white flowers protrude. *Malaxis latifolia* has equally handsome foliage and produces a raceme of tiny pale green flowers which turn purple after a few days.

The compost used for the tropical terrestrial orchids from Australia imitates the humus-rich layer over the rain forest soils in which the wild plants grow. A

Cymbidium madidum, one of three cymbidiums that occur in eastern Australia; it has small flowers on long pendent inflorescences. David DuPuy

mixture composed of leaf mould, peat and loam, lightened with coarse sand, is used at Kew. Repotting is done annually so that the roots never have to suffer stagnant compost. All these plants are grown at Kew in a glasshouse in shady conditions with a winter night minimum temperature of 16°C (61°F).

Epiphytes

The Australian epiphytes, of which there are over 200 species, grow most commonly in the north-east of Australia and along the east coast, with only five species occurring as far south as Victoria. They grow naturally on trees and rocks and have evolved root systems which adhere strongly to the substratum. Those grown at Kew are mainly from the genera *Cymbidium*, *Bulbophyllum*, *Dendrobium* and *Sarcochilus*.

The genus *Cymbidium* contains about 44 species worldwide. There are three species in Australia, each of which has a different habitat. *Cymbidium madidum* grows readily in cultivation in standard cymbidium compost, soon becoming a large plant in a 30 cm pot. It grows in nature in moist open forest or rain forest and needs a winter night minimum temperature of 16°C (61°F) in cultivation and quite shady conditions. Its stout leaves grow up to 35 cm long and are a dark glossy green. The flowers grow on pendulous spikes and are fleshy and long-lasting, varying in colour from yellowy brown to green. *Cymbidium canaliculatum* grows in the drier inland woodland as well as coastal forests. It grows in the clefts of living or dead gum trees, where its roots penetrate deeply into the heartwood finding both moisture and protection from extremes of temperature. The leaves are few, thick, fleshy and grey-green, the flowers variable, ranging from brown and red through purple to green. This species needs the maximum available amount of light in cultivation and is hung close to the glass in the warmest greenhouse with a winter night temperature of 18°C (64°F). Plants are grown in hollow logs made of cork oak bark, which seem to suit them better than plastic pots.

Cymbidium suave has soft, grass-like foliage and a long slender stem. It is unusual in the genus in not forming pseudobulbs. The flowers are greenish in colour and sweetly scented. Like *C. canaliculatum*, *C. suave* is grown in hollow logs rather than pots but it is kept in a cooler glasshouse.

Twenty-seven species of *Bulbophyllum* grow in Australia, 14 of which are grown at Kew. All are grown on slabs of cork oak bark and are kept quite shaded in a greenhouse with a winter night minimum temperature of 15°C (60°F). Over the years, these plants form mats of small, green pseudobulbs joined by short rhizomes. In Australia, bulbophyllums grow mainly in the rain

forests close to the coast. *Bulbophyllum baileyi* is the largest species with solitary flowers up to 4 cm across, white or yellow with purple spots.

The genus *Dendrobium* has over 70 species in Australia in a wide range of habitats. More than half this total is cultivated at Kew in three different glasshouses. *Dendrobium bigibbum*, the Cooktown orchid, is the floral emblem of Queensland. Its pseudobulbs grow up to 45 cm tall with a tuft of leaves at the top of each and arching sprays of mauve flowers in the autumn. The variety *D. bigibbum* ssp. *bigibbum* var. *superbum* has larger flowers than normal while the var. *compactum* has small flowers in cultivation. *Dendrobium discolor* forms dense thickets of enormous stems up to 3 m tall in the wild and is scarcely less vigorous in cultivation so it needs a high greenhouse. Its glossy new growth is most attractive and its arching racemes can be up to 30 cm long. The petals and sepals are brown and yellow and usually twisting and curled, adding to the interest of the plant. Both these species grow well in the brightly lit and warmest glasshouse at Kew.

The pendulous species, *Dendrobium tetragonum* and *D. teretifolium*, are grown in a shadier, cooler greenhouse with a winter night minimum temperature of 16°C (60°F). They are mounted on slabs of cork oak bark so that the flowers are presented in their natural posture. *Dendrobium teretifolium*, known sometimes as the bridal veil orchid, cascades like a chandelier and is covered with small white flowers each winter. *Dendrobium tetragonum* has distinctive square pseudobulbs with a tuft of dark green leaves at the end of each one. The flowers are yellow and brown or green and white and of spidery appearance. The tiny *D. toressae* grows under the same conditions. Its leaves are similar in size and shape to grains of rice and its yellow flowers are just as small.

A cooler glasshouse, with a winter night minimum temperature of 14°C (57°F), is used for growing the very spectacular *D. speciosum*. This variable species grows on rock outcrops in full sun and also on tree stumps in shade. Some clones flower better than others in cultivation. The best are absolutely magnificent with long spikes of densely packed, creamy-coloured flowers growing from each stubby pseudobulb. *Dendrobium speciosum* grows well in pots of medium grade epiphyte compost. *Dendrobium kingianum* is another lithophyte which grows on cliff faces where its roots become entangled in mats of moss and ferns. Its flowers are usually pink, although a range from white through to mauve has been found. *Dendrobium speciosum* and *D. kingianum* form a natural hybrid, *Dendrobium* × *delicatum*, which has characteristics intermediate between its parents. It grows vigorously in cultivation and has pink or white flowers. Although rare in the

Dendrobium bigibbum, an epiphyte from Queensland which is widely cultivated and a parent of numerous hybrids.
Joyce Stewart

wild, it is quite commonly cultivated, often erroneously labelled *D. kingianum 'album'*.

Seven species of the genus *Sarcochilus* are grown at Kew. They are all kept in a glasshouse with a winter night minimum temperature of 13°C (55°F) but the individual species differ in the amount of shade they prefer. *Sarcochilus ceciliae* is grown in an open position in shallow pans of coarse compost where it forms compact tufts of foliage and dainty racemes of pink flowers. It needs to be grown with the crown of each plant standing proud of the surface of the compost so that it does not rot. *Sarcochilus falcatus* and *S. olivaceus* are both pendulous in habit and are grown mounted on to slabs of cork oak bark. They form large root systems which are misted over daily with water. *Sarcochilus falcatus*, the orange blossom orchid, has pure white flowers with the lip of each striped with yellow and orange, while *S. olivaceus* has olive-green flowers with red markings. *Sarcochilus hartmannii* and *S. fitzgeraldii* are erect in habit and make compact plants. Both have white flowers with red markings at the bases of the petals. The flowers of *Sarcochilus fitzgeraldii* have a larger lip and the plants prefer a shaded position in the glasshouse. The natural habitat of this species is the dark, mossy ravines of the Dividing Range in New South Wales. *Sarcochilus hartmannii* is found in sunnier positions on rock faces and so does better in a more open position on the bench. Both species grow well either mounted on cork oak bark or in pots of medium grade epiphyte compost. *Sarcochilus fitzgeraldii* is now endangered in the wild and plants at Kew are deliberately pollinated so that many more seedlings can be raised and distributed around the world in the hope of reducing the need to remove more wild plants from their natural habitat. The artificial hybrid between these two species, *Sarcochilus* Fitzhart, grows vigorously, and is more common in cultivation than either parent.

Australia's most graceful orchid, *Phalaenopsis amabilis* var. *papuana* occurs sporadically along the Mossman and Daintree Rivers in dense forest. Each plant has several pendulous leaves and is secured to the host tree

Dendrobium tetragonum, an epiphyte from the rain forests of eastern Australia. D R M Stewart

by its long flat roots. Five to ten glistening white flowers are borne on each arching inflorescence. This is the only species of *Phalaenopsis* which occurs in Australia. At Kew it is grown with other species of *Phalaenopsis* in a shady and very humid position in the warmest glasshouse with a winter night minimum temperature of 18°C (64°F). Its flowering period is one of the highlights of the year.

7 Asia

THE GREAT VARIETY OF CLIMATE, land forms and vegetation types in the continent of Asia has made available many different habitats for orchids. Plants which tolerate extremes of light and temperature are common at the high altitudes, while lower down there are many different epiphytes and shade-loving terrestrial plants. They exhibit a great diversity of form, ranging in size from tiny species of *Taeniophyllum*, with flowers smaller than a pin head, to the world's largest orchid plant, *Grammatophyllum speciosum*, whose pseudobulbs can grow up to 10 m long.

Terrestrials

Two of the best known terrestrial orchid genera, *Pleione* and *Paphiopedilum*, are both from Asia and well represented in the Kew collection. There are also many less familiar ones, such as *Acanthephippium*, *Ludisia* and *Tainia*.

The pleiones come from the Himalayan region, from Nepal eastwards, to Taiwan, and grow in the mats of moss and fallen leaf litter that accumulates in the cracks among rocks and on mountain slopes. A few are epiphytes. Their root run is quite shallow, and the drainage is very good in their natural environment so at Kew they are grown in half pots, 6 cm deep, in an open, bark-based compost. For ease of cultivation pleiones can be divided into two groups: the autumn flowering species require somewhat warmer conditions and are grown in a greenhouse with a winter night minimum temperature of 11°C (52°F), whilst the spring flowering species are usually kept in a cold greenhouse, minimum temperature 5°C (40°F).

Pleione praecox is usually the first to flower, just as the leaves on the previous year's pseudobulbs die back at the end of September. The flowers are slightly perfumed and are deep pink with a darker lip which is very frilled. *Pleione praecox* 'Alba' has paler flowers, while in the clone 'Everest' the sepals and petals are a sparkling white. The other two early flowering pleiones are *P. maculata*, which has slightly smaller pink or white flowers about 6 cm across, the lip heavily blotched with purple, and *P. × lagenaria*, which is a deep pink colour with a mauve flush down the centre of each sepal and purple streaks on the lip. The autumn flowering

pleiones finish flowering in December. Their new leaves and roots start to grow by mid-February, so annual repotting is carried out in January.

Because the roots are very brittle and easily broken, the spring flowering species are repotted during February, before flowering and root growth starts. Damage to the roots results in a poor season's growth.

Most of the *Pleione* species are now in cultivation at Kew, the collection having been assembled over many years while Peter Hunt, Phillip Cribb and others have worked on the genus. This research resulted in the publication of the widely acclaimed book *The Genus Pleione*, by Cribb and Butterfield in 1988.

Pleione humilis begins the flowering season at the end of February with its pale pink sepals and petals and a white frilled lip with reddish brown streaks. It is easily recognised by the distinctive conical, pointed pseudobulbs. *Pleione formosana* is a very varied species. The type has rosy pink sepals and petals and a white lip with raised yellow markings and orange blotches; other forms have sparkling white flowers with a few lemon yellow markings on the lip. Several of the named cultivars are grown, including 'Blush of Dawn' and 'Oriental Grace' and also some hybrids bred from *P. formosana* including the grexes Versailles, Alishan and Tongariro. The yellow *P. forrestii* is of great interest to hybridisers looking for a new range of colours but is a charming addition to the display in its own right.

By crossing some of the spring and autumn flowering species, winter flowering hybrids have been produced, such as the deep pink Barcena. These hybrids are grown at the warmer temperatures favoured by the autumn flowering species. The spring flowering pleiones can be gently forced into flower early in the season by moving them to warmer conditions (minimum winter night temperature 13°C (55°F)). By careful management, a succession of pleiones can be displayed, beginning in October and lasting until May.

The lovely jewel orchids in the genera *Anoectochilus*, *Ludisia* and *Macodes* have the reputation of being difficult to cultivate. They require warm temperatures with a winter night minimum temperature of 16°C (61°F), shade from direct sunlight, and a high relative humidity in order to grow well. Their succulent stems are very attractive to slugs and, as a growth of many months can be eaten in one night, constant vigilance is needed. In the wild, the creeping stems of the jewel orchids thread their way through cushions of moss and fallen leaves. At Kew they are grown in shallow seed trays filled with about 4 cm of well drained compost so that their stems can spread naturally over the surface.

Most orchids are grown for their attractive flowers, but the main interest in growing the jewel orchids is for their leaves. *Ludisia discolor* has reddish green leaves overlaid with bronze and a velvety bloom. The veins are a delicate network of pink. This species flowers readily and produces flower spikes up to 30 cm tall throughout the winter and spring. The white flowers have yellow markings and a beautiful, penetrating perfume. Unfortunately the widely grown cultivar, *L. discolor* 'Doris Stein' is not scented, but it has larger flowers and leaves than the wild species. *Macodes cominsii* from the Solomon Islands has a fleshy, heart-shaped leaf, which is a pale green colour with purple veins and markings.

Although not as colourful as the jewel orchids, there are many other terrestrial orchids from Asia that have attractive foliage. *Tainia hookeriana* has leaves about 1 m long, the petiole and lamina each 50 cm long so that the leaf arches gracefully under its own weight and sways in the air currents. The flower spike is also about 1 m tall and carries up to 25 beige flowers which are delicately marked with brown lines. The lip is white. This species grows in the forests of Thailand close to streams and rivers. At Kew it is grown in a semi-shaded position in a warm intermediate glasshouse with a winter night minimum temperature of 18°C (64°F) and a high relative humidity.

Acanthephippium sylhetense, also from Thailand as well as India and the Himalayas, is grown nearby. Its bold plicate leaves rise to 90 cm from the stout conical pseudobulbs. The short racemes grow in early spring bearing up to six flowers which are cup-shaped and waxy in texture. The long-lasting flowers are cream with purple markings and produce a beautiful scent.

The genus *Calanthe* comprises over 120 species which are predominantly terrestrial orchids. Representatives are found throughout the old world tropics (Africa, Asia, Australia and the Pacific area), although the majority of species occur in Asia. The deciduous calanthes all have stout, silvery-green pseudobulbs and lush foliage which grows during the spring and

Grammatophyllum speciosum, the largest orchid in the world, flowers well in the Singapore Botanic Garden. Joyce Stewart

Pleione forrestii, with its bright yellow colour, has brought possibilities for many new and bright hybrids in this popular genus. Ian Butterfield

summer. In the autumn, as the leaves fall, the flower spikes grow rapidly from the bases of the newly completed pseudobulbs. They reach 1–2 m in height and the pretty colourful flowers last for many weeks. New leaf growth begins soon after the flowers fall in spring. During their dormant period these species require no water at all, even though they are in full flower, the moisture in the humid air around them being enough to prevent the pseudobulbs from shrivelling. As soon as the flowers fade, the pseudobulbs are repotted into a compost made of peat and perlite with added hoof and horn fertiliser, for calanthes are heavy feeders. New roots grow rapidly into the compost and the fresh green leaves soon expand.

This group of calanthes is grown in a sunny position in a warm glasshouse with a winter night minimum temperature of 18°C (64°F) and a high relative humidity. *Calanthe vestita* is the most vigorous of the species with leaves and flower spikes of up 1.5 m long. The individual flowers are up to 4 cm across and are white with a crimson lip. This species occurs over a wide range from Burma through Thailand to Borneo. *Calanthe rubens* comes from Thailand and the Langkawi Islands and is rather smaller. Its flowers are dark pink, to 3 cm across, while the centre of the lip is deep crimson fading to pink at the edge.

A number of *Calanthe* hybrids are grown for display in the Princess of Wales Conservatory. *Calanthe* Bryan has large cream coloured flowers with a greeny tinge and a deep crimson blotch in the throat. *Calanthe* Veitchii is one of the earlier hybrids with rosy pink flowers resulting from the cross between *C. rosea* and *C. vestita*. Deep rose red flowers are available on *Calanthe* Diana Broughton and its progeny.

The evergreen calanthes of China, Japan and the Himalayas may retain their leaves throughout the year, although the plants become dormant during the winter.

At Kew they are grown in a semi-shaded position, in a glasshouse with a winter night minimum temperature of 13°C (55°F) and a relative humidity of over 75%. They are repotted in the spring in a terrestrial compost with plenty of leaf mould. Most species flower in the spring and summer. Unlike the deciduous calanthes which have long arching flower spikes, the evergreen species have an inflorescence which grows erect, just overtopping the leaves, and the raceme bears several flowers.

Calanthe arisanense starts the flowering season in February and has white flowers with a hint of mauve, each about 3 cm across. *Calanthe brevicornu* is from Nepal and has pale lilac petals and a purple lip with yellow markings. *Calanthe discolor*, from Japan and Korea, is purple with a pale pink lip.

Calanthe argenteostriata is a warm-growing, evergreen species requiring a winter night minimum temperature of 18°C (64°F) and a high relative humidity. It is named for its deep glossy green leaves which have broad silver stripes running longitudinally along the veins. Each leaf is up to 30 cm long and 15 cm wide and a clump of foliage is a striking sight. The inflorescence grows to a height of up to 60 cm and has about a dozen small white flowers. This species was discovered on Triangle Mountain in Guangdong province in China and is still not common in cultivation.

There are currently considered to be some 60 species in the genus *Paphiopedilum*, most of which are cultivated at Kew. Ever since their discovery and introduction, paphiopedilums have been sought after by collectors and their curious flowers seem to excite more interest than any other genus of orchids. In recent years a representative collection of species and hybrids has been brought together at Kew as a prerequisite for the monographic study of the genus by Phillip Cribb published in 1987.

Most paphiopedilums are terrestrial, although a few, such as *P. parishii* and *P. lowii* are epiphytes and several are lithophytes, for example *P. niveum* and *P. bellatulum*. They grow in forest habitats, rooting among the leaf litter, so in cultivation most species need high humidity and shade from direct sunlight. Although the various species inhabit a wide range in altitude, three glasshouses at Kew accommodate the whole range of species. Most are in houses which are well shaded, heated to a winter night minimum temperature of 16°C (61°F) or 18°C (64°F) and the relative humidity maintained above 75%. Good air movement is achieved by the use of fans, supplemented by ventilation in the summer. The cooler growing species, such as *P. insigne* from north-east India and *P. fairrieanum* from Bhutan, are healthier and flower more easily if grown at lower temperatures, with a winter night minimum temperature of 13°C (55°F).

Although paphiopedilums grow in areas of very high rainfall, at least for part of the year, they flourish in situations where the drainage is good, and in cultivation the compost needs to be free draining at the same time as being moisture-retentive. Several different compost mixes have been used successfully for paphiopedilums, the current favourite being: 5 parts medium grade bark, 2 parts perlag, 1 part horticultural grade charcoal and 1 part fibrous peat.

One gram of crushed dolomite limestone is added to each litre of this mixture to raise the pH slightly and a little chopped sphagnum moss is incorporated for those species known to inhabit very moist areas.

Paphiopedilums are readily recognised by their basal fans of leaves from the centre of which the flower scapes emerge. The leaves vary greatly, some being long, strap-shaped and a uniform deep green, such as those of *P. rothschildianum*, whereas others have shorter leaves which are dark green mottled light green or silver, such as *P. wardii* and *P. delenatii*. The flowers have a conspicuous dorsal sepal, the familiar slipper-shaped lip, two outstretched or pendulous petals and a shield-like structure at the apex of the column called the staminode. Within this form, however, there is great variation in shape and especially in colour.

A tour of the paphiopedilum collection at Kew will reveal flowers at any time of the year. All the mature plants flower regularly at their own season, and the flowers will last for up to two months if they are not pollinated. *Paphiopedilum gratrixianum*, from Laos, is at its best in December and January. It has a shiny, pale brown lip and brown petals with maroon veins. The dorsal sepal is pale green fading to white at the edges and marked with large, raised, maroon blotches. This species is quite distinctive, even when not in flower, for the narrow, pale green leaes are covered in maroon spots at their bases. *Paphiopedilum appletonianum* also flowers at this time on very long peduncles, each bearing a single bloom which has a pale pink lip and petals which broaden out at the tips to resemble rosy pink ears. The dorsal sepal is pale green marked with maroon veins.

The unfortunately named bubble gum orchid, *P. micranthum*, flowers in March and April. Its dark

Paphiopedilum rothschildianum, a rare slipper orchid from Borneo, where the remaining colonies of plants have been greatly reduced by collectors. Phillip Cribb

Phalaenopsis gigantea, so named for its enormous leaves, came to Kew from Borneo and flowers well every year. RBG, Kew

Phalaenopsis schilleriana, a shade-loving epiphyte from the warm forests of Luzon in the Philippines. Joyce Stewart

shaped leaves. *Paphiopedilum philippinense* flowers a little later and also has several flowers in each inflorescence. In this species the petals, which are pale purple and green, hang downwards and twist. The dorsal sepal is white with purple markings, and the lip is a yellowish green with purple veins. *Paphiopedilum concolor* is a Thailand species which flowers in late summer. Its rosettes of mottled leaves are interesting all through the year, and from August onwards it produces its rather solid, heavy-looking cream flowers which rest upon the foliage. The rounded petals and dorsal sepal are finely marked with many purple spots.

The autumn brings the cooler-growing species into flower. *Paphiopedilum insigne* from India has pale, narrow leaves, a broad, pale brown lip and pale brown petals with wavy edges. The dorsal sepal is white and green and heavily marked with purple blotches. *Paphiopedilum fairrieanum* has the most elegant white petals, boldly marked with maroon veins and hairs; the petals turn backwards at their tips. The dorsal sepal is white with a network of maroon veins and the lip is pale green. Every month brings different paphiopedilums into flower and, on the rare occasions when the collection can show no flowers, the many superbly mottled and shiny leaves give ample interest.

Epiphytes

The epiphytic genus *Taeniophyllum* has diminutive flowers, scarcely larger than a pin-head. There are some 200 species, most of which occur in Asia. Like the members of the African genus *Microcoelia*, taeniophyllums have small brown scales instead of leaves and the process of photosynthesis is carried out in the green roots. Most members of this genus grow upon the twigs of rain forest trees and in cultivation they respond well to constant air movement, a high relative humidity, and a warm greenhouse with a winter night minimum temperature of 18°C (64°F).

The moth orchids, of the genus *Phalaenopsis*, are far more common. At Kew they are grown with equal success in pots of medium epiphyte compost or mounted on bark, but the mounted plants need more frequent watering and misting as their exposed roots dry out more quickly. *Phalaenopsis* enjoy shady warm conditions in a greenhouse with a winter minimum night temperature of 16°C (61°F). Their healthy, shining foliage is a pleasure to see at any time of the year, and the arching sprays of flowers are a welcome reminder that spring is on the way.

Phalaenopsis amabilis is known from a very wide area of Indonesia, New Guinea, Malaysia and northern Australia. At its best each inflorescence can reach up to 1 m long and carry 20 flowers each 10 cm across. The

green leaves, finely chequered with pale, silvery green, are stiff but very attractive, and the flower is delightful. The petals and sepals are short and wide, rounded, pale green tinged with pink and veined with maroon. The lip is very large, almost spherical, and is white with a rosy pink blush. *Paphiopedilum micranthum* originates from the limestone hills of Yunnan in China, not far from where the golden *P. armeniacum* occurs. Sadly, both these species come from restricted areas in China and may now be very rare indeed due to over-collecting. This places an obligation upon growers to propagate new plants from seeds and divisions, so that collectors do not need to remove more plants from the wild to supply the increasing demand for such attractive orchids.

The early summer brings *P. rothschildianum* into flower. Its petals may span 30 cm and are a creamy colour with maroon veins and maroon warts and hairs. The dorsal sepal is also cream, veined with maroon, and the lip is rosy pink veined with maroon. This spectacular species bears up to five flowers on each inflorescence about 60 cm above the waxy, strap-

Vanda coerulea, a spectacular epiphyte from the forests of the Khasi hills and the slopes of the Himalaya range; now rare in the wild, it is widely cultivated. Joyce Stewart

flowers are a glistening white with a yellow flush on the lip and red markings. *Phalaenopsis stuartiana* and *P. schilleriana* both originate in the Philippines and are similar in that they have long, narrow, deep green leaves which are marbled with silver. *Phalaenopsis stuartiana* has white flowers which are marked with yellow on the lip and liberally peppered with maroon spots. *Phalaenopsis schilleriana* has pale pink flowers with yellow markings and red spots on the lip.

Phalaenopsis mannii has plain green leaves and a short inflorescence containing up to six flowers which are star shaped and pale yellow in colour with brown bars across the segments. This species has a sweet fragrance and originates from Assam. *Phalaenopsis cornu-cervi*, from Indonesia and Borneo, has flowers of a similar colour but differs in its distinctively flattened rachis and orange markings on the lip.

The heavy hanging leaves of *Phalaenopsis gigantea* from Borneo can grow up to 60 cm long under the very humid conditions of their native habitat. Their rounded shape and waxy, grey-green colour make them instantly recognisable, while the inflorescence hangs like a bunch of grapes underneath the foliage. The large buds keep the grower in suspense for a week or more, then open to reveal a pale yellow or pink ground nearly obscured by heavy brown blotches.

The sad story of *Vanda coerulea* is typical of many beautiful orchids. First discovered in Assam in 1857, its white or pale blue flowers with their bold network of royal purple markings made this species greatly sought-after by collectors. It is now a rarity, where once it grew in profusion, and such colonies that do exist are probably too small to maintain themselves naturally as their habitats have also been greatly diminished. This tragedy will be repeated for countless other species of orchids unless every effort is made to satisfy demand by propagating from cultivated plants rather than importing more plants collected in the wild.

Vanda coerulea, like many other vandas, requires a lot of sunlight in order to induce flowering. Even at the height of summer only very light shading is needed. At Kew vandas are grown in slatted pots hanging from overhead wires because mature plants produce a profusion of aerial roots hanging down from the stems. A very coarse epiphyte compost is used. They are grown in the warmest greenhouse, with a winter night minimum temperature of 18°C (64°F), but many species, especially *V. coerulea*, would grow equally well in cooler conditions; they are kept in a warmer house than necessary at Kew because it is the only house where the

Dendrobium decockii, one of the jewel-like dendrobiums that grow at high altitudes in the forests of New Guinea. N Cruttwell

maximum amount of light is available. *Vanda tessellata*, from Bengal, has pale green flowers up to 4 cm across which are tessellated with pale brown markings. *Vanda tricolor* var. *suavis* has white flowers marked with magenta blotches. The heady perfume from this species is almost overpowering at close range. *Vanda lamellata* from the Marianas Islands has rather slender flowers of a pale lemon colour in which the lateral sepals are ·streaked with red. *Vanda dearei* from Borneo is also a lemon colour but the petals are much fuller and more rounded than those of *V. lamellata*. The lip is a more intense yellow around the tip and white at the base.

The genus *Aerides* is closely related to the vandas, and vegetatively the plants are rather similar. At Kew these two genera are grown under the same conditions and in similar pots and compost. The waxy flowers of the *Aerides* species cluster along a short and pendulous rachis. They open simultaneously and are delightfully fragrant. *Aerides falcata* from India and Thailand has white flowers marked with striking magenta spots, while the Himalayan *A. fieldingii* has purple flowers with white markings. *Aerides houlletiana*, from Vietnam, has browny yellow flowers with orange markings at the tip of each segment.

One of the most widely grown genera of orchids is

Dendrobium, which, at a conservative estimate, has at least 900 species, most of them in Asia. At Kew the Asiatic dendrobiums are grown in three different environments. The warmest and lightest greenhouse, with a winter night minimum temperature of 18°C (64°F) and a high relative humidity, houses the lowland tropical epiphytes which, in time, produce mighty clumps of tall canes. They are grown in clay pots filled with broken crocks and coarse epiphyte compost, and their white roots quickly encrust the whole pot. *Dendrobium discolor*, which comes from New Guinea, produces canes up to 2 m tall and inflorescences 30 cm long. The flowers are cream, gold or brownish and the petals have wavy margins. *Dendrobium lasianthera*, also from New Guinea, grows even taller, and each inflorescence has up to 20 flowers which are bronze with purple markings on the lip. *Dendrobium antennatum* is very small by comparison and has densely crowded pseudobulbs, 30 cm tall, with light green lanceolate leaves. The arching inflorescences grow up to 30 cm long and carry up to a dozen graceful white flowers. They have pink markings on the lip and the pale green petals form two upright 'antelope horns' above the flower.

Dendrobium nobile and its allies grow under

Cymbidium dayanum is widespread in Asia; it flowers and fruits readily in the wild but is rarely seen in cultivation. RBG, Kew

intermediate conditions in a light, airy greenhouse with a winter night minimum temperature of 15°C (60°F). These species are grown in small clay pots of medium epiphyte compost. *Dendrobium nobile* has a wide range from China and Nepal to Thailand. Each pseudobulb grows up to 60 cm tall and its leaves are deciduous. The older canes remain leafless at any time of the year. The fragrant, long-lasting flowers are white with magenta tips to each tepal and a deep purple blotch in the throat. *Dendrobium farmeri*, which comes from the Himalayas, also grows well under these conditions, and has flowers up to 4 cm across which are pale pink with a soft yellow lip. *Dendrobium primulinum*, also from the Himalayas, as well as China, Burma and Thailand, grows in a hanging basket for it has a pendulous habit. It flowers on the old leafless canes and has white flowers tinged with pink and a pale yellow lip.

The third set of environmental conditions, cool intermediate, with a minimum temperature of 14°C (57°F), a relative humidity above 80% and very good air movement, is suitable for the 'alpine' dendrobiums from the mountains of Papua New Guinea. These form small creeping tufts of foliage among the surrounding moss on the cork oak bark on which they are mounted. The disproportionately large flowers peep out from amongst the leaves. *Dendrobium subuliferum* has fine grassy foliage with white flowers up to 1 cm across. *Dendrobium alaticaulinum* has flowers which are an intense orange colour at the tips, while the flowers of *D. simplex* are white dotted with purple on the outside and suffused with pale green inside. *Dendrobium cuthbertsonii*, which occurs in a wide range of pinks, orange, and scarlet, is probably the best known of this section.

There are about 44 *Cymbidium* species currently recognised, three of which are native to Australia and the rest range in habitat from the Himalayas to the humid forests of the Philippines. Cymbidiums are known to have been cultivated in China before 551 BC and became a symbol of superiority much admired by the nobility of the day. The first species to be grown in Europe was *C. ensifolium*, from China, introduced in 1778 by James Fothergill. The first hybrid to be shown at the Royal Horticultural Society was a cross between two Himalayan species, *C. eburneum* and *C. lowianum*, one clone from which received a First Class Certificate in 1889. Since then a huge range of hybrids has been bred and enjoyed. At Kew a small selection of hybrids is grown to provide displays of colourful flowers in the Princess of Wales Conservatory. These are grown under cool, light, airy conditions to give strong, hard foliage and regular flowering. The collection of *Cymbidium* species at Kew has been assembled in the last ten years for the research carried out by David DuPuy and Phillip

Cribb which was published in 1988 and is described in more detail in chapter 14. The collection is also of considerable interest to the hybridiser, for the possible introduction of desirable new characteristics, such as fragrance, into future hybrids.

A very warm greenhouse, humid and quite light, with a winter night minimum temperature of 18°C (64°F), suits the small group of lowland tropical species, which are mostly epiphytes. They are grown tightly potted in coarse epiphyte compost or in hollow logs made of cork oak bark which are then hung from the roof of the greenhouse. This method allows the pendulous flower spikes to be appreciated fully. *Cymbidium finlaysonianum* grows under these conditions and has clumps of hard, leathery, dark green, strap-shaped foliage. The pendulous flower spikes grow up to 1.5 m long and carry many flowers each up to 3 cm across. The flowers are a yellowy green shade with purple markings on the lip. *Cymbidium aloifolium*, from Sri Lanka, India, China and south-east Asia, has shorter leaves and a flower spike up to 60 cm long. Each flower is pale green, with brown markings down the middle of each segment, and has a red-brown lip.

The majority of *Cymbidium* species are grown under cool conditions with a minimum temperature of 11°C (52°F) and good air movement. Their colours, shapes and perfumes often surprise people who are only familiar with the larger flowered hybrids. *Cymbidium insigne*, from China, Thailand and Vietnam, has an erect flower spike up to 1.5 m tall with up to a dozen flowers at the top. Each flower measures up to 6 cm across and is white suffused with the palest pink. The lip is marked with deeper pink blotches. *Cymbidium tracyanum*, from Burma, is the first to flower, in October, and has an arching inflorescence up to 1.5 m long, densely crowded with large flowers which are a pale browny yellow colour greatly enlivened by deep red markings on the petals and lip. These flowers produce a heady perfume which easily pervades the whole greenhouse. *Cymbidium devonianum*, from the Himalayas, has characteristically rounded leaves and pendulous flower spikes of pale yellow flowers thickly streaked with purple. *Cymbidium faberi* var. *szechuanicum* from Nepal has slender grassy foliage with flower spikes up to 30 cm tall carrying several flowers which are a very pale green colour with red markings and a deep green lip with crimson streaks. *Cymbidium dayanum* from Thailand holds its flowers on short spikes close to the base of the leaves. The flowers are a starry shape and pale cream in colour with a bold red line along the centre of each petal and sepal and a red lip with yellow markings. One of the most striking species is *C. elegans*, which bears many flowered racemes of pale yellow, funnel-shaped flowers.

8 The Americas

THE MENTION OF CENTRAL and South America immediately conjures up images of exuberance and flamboyance, qualities which are also true for the colourful orchids of these regions. Many species from these areas, particularly in the *Cattleya* alliance, *Brassavola, Laelia, Epidendrum, Broughtonia, Sophronitis, Schomburgkia* and others, and in the *Odontoglossum* alliance, which includes *Brassia, Ada, Oncidium, Cochlioda, Miltonia* and *Miltoniopsis*, have been used intensively in hybridising programmes in the quest for larger, more vigorous and more colourful flowers. The hybrids are not well represented in the Kew collection, where priority is given to natural species of wild origin, but some are welcome additions and are used for the display in the Princess of Wales Conservatory.

Terrestrials

As in other parts of the world, the proportion of terrestrial orchids in the flora is lower nearer the Equator and greater in temperate regions. The dove orchid, *Peristeria elata*, is the national flower of Panama. The plants are robust with fat, round pseudobulbs, and the deciduous leaves are wide and plicate. The waxy, white flowers are cup-shaped, about 4 cm across, and

Phragmipedium caudatum, the largest of the South American slipper orchids, has very long petals. G C K Dunsterville

have a wonderful fragrance. In cultivation *Peristeria* needs conditions similar to those of its natural habitat. It is grown in a semi-shaded position in a glasshouse with a winter night minimum temperature of 18°C (64°F). In its native forests this species grows among the surface litter, so it is grown at Kew in shallow clay pans half filled with broken crocks to give perfect drainage, and a compost containing a high proportion of leaf mould.

Stenorrhynchos speciosum is grown in a similar way as it has been recorded growing as a terrestrial as well as lithophytically and as an epiphyte in the damp forests of Mexico. It is not commonly cultivated and deserves to be much better known. Its low growing, dark green leaves surround the scarlet flower spikes during the winter. The small red flowers are enhanced by the long, scarlet bracts, so that the inflorescence as a whole creates a very fine display.

Some of the South American slipper orchids in the genus *Phragmipedium* are terrestrial whilst others are lithophytic or epiphytic plants. *Phragmipedium schlimii* grows in earth and on rocks in the forests of Colombia. Its grassy leaves attain 30 cm in length, and the flower spike is about 30 cm tall. The flowers are white and quite downy in texture, about 4 cm across, with a deep pink lip that nearly hides the yellow staminode. *Phragmipedium longifolium* forms a tussock of glossy, dark green foliage with arching leaves up to 1 m long. The flowers on each spike open in succession so a mature plant with several flowering growths is rarely out of flower. Each flower is about 6 cm across, suffused with a pale apricot colour and veined with green. The margins of the petals are touched with pink and white and the staminode is yellow. This species grows in Ecuador, Colombia, Panama and Costa Rica, and is terrestrial or occasionally epiphytic.

Phragmipedium caudatum is one of the most interesting species, with incredibly long petals. After the flowers open the petals continue to grow downwards, twisting as they do so, and may reach a length of 1 m. Early illustrations of the species in cultivation show heaps of coiled petals lying on the table. It is said that in the wild the petals continue to elongate until they touch a solid surface from which pollinating insects can crawl up and into the flower. The flowers are greenish yellow with darker green veins and a red hairy margin to the petals. This species grows as an epiphyte in Peru, Ecuador and Mexico. In cultivation, *P. caudatum* and *P. schlimii* are grown in a semi-shaded position in a cool-intermediate glasshouse with a winter night minimum temperature of 14°C (57°F) and plenty of ventilation. *Phragmipedium longifolium* is grown under warmer and more humid conditions with a winter night minimum temperature of 18°C (64°F). They are all grown in pots in a medium

grade epiphyte compost to which has been added peat, chopped sphagnum moss and dolomite chippings to give a slightly alkaline medium. Plants of *P. longifolium* planted out in the Princess of Wales Conservatory grow more vigorously than those which are pot grown.

Epiphytes

The epiphytes of Central and South America present an eye-catching, colourful display of flowers throughout the year.

The genus *Cattleya* contains over 60 species, many of which have been used to breed hundreds of hybrids. In order to flower well, cattleyas require a great deal of sunlight. They are grown in pots of medium or coarse compost which allows very good drainage and are repotted before the compost starts to break down. Their flowering season begins in the autumn, when *C. bowringiana* comes into flower. This species has an arching spike of up to 10 flowers each 6 cm across, rosy mauve with darker markings on the lip and a white throat. *Cattleya skinneri* is very similar but flowers in the summer. *Cattleya mossiae*, from Venezuela, flowers in spring and has much larger pale pink flowers with a splash of orange and deep pink veining on the lip. *Cattleya percivaliana* has narrower petals with a deep pink lip. *Cattleya maxima* seems to have rather weak stems which need staking but its intricate pattern of deep pink veins along the lip makes a very attractive flower. *Cattleya warscewiczii* is also pale pink with a darker pink lip but the form 'Frau Melanie Beyroudt' is more interesting with almost white petals and sepals and a deep pink lip. *Cattleya iricolor* from Ecuador is rare, both in cultivation and in the wild. Its petals and sepals are long and narrow and open rather rolled back at the margins so as to appear even narrower. They are a golden colour except for the lip which is cream on the outside and bright gold with red markings inside.

Both the Brazilian and the Mexican laelias are grown with the cattleyas, although the latter would grow well at lower temperatures. They have a similar requirement for bright sunlight, and flower most prolifically if their leaves are illuminated to the extent that they become suffused with purple. The Mexican laelias have a distinct resting period when they need to be kept dry and they seem to grow best in shallow, slatted wooden baskets. A number of species have been tried on cork oak bark and *Laelia rubescens* flowers well in this way. This species is an epiphyte of dry woodland in Mexico, Costa Rica and Panama and is usually found growing at quite high altitudes and in very exposed positions. Its flower spikes form in the autumn and a cluster of up to seven flowers is produced at the end of each one. The flowers range in colour from white through pink and

Rhyncholaelia digbyana var. *fimbripetala*; this large-flowered species grows wild in Central America and is the parent of a large number of frilly-lipped hybrids. RBG, Kew

Laelia anceps, an epiphyte from Mexico, grows easily in cultivation and flowers in December every year. (Illustration from Warner and Williams' *The Orchid Album*, 1888.) RBG, Kew

lavender to mauve. Sadly they seem to last for only a few days under Kew conditions.

Laelia anceps has been found in both cool and warm areas of Mexico and seems to be tolerant of various methods of cultivation. It is easily recognised by its one-leaved, angled pseudobulbs and flower spikes up to 1 m long which are produced early in winter. There are one or several flowers, each about 10 cm across, rosy pink, rich pink inside the velvety lip and with deeper coloured veins and a yellow callus. Many different colour variants have been described, including a number of white forms, sometimes with coloured markings in the lip. *Laelia gouldiana* is rather similar, but the pseudobulbs bear two or three leaves and the flowers are more rounded. This orchid has sometimes been thought to be a natural hybrid between *L. anceps* and *L. autumnalis* but is now regarded as a distinct species. The petals are rosy pink with a darker pink stripe down the centre, while the lip is dark pink with even darker veins and a central yellow spot.

At Kew stanhopeas and gongoras are grown in semi-shaded positions in a glasshouse with a winter night minimum temperature of 16°C (60°F) and high relative humidity. All the species are vigorous growers and seem to benefit from frequent foliar feeds. On

completion of the growth of the new pseudobulb, a short, dry rest is given to the plants but otherwise they like liberal amounts of water. Early attempts to grow stanhopeas were disappointing because, although the plants produced lush foliage, no flowers were seen. Once it was discovered that the plants had flowered, but their flower spikes grew vertically downwards into the compost, success was assured by growing the plants in slatted wooden baskets. The flower spikes can easily push between the slats and the mature flowers hang below the basket. The gongoras seem to thrive best in mesh plastic pots. Their pendent inflorescences arch outwards from the base of the pseudobulbs. A medium grade epiphyte compost is suitable for plants in both genera.

The fat buds of the stanhopeas spring open with an audible popping sound to produce the extraordinary waxy flowers, which have an overpowering fragrance. *Stanhopea ecornuta* has creamy yellow coloured flowers with purple spots and a strong scent of pinewoods in spring. This species, which originates from Costa Rica and Guatemala, has individual flowers up to 9 cm across. *Stanhopea wardii* has cream-coloured flowers with red spots and comes from Mexico. *Stanhopea tigrina* is possibly the most striking species in the genus with cream-coloured flowers in which, again, the cream is nearly obscured by the large red blotches all over the flower. Sadly the *Stanhopea* flowers do not remain fresh for more than about three days, though they are very spectacular while they last.

The gongoras have smaller flowers but there are usually at least a dozen on each stem and they last for several days longer than stanhopeas. *Gongora galeata* is a pale brown colour with a vivid orange lip. This species, which comes from Mexico, has a fragrance of oranges. *Gongora quinquenervis* from Colombia and Ecuador is also scented and has yellow flowers covered in a profusion of red spots.

Stanhopea wardii, a Mexican species whose large waxy flowers only last for a few days. Peter Taylor

Paphinia cristata from Colombia is closely related to the gongoras and stanhopeas and is grown in similar conditions. The flowers are large compared with the size of the plant and last for several weeks. They are purplish brown with yellow stripes and very eye-catching.

Oncidium is one of the largest Central and South American genera containing about 750 species. Some of these are highly specialised in their range and habitat requirements. *Oncidium onustum*, for example, grows as an epiphyte only on certain cacti in the coastal desert of Peru and Ecuador. Others are more widespread and tolerant. At Kew most of the oncidiums are grown under intermediate conditions, with a high humidity and high light levels.

The tiny flowers of *O. parviflorum* are 1 cm across but cluster thickly around a flower spike about 1 m long and make a pretty display. This is a species from the higher altitudes of Panama. *Oncidium cheirophorum* from Colombia and Panama is tiny in every way. Its leaves grow up to 6 cm long and its flower spikes arch out, up to about 20 cm long. The tiny, frilly, yellow flowers have the delightful scent of wintersweet. *Oncidium splendidum* from Mexico, Honduras and Guatemala has thick hard leaves and a tall branching flower spike that carries a striking display of red and yellow flowers. It is short, however, in comparison with *O. cocciferum* from Ecuador, in which the flower spike, even on a small plant, is several metres long and frequently twists around the internal struts in the glasshouse on its way to the roof. Its flowers are rather small and widely spaced and are reddish brown in colour with yellow tips to each sepal and petal.

The most spectacular flower is borne by *Psychopsis papilio*, formerly known as *Oncidium papilio*, and commonly called the butterfly orchid. In this species from Trinidad and western South America the lovely red and yellow lip and sepals are thought to resemble the wings of the butterfly and the narrow petals its antennae. The flower is held aloft on a slender stem and flutters in the air currents. Each flower is about 10 cm across.

One of the very tiniest orchids in the Kew collection, *Psygmorchis pusilla*, is closely related to the genus *Oncidium*. This delightful plant forms a fan of foliage about 4 cm across and up to four flowers grow on each short flower spike. Each flower is 2 cm across and pale yellow with brown spots towards the centre. This species is a twig epiphyte in the humid forests and plantations of Mexico.

The *Odontoglossum* alliance includes the genera *Lemboglossum, Osmoglossum, Rossioglossum, Cuitlauzina,* and *Miltonia* as well as *Odontoglossum,* and others, which have all been hybridised intensively. At Kew the original species are cultivated together with a few

Dichaea neglecta, a small epiphyte from Mexico which is remarkable for its delicate flowers. RBG, Kew

hybrids which enhance the displays in the Princess of Wales Conservatory. The lemboglossums all come from high altitudes in Mexico and Guatemala and at Kew are grown in a cool airy glasshouse with a winter night minimum temperature of 14°C (57°F). They are potted in the smallest containers able to accommodate their roots, using a medium epiphyte compost. *Lemboglossum cervantesii* has white or pale pink flowers about 6 cm across with concentric circles of maroon bars around the column. *Lemboglossum bictoniense* has a broad pink lip with green and red mottled sepals. There are some fine and distinctive colour forms including *L. bictoniense* var. *alba* in which the lip is white and the sepals pale green. The star-shaped flowers of *L. maculatum* have red sepals and white petals spotted with red. *Rossioglossum splendens*, another Mexican species, is variable in colour but in some forms has flowers of a blazing orange colour with a yellow lip marked with red spots.

One of the largest genera, whose species occupy a wide range in the Americas, is *Epidendrum*. It is

Psychopsis papilio (widely known as *Oncidium papilio*) was first sent to Kew from Trinidad early in the nineteenth century and captured the interest of many enthusiasts. (Illustration from *Curtis's Botanical Magazine*, 1828.) RBG, Kew

extremely variable in size and form and contains many species with very attractive flowers. *Epidendrum ilense* was discovered in 1976 in the Montanas de Ila of Ecuador in an area of felled woodland. Four plants were rescued from the area and seeds and seedlings from these were distributed from the Marie Selby Botanic Garden, Florida, in 1980. Some of these were sent to Kew where, in turn, the numbers of plants are being increased so that they can be distributed. Recently this species has been rediscovered in Ecuador but it is considered to be very rare and it is likely that its remaining habitat will be destroyed before the orchid's ecology is fully understood.

Habitat destruction in Central and South America also threatens the future of many of the thousand or so *Epidendrum* species, only a small proportion of which are in cultivation.

The pale green flowers of *E. difforme* are curious as they are rather fleshy and appear to be almost translucent. This species is an epiphyte from Florida and Mexico and grows up to 30 cm tall. *Epidendrum ciliolare* grows as a lithophyte or epiphyte in most of Central America and will form huge clumps if allowed to do so. The flowers are like lime-green stars about 8 cm across and the lip is white with a shaggy fringed margin.

The encyclias were at one time not considered distinct from *Epidendrum* but are now kept apart because of various characteristics of the flower and their pseudobulbous habit. *Encyclia fragrans* and *E. cochleata* were among the first epiphytic orchids to flower at Kew, in 1782 and 1787 respectively. The most striking feature of *E. fragrans* is its powerful scent which is very strong from a distance of several metres. Its flowers are whitish green except for the lip on the upperside of the flower which is violet striped. The somewhat similar *E. pentotes* has probably the strongest, sickly sweet smell of any orchid at Kew.

Encyclia cochleata, known as the cockleshell orchid, is widespread from Florida, through Mexico and Central America to Brazil. Its sepals and petals are pale green, slender and reflexed, while the shiny, dark maroon lip stands over the column like a hood. This species grows well in a warm intermediate glasshouse with a winter night minimum temperature of 16°C (61°F) where it rarely stops flowering. *Encyclia citrina*, from Mexico, is grown in the *Cattleya* house, with a minimum night temperature of 16°C (61°F), and is kept very dry during the winter months. It is grown on cork oak bark and is quite distinctive with its pendent, grey-green pseudobulbs and foliage. The buttercup yellow flowers have the fragrance of lemons and appear in spring.

The subtribe Pleurothallidinae is probably the largest single alliance in the American continent. *Restrepia*,

Masdevallia auropurpurea grows and flowers prolifically in damp, mossy, forest habitats in Colombia and western Venezuela.
G C K Dunsterville

Pleurothallis, Scaphosepalum, Masdevallia, Dracula, Stelis and others are included in the Kew collection. The two genera of most horticultural merit are probably *Masdevallia* and *Dracula*. Both are grown in a glasshouse with a winter night minimum temperature of 14°C (57°F) and both benefit from liberal watering. The draculas are grown in hanging baskets of fine epiphyte compost and hung above head height so that their pendulous flowers can be appreciated. They have three large sepals which form a triangle and a pouch-like lip which wobbles in the air currents in a fascinating manner. *Dracula chimaera* has white sepals which are heavily blotched with red and a white lip. The sepals are dotted with short white hairs. This species originated in Colombia, as did *D. bella* which has yellow sepals with deep red spots and long trailing tails at the tip of each sepal. The inflated lip is white. The inflorescences of this species emerge from the base of the plant and hang down below the plant in the sunlight.

Although most of the masdevallias are epiphytes they seem to grow best when grown in pots just large enough to accommodate their roots in a fine epiphyte compost. They form neat tufts of attractive green foliage and have one or more colourful flowers on each inflorescence. The petals and lip of each flower are very tiny but the sepals are greatly enlarged and the tips of each are frequently decorated with a slender pointed tail.

In a brief survey, it is impossible to mention more than a few of these increasingly popular orchids. The scarlet *Masdevallia veitchiana* is probably the best known, and the various colour forms of *M. coccinea*, white, yellow and magenta, are also commonly cultivated. *Masdevallia angulata* from Ecuador is a vigorous grower and has rather tubular flowers which are olive-green with deep red blotches. *Masdevallia barlaeana* from Peru is a vivid magenta colour and flowers over a long period. *Masdevallia macrura* from Colombia has extraordinary orange flowers with red spots and long twisty yellow tails. It is one of the longest *Masdevallia* flowers and can measure up to 30 cm from the tip of the tail of the dorsal sepal to the tip of the tail on one of the lateral sepals.

Several of the North American species of *Cypripedium* are grown amongst the other terrestrial species in a cold glasshouse and also in cold frames in the nursery. The stately *Cypripedium reginae* forms splendid clumps of stems with attractive pink and white flowers. It contrasts with the smaller and slender *C. acaule*, which has a large pink lip but smaller, brownish sepals and petals. There are also several different forms of *Cypripedium calceolus* which have a bright yellow lip and yellow, green or brownish sepals and petals.

Cypripedium acaule is widespread in North America, where it forms large populations on the woodland floor in many areas.
Phillip Cribb

9 Propagation from Seed

THE LIVING ORCHID COLLECTION at Kew is augmented every year by seedlings raised in the Micropropagation Laboratory. The seeds from which the plants are grown come from a variety of sources, including from plants grown at Kew which are pollinated by hand as required. Many species which are rare or approaching extinction in the wild are increased in this way, as are particularly decorative plants for use in displays. Seeds are also obtained from plants used in breeding experiments, both species and new crosses. They are also used simply to increase the number of plants of species which are hard to grow or represented by only one specimen in the collection.

Kew also receives donations of seeds from many sources. Botanists on expeditions are encouraged to collect seeds rather than plants, thus causing less damage to wild populations. Private growers who have rare plants in their collections are often prepared to provide seeds from plants which cannot be divided, while commercial orchid growers sometimes share a crop of seeds. Other botanic gardens in many parts of the world, and organisations like the Australian Orchid Foundation, also exchange seed with Kew. From all these sources, new species are added to the orchid collection every year as young seedlings, the stage at which they are most adaptable to glasshouse culture.

Sending seeds rather than plants around the world has many advantages. They are extremely light and several thousands can be packed in a small envelope. CITES controls apply to seeds of orchids listed in Appendix I (see chapter 16), while European Community Regulations affect the movement of seeds of most European orchid species; seeds of all other orchids are exempt from CITES control. When they are received at Kew, seeds can be stored in a domestic refrigerator for short periods but should be sown as soon as possible.

The Micropropagation Unit

It is now some 30 years since Peter Thompson started working in the Jodrell Laboratory on a new formulation for a medium for the germination of orchid seeds. In the course of this work he succeeded in germinating seeds and raising seedlings of a wide range of genera. His book *Orchids from Seed* is still widely used as an introductory guide to micropropagation. In 1974 a Micropropagation Unit was set up at Kew to make *in vitro* propagation techniques available to the gardens for a wide range of plants including orchids.

The Micropropagation Unit occupies the whole of the ground floor of Aiton House, situated in the Lower Nursery area of the Gardens. The main laboratory has offices, preparation, autoclave and store rooms adjacent to it. There are separate rooms where the laminar flow cabinets are kept at which all sterile techniques are carried out. Next to these are the air-conditioned growth rooms with racks of illuminated shelves where the young plants are grown *in vitro*. Growth cabinets where light and temperatures can be carefully regulated for small batches of flasks are also available. The unit has its own range of glasshouses where all the transfers of young plants to compost are made and the seedlings can be weaned under very humid conditions.

Seed Collection and Storage

Seeds of most orchids take a long time to mature and it is not unusual for many months or even a year to pass, after pollination of the flower, before the capsule is ready. As the green capsules ripen they often change

Packets of seeds and fruits of orchids arrive at Kew from many different sources. Robert Mitchell

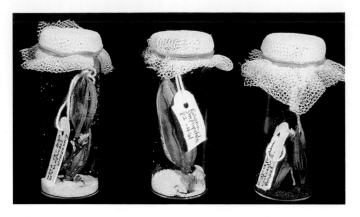

Orchid fruits are allowed to ripen and dry in closed containers before the seeds are collected and stored. Hugh Pritchard

Nutrient Solutions

Orchid seedlings have been grown on many different substrates but best results are obtained where the correct balance of nutrients is present. This varies from species to species, but all the media used contain a carbohydrate source, a range of mineral salts and agar, which solidifies the medium. In addition, many media contain other additives including vitamins, amino acids or plant extracts such as banana pulp or potato extract. Some of the standard media are now available as powdered mixes, which simplifies their preparation. After mixing, the media must be sterilised, normally in an autoclave, to prevent the growth of contaminants.

The minute orchid seeds lack food reserves for their early growth and this is provided by the carbohydrate. Ordinary sugar, or laboratory refined sucrose, is normally used. The young seedlings will only grow satisfactorily if they are provided with a complete and balanced mineral solution as well. The different elements are necessary in various amounts with much higher concentrations of nitrogen, potassium, phosphorus, calcium, magnesium and sulphur, rather less of iron and minute quantities of manganese, copper, zinc, boron and molybdenum. Where prepared mixes are not available, media are made up from the pure chemicals. Where only very small concentrations are used, stock solutions prove to be the most convenient method. Peter Thompson's book, *Orchids from Seed* (see Further Reading) gives full details for the preparation of the medium he developed and other nutrient solutions, some of which are still used routinely at Kew.

colour, becoming yellow or brownish. Narrow slits appear along the sides, or along the ventral surface during the ripening process, and the seeds are usually released gradually over a period which can range from several days to weeks or months. It is therefore important to watch capsules ripening in the glasshouse and harvest them before they split. Each capsule is cut off and stored separately in a small labelled jar until all the seeds can be tapped out in the laboratory. In all cases capsules which have not yet dehisced are preferred and the technique for using them is described later in this chapter.

An important feature of the arrival of new seeds for sowing is the opportunity to record information about them. As much as possible is recorded, from the donor's name to provenance data, while recording the date received and state of the seeds on receipt may prove important later. Accurate identification is of paramount importance. Where possible, seeds from the wild are accompanied by herbarium voucher specimens. Seeds obtained from the glasshouses are backed up by the information already on record for the parent plants. Seeds may be loose and dry or may arrive in the fruit or capsule, sometimes split and sometimes still intact. The latter is always preferable.

Loose seeds from the wild or glasshouse have often been collected under warm, moist conditions and thus may be contaminated by bacteria, fungi or algae. It is therefore important to dry the seeds or capsules as soon as possible after harvest. They are placed in glass vials closed with tissue paper in a desiccator at room temperature and then sown as soon as possible. This method seems to be quite adequate for periods up to three months. For longer term storage the seeds are separated from any debris of the capsule and, after drying, are kept in cold store at 4°C. The reason for the drying period is not only to impede the germination and growth of any fungal spores which may be present on the seed surface, but also to enhance seed longevity.

Sterilising

Orchid seeds are very small. Unlike the nutrient solutions, they cannot be sterilised by heating, because

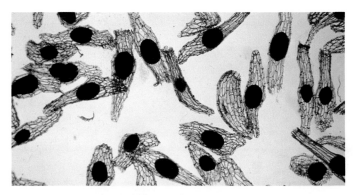

Orchid seeds are tiny, like specks of dust; each seed has a minute, ovoid embryo inside the net-like coat (magnification × 250). Hugh Pritchard

this would kill them, so a chemical method is usually used instead. Sodium hypochlorite, the active ingredient of most domestic bleach, makes a good sterilant. Alternatively, water can be added to fresh calcium hypochlorite which is then filtered after five minutes. A strong solution containing chlorine is thus obtained, which must be used with care.

Small quantities of seeds are sterilised in filter paper packets so that none is lost. A small filter paper is folded twice and stapled shut with the seeds inside. The packets are immersed in the chlorine solution together with a wetting agent for 10 minutes, and then rinsed in sterile water. The seeds can then be transferred to the medium on the opened paper or pressed on the surface of the medium from the paper.

Seeds from young or intact capsules need not be sterilised. In this case only the outside of the capsule is treated. It is then opened in the sterile conditions of the air-flow bench and the seeds, which are naturally sterile, removed and sown. Better results are obtained in this way for many species, and especially in the genera *Cypripedium* and *Paphiopedilum*. A growing volume of evidence suggests that these species germinate better when the seeds are immature, harvested about 50 days after pollination for *Cypripedium* and 120 days for *Paphiopedilum*.

Sowing

The sowing of seeds has become much more reliable since the advent of the laminar flow bench. This is a sterile environment where the air is filtered free of contaminants and the worker can open sterile containers and manipulate sterile seeds without risk of reinfection.

Various culture vessels have been tried at Kew, including test tubes, Petri dishes, conical flasks, Kilner jars and honey jars. For sowing, pre-sterilised Petri dishes are often used because their flat shape means they can be examined easily under the dissecting microscope. Their disadvantage is that the medium they contain dries out more quickly than in a larger container. When germination has begun, the protocorms are replated to a larger container for further growth. Small honey jars with plastic caps are frequently used at this stage.

At Kew, the culture conditions which seem to be suitable for a wide range of species are a 16-hour photoperiod and a temperature range of 22–25°C. Light appears to be useful for the germination of epiphytic species. Terrestrial species are often germinated in the dark, by keeping the cultures in dark polythene bags, and only moved into light conditions once a green shoot has appeared.

Seedlings of *Orchis laxiflora* raised in the laboratory and almost ready for transfer to the greenhouse. RBG, Kew

The dishes and jars are examined regularly and any which become infected with bacteria or fungi are removed. Sometimes very precious seeds of a contaminated culture can be saved by opening the vessel and moving the seeds to a fresh medium, but this can only be done successfully during the very early stages of infection. The contents of vessels must also be watched for drying out. If the agar shrinks away from the sides, the seedlings must be transferred to fresh medium in a new vessel.

After a few months the developing seedlings become crowded inside the vessels and grow less well as a result. It is important to move them on before growth begins to slow down, either to a fresh medium in another vessel, or into compost in the glasshouse. In either case, the gentle separation of the entangled seedlings is a task requiring much time and patience to ensure they are not damaged.

Weaning

Large, well-grown seedlings are removed from their flasks in the laboratory and established in the glasshouse environment. This process is known as weaning, and every precaution is taken to ensure that the seedlings suffer as little stress as possible.

The glasshouse used for weaning seedlings is maintained at a minimum temperature of 18°C (64°F) at night and 23°C (73°F) during the day. Heavy shading is used to prevent the temperature rising above 28°C (82°F) even during the summer. An overhead humidifier fills the air with water vapour and, because it is large in relation to the size of the glasshouse, provides strong air movement.

Deflasking is carried out from February until May. Seedlings then come into an environment when the days are lengthening and they have a full growing

season ahead of them in which to become established.
The largest seedlings are selected from each group in
the laboratory growth room. It is essential that the
seedlings are large enough to grow new roots from their
existing reserves in case of damage during deflasking.
The smaller seedlings can be kept in the laboratory to
provide a useful back-up should the first batch fail,
although this is a very rare occurrence.

The flasks of seedlings selected for establishment
stand out on the staging in the glasshouse and begin to
acclimatise while they await attention. Each seedling is
lifted carefully from its agar substrate and put straight
into lukewarm water containing a dilute fungicide
solution. Any remaining agar is gently rinsed away and
the fungicide prevents any fungal growth in the traces
which may adhere too closely to be removed
completely. The seedlings are dried and potted singly
in 5–6 cm square plastic pots.

Two different seedling composts are used. For
epiphytes the mixture is: 5 parts fine orchid bark, 1 part
perlite and 1 part fine charcoal. For the tropical
terrestrial species the compost consists of: 3 parts grit, 1
part loam and 1 part fine bark.

Terrestrials and epiphytes are arranged separately on
the staging as they need different kinds of
management. After watering-in, the terrestrials require
rather little additional water until they are well
established and growing rapidly. The epiphytes are
also watered-in and then misted-over thoroughly
several times each day for the first few weeks after
deflasking. This is necessary to prevent desiccation for
the leaf cuticle of the seedlings is poorly developed
while they remain in the flasks. The pots are watered
frequently, too, just before the compost dries out. As
the seedlings root more strongly, the misting becomes
lighter and less frequent, until, by the late autumn,

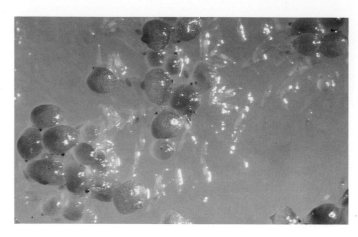

Many protocorms of *Cattleya dowiana* developed successfully
from a tiny pinch of seeds. Blaise DuPuy

misting once a day in the early morning is sufficient.
Seedlings are fed each week with a dilute balanced
fertiliser.

Most of the seedlings remain in the seedling house
for about a year. However, some epiphytes from high
altitudes require a cool, dry winter, and these are
moved in the autumn so that they can experience
conditions similar to those of their natural habitat at an
early stage. All the rest of the orchid seedlings are
moved to the main orchid collection at the end of the
winter. Then the seedling house soon fills up with the
new season's young plants.

Some Successes

The species *Cattleya dowiana* is rare in cultivation
because it requires more humid conditions than many
other cattleyas, and because plants imported from the
wild have been difficult to establish. It has become
rather rare in the wild because its habitat, along cliff
edges in humid forests at medium altitudes, always
where there is high humidity and plenty of air
movement, has become greatly reduced by
development and because plants in accessible places
have been collected for sale. On a short visit to Costa
Rica in 1986, Joyce Stewart was given a small packet of
seeds by Clarence Horich, a resident of Costa Rica who
has sent many specimens to Kew.

The seeds were sterilised and sown on standard
Vacin and Went medium. They germinated without
difficulty and many bright green protocorms developed
very quickly. Seedlings were transferred to fresh
medium to which homogenised banana was added.
They grew rapidly and 12 months after germination
husky young plants were potted into a compost of fine
bark, charcoal and vermiculite. Some are now growing
strongly at Kew and several hundred others have been

Cattleya dowiana, a species which is greatly reduced in Costa
Rica because of loss of habitat and over-collection; wild
collected plants have always been difficult to grow in
cultivation. Joyce Stewart

distributed to other botanic gardens and experienced individuals.

One capsule of the rare species *Dendrobium spectatissimum* was collected in Sabah, Borneo, by Phillip Cribb and Christopher Bailes in 1983. The seeds germinated successfully on Vacin and Went medium and the seedlings grew very quickly. They were transferred to a modified medium as soon as they were big enough to handle and after a further 16 weeks were sufficiently large to be potted in a fine bark, perlite and charcoal mix.

As soon as they were large enough to travel, the first seedlings were returned to the National Park Authorities in Sabah. This work has been repeated with some of the additional seeds and more seedlings have been produced with equal ease. They have been distributed to botanic gardens and other collections as well as incorporated into the collection at Kew.

The beautiful species *Peristeria elata*, sometimes known as the dove orchid, or holy ghost orchid, is the national flower of Panama. Seeds donated to Kew by David Jones in 1983 germinated on a range of media.

After nearly two years in culture, the seedlings were large enough to be potted up and many were subsequently distributed to botanic gardens and scientific institutions around the world. Growers in Britain with facilities for growing this tall terrestrial species were also offered plants.

Epidendrum ilense from Ecuador was known from only six plants in the wild when it was propagated at the Marie Selby Botanic Gardens, Sarasota, Florida, and a small plant given to Kew. The area the species came from was completely deforested and for a few years it was thought to be extinct in the wild. Recently, another small population has been discovered, but even in that area the future of this unusual species is also precarious.

Seeds were collected from the Kew plant in 1986 and 1987. They germinated on several different media. The small seedlings were transferred to half strength Murashige and Skoog medium, supplemented with banana pulp or activated charcoal. They grew well on both these media and plants have since been widely distributed.

Epidendrum ilense, an epiphyte which has been successfully propagated and distributed in cultivation although its habitat in Ecuador has now become farmland. John Gregory

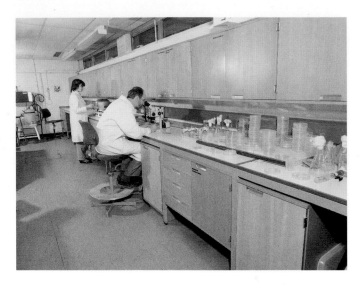

Many orchids have been raised from seeds in the Micropropagation Unit at Kew; Dickon Bowling examines embryo viability before sowing. RBG, Kew

Seeds of *Clowesia rosea*, an endangered and very beautiful orchid, were sent to Kew by Ed Greenwood who lives in Oaxaca and who has been supplying Kew with orchid seeds from Mexico for the last 15 years. This *Clowesia* grew best on Vacin and Went and on half strength Murashige and Skoog medium when these were supplemented with activated charcoal.

Strong plants are now thriving in the glasshouses at Kew and have been distributed to other gardens and growers. Other successes with Mexican orchids include several attractive species of *Encyclia*.

The 'lost' species *Cymbidium rectum* was rediscovered by the botanist Tony Lamb in Sabah. It differs from *C. bicolor* in having an upright raceme, an unusual characteristic in this section of the genus. The habitat where a few plants were rediscovered has since been clear-felled and it is likely that the species is extinct in the area now. Seeds were sown in 1983. The resulting seedlings grew most vigorously on Vacin and Went or half strength Murashige and Skoog medium with activated charcoal. Like the other species discussed above, this *Cymbidium* has now been distributed to many institutions and growers.

Gynoglottis cymbidioides is the only species in this curious genus. It occurs in Sumatra at about 1550 m

altitude and it was unknown in cultivation until seed capsules were collected by Jim Comber in 1988.

The species resembles *Coelogyne* in habit, but has rather small white flowers of distinct structure in a long, many-flowered raceme. The seed capsules were undehisced on arrival at Kew and seeds germinated within two weeks of being sown. Surplus capsules were sent to Richard Warren in Edinburgh who raises a wide range of tropical orchids from seeds for sale.

Seedlings are now growing well *in vitro* and have been distributed in flasks to other institutions with facilities for growing-on plants under *in vitro* conditions.

These success stories are only a sample of the routine work of orchid propagation carried out by Dickon Bowling in the Micropropagation Unit under the supervision of Dr Michael Fay. Though primarily a service to the living collections at Kew, the work is increasingly involved with conservation, either by the return of propagated plants to their place of origin, or by the distribution of surplus seedlings to growers in other botanic gardens and elsewhere. It is likely that this work will become increasingly important as the wild orchids throughout the world continue to disappear and as national and international legislation controls the movement of wild-collected plants.

Seedlings which are surplus to Kew's needs are despatched to other growers, including many botanic gardens. Robert Mitchell

Orchid Taxonomy, the Herbarium and Library

By Phillip Cribb and Joyce Stewart

THE CLASSIFICATION AND NAMING of plants has been a function of Kew for 150 years. It began with the appointment of Sir William Jackson Hooker as the first official Director. Today, there are many other botanical establishments whose staff are engaged in similar work, but Kew still plays a major international role, especially with regard to orchids.

The accurate description, illustration, classification and naming of plants is a continuing task which is facilitated by the wealth of reference material in the Herbarium and Library. The collections of specimens are constantly added to from the live plants in the gardens, from others collected on expeditions and from specimens sent in for naming by the public. Similarly, books, journals and illustrations are continuously enriched by purchase and exchange as well as by donations and bequests.

Together these provide an incomparable resource for the continuation of taxonomic work on the Orchidaceae at Kew.

PL. 51

Aeranthes grandiflora, a beautiful epiphyte from forests on the eastern slopes of Madagascar; this plate is one of the illustrations from *The Orchid Album* by Warner and Williams (1897). RBG, Kew

Overleaf: *Aerangis luteoalba* var. *rhodosticta*. Bob Campbell

10 Taxonomy

DESPITE THE POPULARITY OF ORCHIDS in horticulture they remain to this day one of the families of flowering plants least studied by botanists. The reasons for this paradoxical situation are several, but a few of them are highlighted here.

First of all, orchids are usually considered to be the largest family of flowering plants with between 15,000 and 30,000 species, according to which authority you choose to believe. Indeed, the inexact estimates of the number of species of orchids are a reflection of our inadequate knowledge, and many scientists have tended to steer clear of orchids for this reason alone, for there are other groups of plants that are more manageable. It can take several years before a botanist can even begin to find his way comfortably around the approximately 900 or so orchid genera, let alone the tens of thousands of species!

A second reason is that the majority of orchids are tropical or subtropical. The lands where they abound were often opened up to the prying eyes of European botanists during the 19th and early 20th centuries. The first significant collections from Colombia, which probably has more orchids than anywhere else, were made by Humboldt and Bonpland in the early 19th century. Borneo, with probably in excess of 2,000 species, was only visited on its fringes by collectors such as Hugh Low and James Motley in the last century, while the first significant collections of orchids from New Guinea were those of Rudolf Schlechter between 1902 and 1909. New Guinea alone has an estimated 2,000 to 2,500 orchid species!

During the last twenty years of the 19th century, botanists such as H G Reichenbach, Fritz Kraenzlin and Robert Rolfe were describing new orchids at the astounding rate of hundreds a year. A cursory glance over the literature of the past decade suggests that the rate still exceeds 100 a year (440 species in 1980). Some of these recent discoveries, such as the Bornean scorpion orchid, *Arachnis longisepala*, *Renanthera bella*, the Chinese slipper orchids *Paphiopedilum armeniacum* and *P. malipoense*, and the scarlet Andean slipper orchid, *Phragmipedium besseae*, are spectacular, brightly coloured species which could not have been previously overlooked. It seems likely that new species will continue to be discovered even though the tropical forests are destroyed by man at an ever-increasing rate by logging companies, mining activities, agricultural 'development' and dam-building.

British plants have been studied in depth by generations of botanists since the days of John Ray and yet, every year since the last war, at least one species new to the British Isles has been discovered. In 1989 it was *Serapias parviflora*, a small-flowered species of a genus not previously recorded further north than Brittany, and thus both a new species and a new genus for Britain. The tropics have a long way to go before they receive such close attention. The orchid flora of Borneo can boast almost twice the number of species of all the flowering plants found in the entire British Isles (about 1,500). Perhaps it is not surprising that most botanists have avoided orchids!

The German botanist H G Reichenbach described many new species of orchids at the end of the last century. RBG, Kew

77

Paphiopedilum malipoense, which has scented flowers, is a recent discovery from south-west China. Phillip Cribb

Thus it is both the size of the family Orchidaceae and its extensive tropical component that have been the major factors which have deterred botanists. Plants that are useful to man, such as potatoes, beans and grains, are usually well studied. The orchids are said by some to be largely devoid of useful species, except for the genus *Vanilla*, which produces the essence so widely used as a flavouring. This statement, however, ignores the vast trade in cut-flowers and pot plants, which is nowadays worldwide and benefits countries as diverse as Thailand, Australia and the United States of America to the tune of millions of US dollars per year. Even setting aside the aesthetic and financial appeal of orchids, the enterprising Chinese have used orchids for centuries in materia medica. Over one hundred species are considered by them to have active ingredients useful in curing a wide range of human disorders. It would be foolish, therefore, to ignore the potential utility of a family that comprises over 10% of the flowering plants of the world.

In one sense, however, the aesthetic appeal of orchids has also deterred botanists from studying them. The interest of horticulturists over the past 150 or so years has generated a vast literature on the family. Furthermore, the increasing search for novelty quickly led gardeners to start hybridising orchids, the first artificial hybrid flowering in London in 1857. As Lindley remarked at the time, 'What with heteranthism, dimorphism, pelorism and [now] hybridism our favourite orchids may be found to assume as many disguises as an actor.' Modern hybrids are often quite unlike their ancestral species, but the 100,000 or so registered hybrid grexes, added to the 25,000 or more species, has resulted in a body of literature that is not only amazing in size but also hard to find, in obscure or unobtainable publications. For instance, James Bateman's illustrated work *The Orchidaceae of Mexico and Guatemala*, 1837–43, had an initial print run of 500, and copies now sell for thousands of pounds when they make rare appearances in sales rooms.

Notwithstanding its size and complexity, the orchid family has attracted a number of the finest taxonomic botanists of their day, and sadly also some of the worst! In the orchids they have ample scope for the classification, identification and naming of plants, but, nevertheless, face a daunting task to make sense of a myriad of form and function.

The study of orchids in the field or in a glasshouse can give the taxonomist only an incomplete picture of the diversity of form he hopes to understand. Like most living organisms, from man to the smallest insect, orchid species are variable with no two plants looking quite alike. The degree of variability is usually slight, especially between plants growing in the same population or in neighbouring ones. However, many

Paintings by Miss Drake, reproduced from Bateman's *Orchidaceae of Mexico and Guatemala*; these species are known now as *Artorima erubescens* (above) and *Rhyncholaelia glauca* (below). RBG, Kew

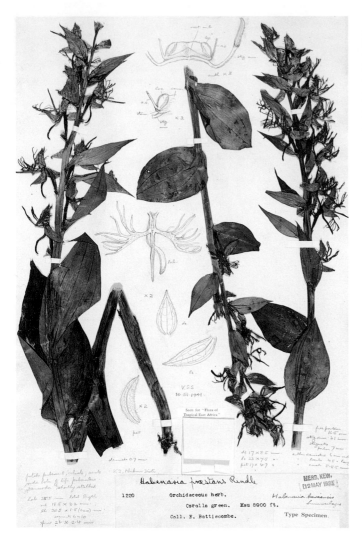

Habenaria keniensis: pressed specimens and the drawings made from one of the flowers by Victor Summerhayes when he first described this Kenyan species. RBG, Kew

plants and their variation, a method that has enabled him to make a permanent record of the plants he is studying. This is the herbarium, a collection of plants that have been pressed flat, stuck on sheets of paper, labelled with their name provenance and other information and arranged in order, rather like the cards in a card index box. The system used to arrange the plants in a herbarium is one that enables a particular plant or species to be easily and quickly found.

The Herbarium at the Royal Botanic Gardens is probably the largest of its kind in the world. It contains in excess of six million specimens arranged, not alphabetically, but following the well-known system of flowering plant classification devised by the gifted botanist George Bentham and Sir Joseph Hooker and subsequently much modified. It is probably the most comprehensive collection of its kind, covering the plants of all parts of the world. The main Herbarium was based on the private collections of Sir William Hooker and George Bentham. Their collections, together with the orchid herbarium of Professor John Lindley (see below), also formed the basis of the present collection of preserved orchids at Kew, thus making it probably the richest in the world. Since 1969 this has been housed in its own room, overlooking the Thames, in the new wing of the Herbarium directly below Kew's incomparable library.

Since the acquisition of Lindley's herbarium, the Orchid Herbarium has continued to grow and now contains more than 250,000 dried specimens. These are housed in fireproof metal cabinets in tiers, four high and 10 broad, in a room with additional space for working benches and the library of orchid books and other publications. Herbarium specimens, if well curated and kept in an insect-free and stable environment, are more or less permanent. The oldest orchid specimens at Kew are over 200 years old, while specimens almost twice as old can be found in the Natural History Museum in London.

Herbarium specimens are often criticised by those unfamiliar with working with them as being of little use and incapable of providing information about plants and flowers that were three-dimensional in their living state. While there is some truth in this, in the sense that the flattened flowers are difficult to interpret, it is possible for an experienced botanist to reconstruct the three-dimensional form of a pressed flower with little difficulty. The simple expedient of boiling a flower will often be sufficient to resurrect the original form. Failing that, fleshy flowers respond remarkably to a concentrated solution of ammonia which swells their fleshy structures to their original proportions. Neither method recreates the original coloration of the flowers, but this is usually recorded on the data label attached to the bottom right-hand corner of the sheet.

orchids are very widespread, for example, the epiphytic orchids *Bulbophyllum longiflorum* and *Liparis caespitosa* range from tropical Africa to the Pacific islands. To examine them in the living state in all parts of their ranges is scarcely feasible. Even if the plants were transported to a glasshouse, the scientist could only ever examine a small fraction of the species. A complicating factor is that the survival of plants in cultivation is often a matter of luck. At Kew, we have a few plants that have been in cultivation for nearly one hundred years, but the average life expectancy in most collections is probably ten years or less.

The Herbarium

The taxonomic botanist has therefore been forced to resort to a different method to enable him to study

As has already been mentioned, the collection of dried plants in the Orchid Herbarium allows a botanist to study a range of specimens of any particular species. This enables him to build up a description of an orchid species, to assess the variation within that species, its distributional and altitudinal range, habitat and the associated vegetation. From such information floristic accounts, monographs of particular genera and other taxonomic accounts can be compiled.

All scientific research depends on the repeatability of the results. The Herbarium allows for the repetition of taxonomic research by preserving the specimens which form the basis of any particular project.

Taxonomy is also concerned with the identification and naming of plants. The Herbarium has a very specific role in these activities. Identification of plants in the Herbarium is usually by direct comparison of the unknown material, whether living or preserved, with named herbarium specimens. A knowledge of the herbarium system usually enables an unnamed plant to be identified and named within minutes.

One might well ask, 'How do we know if the herbarium specimens are correctly named in the first place?' The answer lies in the type system. When a botanist describes and names a specimen new to science, he must do so in accordance with the International Code of Botanical Nomenclature, a quasi-legal document which lays down rules and recommendations for naming plants. This states that the botanist, when describing a species new to science, must cite a herbarium specimen as the type of the new name and record where it is kept. This will usually be the specimen from which he has drawn his original description. The new name will relate to the type specimen and anyone wishing to check the correct assignment of that name can do so by looking at the type.

It not infrequently happens that a species can acquire more than one name during the course of time. For example, the south-east Asian slipper orchid, *Paphiopedilum appletonianum*, was given that epithet by Gower in 1893 but was also described in 1895 as *P. wolterianum* by the German botanist Fritz Kraenzlin, who thought it was distinct. The International Code of Botanical Nomenclature states that the first name given to any species is the correct one, while the later names should be considered synonyms. Reference has to be made to the type specimens to check that these names were indeed applied to the same species.

Needless to say, the Kew Orchid Herbarium has the most extensive collection of orchid type specimens. In truth, it had a head start on other herbaria through the prescient acquisition of Lindley's orchid herbarium by Sir William Hooker in 1865.

The Lindley Herbarium

John Lindley (1799–1865) was a remarkable man. He was the first Professor of Botany at the University of London and might easily have been the first Director of Kew if he had been as astute politically as William Hooker. Perhaps as important, however, were his efforts in establishing Kew through the work of a Commission he led which reported to the Government in 1840 that Kew Gardens should be saved for the nation and become a centre for research into plants and plant products.

Lindley had hoped that he might become the first Director of Kew, but when Hooker was appointed he remained at his post at London University. Lindley's early career as Assistant Secretary and later Secretary to the Royal Horticultural Society (from 1822 onwards) had brought him into contact with tropical orchids at an early age and at a time when the rich orchid flora of the tropics had scarcely been guessed at. Those orchids that had appeared in Europe were considered to be parasites and almost impossible to grow. A few had

This specimen of *Anguloa uniflora* shows how a dried flower which has been treated with ammonia solution regains its original shape, but not its colour. RBG, Kew

flowered at Kew and elsewhere but most had perished soon afterwards.

The rapidly expanding British Empire, and the wealth it and the rise of industry created, gave the landed gentry access to the plants of the tropics and the money and time to try to grow them. From the 1820s onwards, tropical orchids began to flood into Britain, mostly to perish in the steamy pit greenhouses of the day. Through his energy and enthusiasm, Lindley rapidly established himself as the leading orchid expert of his day. His advice was sought on both taxonomic and horticultural matters. He published extensively on the family and his *Genera and Species of Orchidaceous Plants* (1830–40) is usually taken as the starting point of modern orchid classification. The outlines of Lindley's classification of the family can clearly be seen in the most up-to-date classifications of the present day.

By the time of his death in 1865, Lindley had described several thousand new orchid species and established dozens of new genera. These appeared in the *Botanical Register*, of which he was editor for over

20 years, the *Gardeners' Chronicle*, *Paxton's Flower Garden*, *Folia Orchidacea* (1862–9), and such beautifully illustrated works as his and Bauer's *Illustrations of Orchidaceous Plants* (1830–8) and *Sertum Orchidaceum* (1838). Lindley received his specimens from all over the world, from collectors such as William Lobb in Java, Nathaniel Wallich in India, and William Gardner in Brazil; from orchid growers and nurseries such as Messrs Loddiges of Clapton, William Cattley of Barnet and Mrs Harrison of Liverpool; and by exchange with other botanists such as Hooker and Reichenbach.

In 1864 Sir William Hooker wrote of John Lindley's orchid herbarium: 'It is unique, its value can never diminish for it is a standard of reference, it can neither be imitated nor replaced. It must instantly be consulted as long as orchids are cultivated and Botany is a science.' The collection contained upwards of 3,000 specimens, many of them illustrated by Lindley's

John Lindley, Professor of Botany at the University of London and Secretary of the Royal Horticultural Society, whose orchid herbarium is treasured at Kew. RBG, Kew

Dactylorhiza foliosa, coloured drawing by Miss Drake for Lindley's *Sertum Orchidaceum*. RBG, Kew

Bollea violacea (first known as a *Huntleya*): the type specimen of a species first described by Lindley, with accompanying illustrations. RBG, Kew

Esmeralda cathcartii, a plate made by W H Fitch for J D Hooker's *Illustrations of Himalayan Plants* (1855) from the original drawings by J D Cathcart. RBG, Kew

dissections and drawings, and most of which are types of the many new species that he described. This treasure-house was purchased for Kew, on Hooker's advice, from Lindley's widow in 1865 for £500. The remainder of Lindley's herbarium went to the University of Cambridge and his library to the Royal Horticultural Society in London. Lindley is now remembered as the 'Father of Orchidology' but it should not be forgotten that he was interested in a far wider range of plants and published standard texts on many subjects ranging from agriculture to roses.

The Hooker and Bentham Collections

Sir William Hooker, who also died in 1865 after serving for nearly 25 years as Kew's first Director, had a long-standing interest in tropical orchids. Some were grown at his home in Suffolk before he took up the Professorship of Botany at the University of Glasgow in 1820. While in Glasgow he described several species in his *Exotic Botany* and others in *Curtis's Botanical Magazine*. After his arrival at Kew he greatly encouraged the Curator, John Smith, to enlarge the living orchid collection. He was succeeded as Director at Kew by his son, Joseph Dalton Hooker (1817–1911), who had served as Assistant Director since 1855.

Joseph Hooker was already an established botanist of broad interests and immense ability. He was a friend and inspiration to Charles Darwin. His travels in the Sikkim Himalaya had provided him with first-hand experience of tropical orchids and an interest that culminated in his seminal account of Indian and Burmese orchids in his *Flora of British India* (1891). Both father and son built up herbarium collections which are now at Kew.

Lindley's herbarium was soon put to good use by George Bentham, who, in association with Sir Joseph (he was knighted in 1877), published the first detailed classification of the family down to generic level in their *Genera Plantarum: Orchideae* (1883). Bentham's own herbarium and that of Sir William Hooker contained many orchid specimens sent, for example, from India by Wallich, Joseph Hooker and Thomas Thompson; from Australia by Robert Brown and Alan Cunningham; and from Africa by Livingstone and Kirk. Added to Lindley's collection, these formed a unique collection for Bentham and later botanists to study.

The Spirit Collection

At Kew, there is an additional aid to the understanding and interpretation of orchid flowers. This is the extensive collection of flowers preserved in a spirit preservative in glass bottles. The collection approaches 60,000 items, of which nearly half are orchids. Robert Rolfe, Kew's first orchid taxonomist, preserved many flowers in spirit, but his collection did not survive his death in 1924. The present collection was founded by his successor, Victor Summerhayes, in 1930 and is currently housed in a ground floor room directly below the Orchid Herbarium and linked to it by a dumb-waiter lift. The card index records for the spirit collection have been computerised and are accessible on terminals placed throughout the Herbarium. The collection is used extensively by botanists both at Kew and elsewhere.

Naming Orchids

As well as carrying out research, describing and illustrating new species, and writing floras and monographs, the staff of the Orchid Herbarium provide an important service by naming a wide variety and considerable numbers of specimens, living and dead, which are submitted for identification.

Every day, as they come into flower, a few plants are brought in from the Living Collection. Some of these are already named, but it is important to check that the names attached to them when they were accessioned were correct or that they have not been changed as a result of recent studies. Other plants have been added to the collection without names and these are identified by comparison with the reference collection.

Living specimens are also sent in by members of the Royal Horticultural Society, often after the regular flower shows and meetings of the Orchid Committee in Westminster. Plants which are unidentified or thought to be incorrectly named are submitted to Kew botanists for naming.

Most of the naming is carried out on dried specimens which come from a variety of sources. They may be duplicates presented by another herbarium which does not have an orchid specialist on its staff. This helps to augment and improve the collection at Kew and also makes the expertise of the staff more widely available. It can also be an important safeguard against loss or destruction, such as occurred in Berlin when most of the orchid collections maintained there were destroyed by fire in 1943.

Other dried specimens come in from botanical expeditions, sometimes to areas which have not been explored by botanists before. Visiting botanists from other continents often bring material with them, primarily for their own use, but it is often presented to the Kew collection when they leave. All this material has to be treated before it enters the building to ensure beetles and other insects that feed on dried plants are not being introduced. Today, this is easily done by deep-freezing the bundles of specimens for 48 hours.

Name Changes

Amateur botanists and horticulturists are not alone in finding the changing of orchid names a nuisance. When it has to be done, as a result of reassessing old specimens and publications in the light of new studies or new collections, it must conform with the rules laid down by the International Code of Botanical Nomenclature. The Code itself is changed or amplified at the meetings of the International Botanical Congress, held every six years, but only after considerable publicity and discussion.

Some name changes are simply a matter of opinion however, and depend on an individual botanist's interpretation of the limits of the categories employed in taxonomy. Where one botanist recognises the single genus *Dendrobium*, for example, albeit a very large one, others have suggested that it should be split up into a number of smaller genera. Similarly at the species level and below, some botanists have a wider concept of what constitutes a species and how variation, which is quite natural, should be recognised nomenclaturally, if at all. The 'lumpers' and 'splitters' are as well known in orchid taxonomy as they are in groups studying other plants. Most botanists are aware that taxonomy is a discipline devised by man for his convenience and that names are useful as a means of referring to individual plants. They are therefore reluctant to change names, except when obliged to do so in accordance with the international rules.

Dendrobium lawesii, an epiphyte from Papua New Guinea which has been raised from seeds at Kew and widely distributed. RBG, Kew

11 Publications and Illustrations

THE ORCHID HERBARIUM IS UNIQUE at Kew in being accompanied by a superb collection of books, journals and pamphlets on the family Orchidaceae which is housed nearby. The sheer number of publications on orchids is immense and grows at an increasing rate every year, indeed probably no other family of plants has spawned so many published words, and the fascination for generations of gardeners and botanists in the family is reflected in this mass of literature on the subject. The Orchid Library at Kew reflects the whole range of interest in orchids from the purely taxonomic through to their biology and cultivation.

The library contains many rare and a few unique works. Kew's copy of Bateman's folio volume *The*

Orchidaceae of Guatemala and Mexico is inscribed on the first page 'Sir W.J. Hooker from the author'. Indeed, Kew's library was partly founded by the acquisition of Sir William's own library, and many of the older works come from it.

Outstanding Works

A few of the noteworthy books that appeal especially to the orchid botanist deserve mention. There is a rather slim folio volume by the French botanist Aubert du Petit Thouars entitled *Cahier de Six Planches* (1804–19) comprising six finely engraved plates of Madagascan

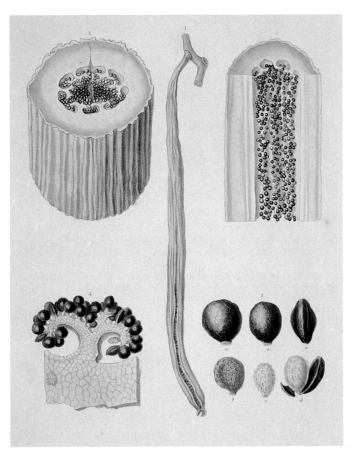

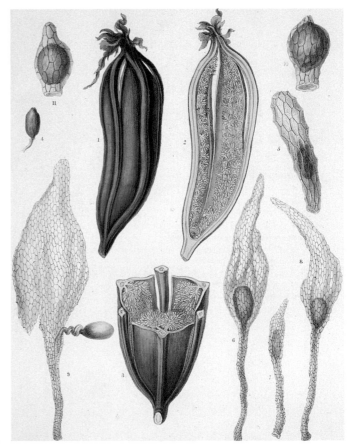

Drawings of dissections of orchid fruits and seeds executed by Francis Bauer at Kew and published in *Illustrations of Orchidaceous Plants* by Lindley and Bauer (1830–8). RBG, Kew

Florence Woolward's painting of *Masdevallia veitchiana*, a species from Machu Picchu, Peru, reproduced in her book *The Genus Masdevallia* (1890–6). RBG, Kew

orchids. This was the only known copy of the work until a second was discovered in 1975, in Geneva, by Ib Friis and Finn Rasmussen. The two plates of the comet orchid *Angraecum sesquipedale* must have excited any botanist who was fortunate enough to see them. One may well have been Sir Joseph Hooker's good friend, Charles Darwin, who spent many years during the preparation of *Origin of Species* in the study of orchids and their pollination. Hooker sent orchid flowers to Darwin from the Kew collection of plants. One of these may have been *A. sesquipedale*, which Darwin predicted, in his book *On the various contrivances by which British and foreign orchids are fertilised by insects* (1862), should be pollinated by a hawk moth with a tongue as long as the foot-long spur of the orchid (see chapter 5).

The superb craftsmanship of Francis Bauer is commemorated in the outstanding illustrations of his and Lindley's *Illustrations of Orchidaceous Plants* (1830–8). Here a variety of orchid flowers has been dissected and drawn in exquisite detail by Bauer. The quality is amazing considering the primitive nature of microscopes in the early 19th century.

Florence Woolward's *The Genus Masdevallia* contains a selection of the most spectacular and grotesque species of this popular genus illustrated by her own watercolours. The double page plate of *Masdevallia chimaera* illustrates well the sinister appearance of this orchid, which is now considered to belong to the genus *Dracula*. Many of the plants illustrated here were sent to England by Consul Lehmann, the German consul in Colombia. On his death, his herbarium specimens, notebooks and accurate watercolours were purchased by the Royal Botanic Gardens and are now incorporated into the collection at Kew.

Not all of the rare books are illustrated in colour. One of the few surviving original copies of a delightful little book by the Irish gardener J C Lyons, *Remarks on the Management of Orchidaceous Plants* (1843), is to be found here. It has fortunately been reprinted by the Boethius Press of Kilkenny, Ireland.

Unpublished Work

The wisdom of many orchidologists is sadly never published. Some have indeed produced substantial contributions to our knowledge without ever appearing in print. The unpublished work of two outstanding orchidologists can be seen in the Kew orchid library.

Charles Samuel Parish (1822–97) was a chaplain who took up an appointment in Moulmein in Burma in 1852. For the next 19 years he devoted his spare time to collecting and illustrating the wealth of orchids he found there. Parish discovered many species new to

The Reverend Charles Parish spent many years in Burma, where he collected, cultivated and carefully illustrated many orchid plants; his unpublished work is now at Kew. RBG, Kew

Paphiopedilum parishii, from Burma and Thailand, is one of the orchids illustrated meticulously by Parish and named in his honour by Reichenbach. RBG, Kew

Two illustrations from John Day's scrapbooks, which are preserved in the Library at Kew: left, *Cymbidium canaliculatum*, from Australia; right, *Coelogyne pandurata*, from Malaysia. RBG, Kew

science, several being named in his honour including the attractive orchids *Paphiopedilum parishii*, *Dendrobium parishii* and *Cymbidium parishii*. He sent many orchids to Kew where they were figured in the pages of *Curtis's Botanical Magazine* when they flowered in cultivation. It fell, however, to H G Reichenbach to describe and name most of Parish's novelties. Parish's published contributions appeared in the *Journal of the Asiatic Society of Bengal* and in Mason's *Burma* (1882–83) where he enumerated 350 Burmese species, many of which had grown and flowered in his own garden. In 1871, on his return to England, Parish gave a complete set of his exquisite drawings, all made from living plants in Burma, to Kew where they are now preserved in the Orchid Herbarium in two folio volumes. They have provided invaluable information for other botanists, most recently Dr Gunnar Seidenfaden, who has just completed a detailed account of the orchids of Thailand.

The largest collection of unpublished illustrations of orchids at Kew is that of John Day, who lived at Tottenham in north London. He was a wealthy amateur orchid grower who painted orchids in his own collection as they came into flower. He also painted the flowers of orchids at Kew and in the leading nurseries of James Veitch of Chelsea, Stuart Low of Clapton and William Bull of Chelsea. Beside each watercolour is a description of the orchid and an account of its provenance in Day's distinctive copperplate script. Attractive as these illustrations are, their importance relates more to John Day's friendship with H G Reichenbach. Day had access to many novelties which he drew from January 1863 onwards as they flooded into England from the tropics (one nurseryman, Frederick Sander of St Albans, had, at one time in the

1880s, 23 collectors sending orchids to him from all over the world). When Day was unable to name a plant he sent preserved flowers and often a sketch to Reichenbach, who described them as new species in the pages of the *Gardeners' Chronicle*. Day's drawings and watercolours are, therefore, often illustrations of the type specimens of Reichenbach's species. Reichenbach dutifully named several species after John Day, including *Paphiopedilum dayanum*, *Coelogyne dayana* and *Cymbidium dayanum*.

A more recent set of illustrations of orchids in Kenya and Uganda was prepared by an amateur botanist, the late Marjorie Tweedie. During her many years' residence on farms on the slopes of Mount Elgon she collected and illustrated native plants, and had a particular interest in orchids. In due course, most of her specimens were presented to the Orchid Herbarium at Kew, and these were later followed by her paintings. Many of the specimens and their matching paintings are of historic interest now that the areas where she lived and worked have been developed for agriculture.

Nineteenth-Century Colour Plate Books

In addition to the remarkable volumes of Parish and Day, the Orchid Herbarium contains an incomparable set of the major colour plate works devoted to orchids that were produced towards the end of the last century. Supported by orchid growers and nurserymen and their patrons, the publication of these works over a period of several, even many years, provides a tantalising record of the discovery and cultivation of

Coelogyne speciosa, a beautiful species from Java and Sumatra; this plate is one of the illustrations published in *The Orchid Album* by Warner Ind Williams in 1897. RBG, Kew

Oncidium splendidum, a Central American species, was one of H G Moon's illustrations published in the *Reichenbachia, Orchids Illustrated and Described* by Frederick Sander (1888–94). RBG, Kew

Paphiopedilum philippinense, a lithophytic slipper orchid which is widespread in the Philippines, is one of more than 800 orchids illustrated in the series called *Lindenia*. RBG, Kew

some of the more spectacular orchid species and their varieties which were cultivated in Europe at that time. The books contain full-page, life-size illustrations, often hand-coloured, each accompanied by a page or two of descriptive and informative text. Several works also include the man-made hybrids which began to appear in glasshouses at this time. Complete sets of most of these works have now become very rare because so many copies have been broken up to provide prints for framing.

One of the largest of the colour plate books of orchids was published by Frederick Sander between 1888 and 1894. The *Reichenbachia, Orchids Illustrated and Described* was illustrated with life-size coloured paintings by the well known painter, H G Moon. Though not in the usual style of botanical illustration, these paintings have individual charm, and the accompanying text is of historical value.

Two fine series of colour plate works, three volumes of *Select Orchidaceous Plants* (1862–91), and 11 volumes of *The Orchid Album* (1882–97) were produced by the partnership of Robert Warner and Benjamin S Williams

together with several other contributors and various artists. An experienced nurseryman and orchid grower, Williams provided the cultural notes on the plants. He is better known, perhaps, for a series of articles in the *Gardeners' Chronicle* entitled 'Orchids for the Millions' which formed the basis for his book *The Orchid Growers' Manual* first published in 1852. It became so popular that seven editions, each larger and more informative than the last, had appeared by 1894, and the seventh has been reprinted several times.

Jean Linden (1817–1898) was born in Luxemburg but moved to Belgium when still young. He spent 10 years travelling in the New World collecting orchids and other plants while in the course of various missions, and many orchids from these regions are named after him. At one point he was hired by Clowes and other English growers to collect orchids for them in Colombia and Venezuela, and it was his collections of *Anguloa clowesii* and *A. ruckeri* which flowered first in Europe. His herbarium specimens are in Lindley's Herbarium at Kew. However he is best known for the illustrated works which he contributed to the horticultural press after he returned to Belgium. Volumes 17–43 of *L'Illustration Horticole*, (1870–96) contain a variety of articles and illustrations, but the 17 volumes of *Lindenia, iconographie des Orchidées* (1885–1906) contained 813 plates of orchids only. Complete sets of this work in good repair are highly sought after.

Another Belgian botanist who made an enormous contribution to studies of the Orchidaceae, particularly those of the New World, was Alfred Cogniaux (1841–1916). He worked for many years on the *Flora Brasiliensis*, which is also a valuable reference for the orchids of the whole of the northern part of South America. After his 'retirement' he collaborated with A Goossens in producing the work *Dictionnaire iconographique des Orchidées* (1896–1907), a work in which a large number of cultivated orchids were illustrated by chromolithography from watercolour paintings by Goossens. The set at Kew is beautifully bound in 17 volumes. Because the usefulness of this

work is still appreciated it has recently been reprinted, in France, in two volumes.

Colour plate books on orchids have also appeared in other parts of the world, the most famous and rarest of which is probably Robert D FitzGerald's *Australian Orchids*, in which the drawings were all made by the author. Published in Sydney, in parts, between 1875 and 1894, the set at Kew is bound in two volumes and contains 118 coloured lithographs whose colours are still bright and clear.

Modern Works and Reproductions

Many books containing excellent colour photographs which aid the identification of orchids are now published in many parts of the world. Of particular note is Kohji Karasawa's *Orchid Atlas*, the first volume of which was published in Tokyo in 1987. This is a

Renanthera storiei, from the Philippines, painted by A Goossens for his joint work with the botanist A Cogniaux, *Dictionnaire iconographique des Orchidées* (1896–1907). RBG, Kew

beautiful photographic record of orchid species in cultivation now, with bilingual descriptions and notes on cultivation. It will be completed in eight volumes, of which three have appeared so far.

The most famous colour plate work of recent years is *Orchidaceae*, a sumptuous volume with 40 plates by the artist Mary Grierson and text by Kew's orchid specialist Peter Hunt. Published in a limited edition by the Bourton Press in 1973, it is already a collector's item.

The rarity of many of the older publications on orchids and their inaccessibility to many orchid botanists and enthusiasts is a concern which is now being addressed at Kew. The orchid plates from *Curtis's Botanical Magazine* are the richest source of coloured illustrations of orchids. Samuel Sprunger, a Swiss enthusiast, and Phillip Cribb edited *Orchids from Curtis's Botanical Magazine 1787–1948*, which includes 1,200 illustrations of orchids and an updated nomenclature. The same authors, together with William T Stearn, have recently compiled *Orchids from the Botanical Register* along similar lines. The addition of Stearn's authoritative and entertaining appreciation of the life and work of John Lindley, who edited the journal from 1827 to 1843, sets the work in context.

Illustrations

Besides the Herbarium and Library, the other main collection housed in the Orchid Herbarium is a collection of some 100,000 illustrations of orchids. These are attached to herbarium sheets and are arranged in

Dendrobium unicum from Laos and Thailand, painted for *Curtis's Botanical Magazine* by Margaret Stones (1972), has become more widely available in cultivation recently. RBG, Kew

the same systematic order as is the Orchid Herbarium. The illustrations in this collection derive from a wide variety of sources. Pride of place must go to the large number of original watercolour paintings and gouaches. Over one thousand of the watercolours are the original illustrations from *Curtis's Botanical Magazine* (1787–1983) and its successor *The Kew Magazine* (1984 onwards). The cream of botanical artists are represented here: notably Walter Hood Fitch, Francis Bauer, and more recently Lilian Snelling, Mary Grierson, Margaret Stones and Pandora Sellars. The original watercolours by Fitch for James Bateman's *Monograph of the Genus Odontoglossum* and those of Miss Drake for Lindley's *Sertum Orchidaceum* are also to be found here.

Two of the most important collections of illustrations at Kew are of South American orchids. Those of Consul Lehmann have already been mentioned. The other collection of Brazilian orchid paintings has a strange provenance. When Martius was preparing his monumental *Flora Brasiliensis* he had asked the Brazilian botanist Joao Barbosa Rodrigues to write the account of the orchids, the largest family in the Brazilian flora. In preparation, Barbosa Rodrigues produced a preliminary account which he published as *Genera et Species Orchidearum Novarum* (1877–82). He

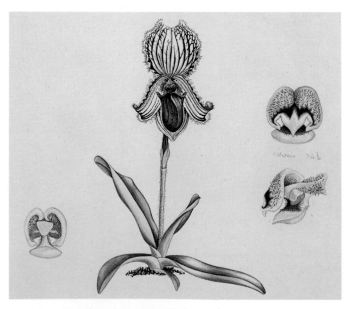

Paphiopedilum fairrieanum, a cool-growing lithophyte from Sikkim, Bhutan and north-east India, painted for *Curtis's Botanical Magazine* by Mary Grierson (1969). RBG, Kew

A group of Bornean orchids, including the purple *Dendrobium anosmum* and the white *Calanthe vestita*, painted by Marianne North in the Philippines; one of 848 oil paintings which are on display in the Marianne North Gallery at Kew. RBG, Kew

Many orchids have been depicted on postage stamps, and some enthusiasts make special collections of orchids on stamps. Joyce Stewart

also prepared watercolours of many orchids which were subsequently bound in four volumes. In the event, in 1893, Martius eventually asked the Belgian botanist Alfred Cogniaux (1841–1916) to prepare the orchid account which he duly published in three volumes (1904–06). Cogniaux borrowed Barbosa Rodrigues' illustrations while preparing the text and these were in turn lent to Sir Joseph Hooker so that his daughter, Harriet Thiselton Dyer, could copy them. Harriet had been trained by Walter Fitch and was a competent if not inspired illustrator. Her copies, in pristine condition, are in the Kew collection. The originals were eventually returned to Brazil, where three of the volumes are now at the Rio de Janeiro Botanical Garden. The fourth

volume is in the possession of the Oakes Ames Herbarium of Harvard University. The only complete set, therefore, is at Kew, where it is regularly consulted by Kew staff and visitors.

Original watercolours, often of plants grown and flowered at Kew, and line drawings, photographs and transparencies are added regularly to the illustrations collection. Other illustrations of various kinds are added from all possible sources in order to make the collection as useful as possible for the identification and naming of orchids. Orchids on postage stamps, postcards, posters and other publications are incorporated. A set of Wills' cigarette cards of orchids, issued in the early 1900s, has also been added to the collection. The criteria for inclusion of illustrations in the collection are simple – they must be accurate and of identified orchids. This collection is essentially utilitarian, as well as being attractive, and using it is one of the quickest ways of naming an orchid brought in for identification.

Elsewhere in the gardens orchid paintings are often on show to the public. Exhibitions of botanical art are arranged several times a year in the Kew Gardens Gallery housed in Cambridge Cottage. Several of these have included orchids by recent artists of note, including Christabel King, Marjorie Blamey, Mary Grierson and Pandora Sellars.

At the other end of the gardens, the Marianne North Gallery houses 848 oil paintings produced by this indefatigable lady during her travels between 1871 and 1885. She not only presented the entire collection to Kew, but provided the building and arranged the paintings in it. It was first opened to the public by Sir Joseph Hooker in 1882. The paintings are arranged geographically and together present a remarkable assembly of mainly tropical plants. Oil is not a medium which is frequently used to illustrate orchids, but Marianne North's uninhibited use of it, often in mixed compositions, presents a colourful and memorable display in which the orchids are easily identified.

Probably nowhere else in the world is it so easy to find any published reference on orchids as at Kew. The Orchid Library is the most comprehensive of its kind anywhere. Allied to the ready accessibility of the main library, situated on the floor directly above the Orchid Herbarium, a more amenable environment for the study of the orchid family would be difficult to find.

12 The Contribution of Taxonomists

SIR JOSEPH HOOKER'S ADMINISTRATIVE duties as Director, and his broad spectrum of interests, gave him little time to indulge his interest in orchids and led him to appoint, in July 1880, Kew's first orchid taxonomist. He chose Robert Allen Rolfe for this role.

R A Rolfe (1855–1921)

Rolfe began his career as a horticulturist, joining the Kew staff in 1879 as an apprentice gardener. His interest in the horticultural side of orchids proved lifelong and led to the foundation, in 1893, of the world's longest surviving orchid journal, *The Orchid Review*.

From the time of Lindley's death until nearly 10 years after Rolfe's appointment, the role of premier orchid taxonomist had been assumed by the German botanist H G Reichenbach (1823–1889), himself the son of a famous father of the same name. Reichenbach worked for many years in close collaboration with British nurserymen such as Frederick Sander of St Albans, amateurs such as John Day of Tottenham, and collectors such as Charles Parish. They sent him flowers and plants for identification and many of these Reichenbach described as new to science. During this time he visited Kew and was given free access to the Kew collections. He liberally annotated many of the specimens and obtained material from them. Rolfe's appointment in 1880, and his independent and rapid development as an orchid taxonomist, appear to have been resented by Reichenbach.

Reichenbach had promised that his own extensive orchid herbarium would come to Kew on his death. However, when he died in 1889, the botanical world was stunned to find that a new will dictated that his herbarium would be donated to the Naturhistorisches Museum in Vienna, on condition that it should remain sealed for 25 years after his death. The exclusion of Kew from his will seems to have resulted partly from his resentment of Rolfe but more so from his antipathy to Bentham, whose *Genera Plantarum* account of the orchids had aimed some well directed darts at Reichenbach's own work.

Among the important collections to arrive at Kew during Rolfe's reign were the herbarium specimens and illustrations made by Consul Lehmann in Colombia and Ecuador, Rudolf Schlechter's collections from New Guinea, Indonesia and Africa, and Henry Ridley's types and illustrations from peninsular Malaya and Singapore. Rolfe laboured under a handicap of monumental proportions because Reichenbach had described, by the time of his death, almost half of the then known orchid species and genera. The proviso to close his herbarium for 25 years, thereby setting back orchid taxonomy by probably half a century, may be explained in part by Reichenbach's fear that potential users would discover the large number of specimens he had removed from other herbaria during his career. Sadly, the advent of the First World War meant that Rolfe never saw Reichenbach's herbarium even though he survived beyond the end of the edict in the will. Needless to say, many Reichenbach species were subsequently redescribed by Rolfe and his

Robert Allen Rolfe was the first botanist who specialised in the study of orchids in the Herbarium at Kew. RBG, Kew

Pleione formosana; modern authors have all followed Rolfe in making *Pleione* distinct from *Coelogyne*. (Illustration by Margaret Stones for *The Genus Pleione* (1988).) RBG, Kew

contemporaries adding immensely to the synonymy that later botanists have had to resolve.

Rolfe's major contributions to orchid taxonomy were his accounts of the family in the *Flora of Tropical Africa* (1897–8) and *Flora Capensis* (1912). In 1905 he also took over from Joseph Hooker the commentaries on orchids in *Curtis's Botanical Magazine*, still the richest source of illustrations of orchid species. He also published extensively in journals such as the *Kew Bulletin*, the *Gardeners' Chronicle*, the *Journal of the Linnean Society*, *Lindenia* and *Reichenbachia*. However, Rolfe's claim to a special place in the pantheon of orchidologists remains his pioneering work on the interface between orchid science and horticulture. *The Orchid Review*, whose early numbers he largely wrote, is still consulted as a rich source of orchid lore. For example, his account of the slipper orchids published in 1896 was a milestone of orchid literature, establishing once and for all the distinction of the tropical from the temperate slipper orchids, and placing the distinction of *Paphiopedilum*, *Phragmipedium* and *Selenipedium* from *Cypripedium* on a sound scientific basis.

He was fascinated by orchid hybridisation and was among the first to realise that family trees were essential if breeding was to proceed along sound scientific lines. With Charles Hurst, he produced *The Orchid Stud Book* in 1913, an enumeration of all man-made orchid hybrids and their ancestry. This book led ultimately to Sander's renowned *List of Orchid Hybrids* which is still kept up to date by the Royal Horticultural Society in its role as International Registration Authority for orchid hybrids. This constitutes the largest, oldest and most useful compilation of the pedigrees of any group of plant hybrids. Its computerisation is a sign not only of the times and its universal applicability but also of its size, with approaching 100,000 hybrid grexes now in registration.

Rolfe, like his mentor Joseph Hooker, was also interested in other plants and published writings on several families. His productivity over 40 years at Kew was prodigious, helped perhaps by his deafness and the lack of modern interruptions such as the telephone. However, his fine example was matched by that of his successor, Victor Samuel Summerhayes.

Examples of the genera *Paphiopedilum*, from tropical Asia (*P. barbigerum*, left), and *Cypripedium*, from cool temperate regions (*C. reginae*, right); Rolfe established the differences between these genera of slipper orchids. RBG, Kew and C Luer

V S Summerhayes (1897–1974)

Summerhayes arrived at Kew in 1924, an experienced ecologist and botanical author with a broad interest in plants in general. His name is familiar to two generations of modern botanists and naturalists as the author of the seminal *Wild Orchids of Britain*, published in 1951 in the New Naturalist series. The significance of this book was its combination of a sound taxonomy based on Summerhayes' long experience as a herbarium botanist, curating Kew's incomparable collection, and his knowledge of the biology of orchids gained from many hours spent studying them in their natural habitat. *Wild Orchids of Britain* remains the standard text for those interested in British orchids as well as for those requiring a well-written lucid account of the complexities of orchid biology and ecology.

Throughout his career at Kew, Summerhayes specialised in the study of tropical African orchids. The opening up of tropical Africa in the 20th century led to a flood of new material from the interior of the 'Dark Continent' that rendered Rolfe's account in the *Flora of Tropical Africa* inadequate. Rudolf Schlechter, in describing his own collections from Cameroun, Mozambique and South Africa and those of Adolf Stolz in Tanzania and H Baum in Angola, not to mention others, realised that the generic concepts of the 19th century were far too broad. By his death in 1921, he had produced a framework that would enable Summerhayes to produce in 1936 the account of the orchid family for the *Flora of West Tropical Africa* as well as to write the first of three parts of the Orchidaceae for the *Flora of Tropical East Africa* (1968).

Reichenbach's vindictive will was a major setback for orchid taxonomy, but it was nothing compared to the destruction of the orchid herbarium collections in the Berlin Natural History Museum in 1943. This almost rivalled Kew in its richness and held all the type specimens of orchids described by, among others, Rudolf Schlechter, the most prolific of all orchid taxonomists, as well as those of Fritz Kraenzlin and R Mansfeld. Some idea of the scale of the loss can be gained from the recent attempts to trace duplicates of Schlechter's thousand or more New Guinea orchid types. Examination of almost 20 herbaria worldwide has revealed duplicates of only about 40% of the specimens. Kew probably has one of the richest collections of these, but it is still a woefully inadequate selection for those working on the orchids of New Guinea. Schlechter described hundreds of species and many new genera from South and East Africa, the Pacific islands, Asia, and tropical and South America. The loss of his herbarium was a tragedy whose repercussions continue to be felt.

Fortunately, for botanists working on African plants,

Victor S Summerhayes worked at Kew for 40 years and specialised in the study of British and African orchids. RBG, Kew

Mrs Mary Richards collected many plants for Kew in remote parts of Tanzania for nearly 30 years. RBG, Kew

Summerhayes had borrowed most of Schlechter's and Kraenzlin's African orchid types before the Second World War and had drawn and photographed them. These illustrations in the Kew collection represent, in many cases, our only knowledge of those types.

Edgar Milne-Redhead, Deputy Keeper of the Herbarium from 1959–71, encouraged an army of amateur collectors in tropical Africa, mostly ladies, and their efforts greatly enriched Kew's Orchid Herbarium during these years. Milne-Redhead's own collections in north-west Zambia, and later, in 1956, with Peter Taylor in Tanzania, are among the finest herbarium collections at Kew. The plants were carefully arranged and pressed and detailed notes made of their provenance, habitat and appearance. Flowers were also collected in spirit for the rapidly expanding Kew spirit collection. Notable amongst Milne-Redhead's collectors were Mary Richards, who collected over 30,000 numbers in Zambia and Tanzania (all after her sixtieth birthday); Winifred Moreau in the Usambara mountains of Tanzania; and Marjorie Tweedie who collected in Kenya and Uganda.

Summerhayes never visited tropical Africa, where his main taxonomic work was concentrated, but he did travel widely in Europe and became the foremost authority on European orchids in his day. He also maintained Kew's horticultural links, serving throughout his Kew career on the Orchid Committee of the Royal Horticultural Society. On Rolfe's death, control of *The Orchid Review* had left Kew, but Summerhayes continued to contribute to it and to advise a succession of editors whose spiritual home remains at Kew to the present day.

P F Hunt

Summerhayes retired from Kew in 1964 and was succeeded by his assistant Peter Hunt. Over the next eight years, Hunt developed Kew's links with orchid horticulture through the Orchid Committee of the Royal Horticultural Society. He is still one of the editorial board of the *Handbook on Orchid Nomenclature and Registration* and, as well as serving as a member of the Orchid Registration and Advisory Committee of the Royal Horticultural Society, is the Registrar of Orchid Hybrids.

P Taylor

Peter Taylor, the world's foremost authority on bladderworts (*Utricularia*), was appointed Curator of the Orchid Herbarium in 1973. Under his direction, the taxonomic work of the Orchid Herbarium was revitalised and its horticultural contacts strengthened.

R E Holttum, seen here at an orchid conference in Thailand, was an expert on south-east Asian orchids; he worked at Kew for many years after his retirement. Phillip Cribb

He retired in 1988. From 1973–83 he served on the Orchid Committee of the Royal Horticultural Society.

R E Holttum (1894–1990)

No account of the Orchid Herbarium at Kew would be complete without mention of Professor Holttum who, though never a member of the staff, worked at Kew for 40 years. His founding of the Singapore orchid industry in the 1930s resulted in what is today a multi-million dollar business. His much admired account of the *Orchids of Malaya* was written while he was interned in Singapore during the Second World War and much of his subsequent work was on ferns rather than orchids. However, he continued to take a lively interest in orchids and at the time of his death was the longest serving member of the Royal Horticultural Society's Orchid Committee, where his expertise on orchids of south-east Asia was much appreciated. He was an inspiration to generations of orchid growers and botanists, including the present members of staff at Kew.

The Staff Today

The staff of the Orchid Herbarium since 1974 has comprised Phillip Cribb, who took over as Curator in 1983, Jeffrey Wood since 1973, and Sarah Robbins who joined as an assistant in 1987. They have continued Summerhayes' work on African orchids, sometimes with the help of visiting botanists from Africa and Europe. The account of the family Orchidaceae for the *Flora of Tropical East Africa* has been completed, and checklists of the orchids of various countries have appeared, including the Ivory Coast (1975), Nigeria (1983), and the Central African Republic (1987). Jeffrey Wood's interest in European and Middle Eastern orchids has resulted in orchid accounts for the *Flora of Cyprus* (1985) and the *Flora of Iraq* (1985). Summerhayes would undoubtedly have approved of the establishment at Kew in 1983 of a project aimed at growing endangered native orchids with a view to their eventual reintroduction into the wild (see chapter 15).

The relationship with the horticultural world has been continued and extended. Phillip Cribb has served on the Orchid Committee of the Royal Horticultural Society since 1980, and also represents Kew on the International Orchid Commission, a guiding body on technical and scientific aspects of orchid cultivation and nomenclature which meets every three years at the World Orchid Conferences.

Phillip Cribb has also begun a notable contribution to the literature on orchids of horticultural merit. He has been involved with the production of several monographic treatments of popular genera, including *Paphiopedilum*, *Pleione*, *Cymbidium* and some sections of *Dendrobium*. His *The Manual of Cultivated Orchid Species*, a popular account with a sound scientific background, covers many genera and is intended as a modern equivalent of Schlechter's classic *Die Orchideen* – a book intended to enable growers to identify the orchid species in their collections. It is currently being revised for a third edition.

Throughout this period, the Orchid Herbarium collections have continued to grow. The influx of herbarium specimens averages about 1,500 per annum with an almost equal number preserved in spirit. These specimens come from a wide variety of sources: from Kew expeditions, from other institutions and scientists throughout the world, from orchid growers and nurseries, and last but not least from Kew's own collection of living orchids. They are sent to the Orchid Herbarium for identification and naming, a process made relatively easy in most cases because of the comprehensive nature of the Herbarium collection and its history of first class curation over the last century or more. The advent, in 1976, of improved microscopes with high quality *camera lucida* attachments has not only greatly speeded up the routine identification and naming work of the herbarium but has also made possible the addition of substantial quantities of accurate illustrations to the herbarium collection.

Visiting Botanists

In addition to the daily use by the staff of Kew, the orchid collections of the herbarium and library are

Phillip Cribb has studied orchids at Kew and on his many travels since 1974; orchid hunting on tropical mountains is one of his special delights. Phillip Cribb

much in demand by visiting botanists. Hardly a day goes by without one or more visitors enjoying and making use of the wealth of material that is housed here. Many books and publications result, in various languages in different parts of the world, and all acknowledge the hospitality they have received at Kew and the value that study of the priceless collections adds to their work. All of the most familiar names in orchid botany of recent years have visited Kew, including Gunner Seidenfaden, Carlyle Luer, Robert Dressler, Leslie Garay, Ed de Vogel, Jaap Vermeulen, Cal Dodson, Carl Withner, and many others.

Nowadays, Kew's Orchid Herbarium has an increasing role to play in a world that is losing its wild vegetation. Orchids are amongst the first plants to suffer when habitats are disturbed or desecrated and they are, therefore, an ideal barometer of the health of their environments. The study of the past and present orchid flora of many parts of the world can begin in the herbarium. Once checklists and floras have been compiled and distributions understood, decisions can be taken about areas and regions that need protection. Sadly, there is an increasing number of orchid species that are known only from the dried collections in the herbarium because they are already extinct in the wild.

Research and Conservation

By Joyce Stewart, with contributions from
Peter Brandham, Sean Clifford, David Cutler, David DuPuy,
Noel McGough, Robert Mitchell, Simon Owens
and Hugh Pritchard

MANY KINDS OF ORCHID RESEARCH are undertaken in the Herbarium, the Jodrell Laboratory and in the Living Collections Department at Kew. The techniques that are traditionally carried out in each area have often been combined to elucidate particular problems, for example, to provide more evidence in taxonomic studies. A monographic study that was carried out recently on the genus *Cymbidium* (see chapter 14) involved the study of both living and preserved specimens in many different ways.

Anatomical and cytological studies have always depended on the accurate identification of the plants in the Living Collection. The preparation of voucher specimens is a routine procedure. They provide a permanent record in the Herbarium of the material, often from the Living Collection, studied in the Jodrell Laboratory. Specimens are also prepared, or collected for the Spirit Collection, from the living plants which are used as a germplasm resource for propagation and conservation. The accurate identification of this material is of critical importance.

There are also close associations between scientists in other sections at Kew. The techniques of micropropagation are used in studies of pollen and seed longevity and breeding systems, while the regular routines of plant physiology are used to prepare media and determine seed viability in the course of work on germination.

Many other examples could be cited, but these are enough to show that work on and with the orchids at Kew does not fall neatly into separate departments. There is much interdependence between scientists and horticulturists and between scientists of different disciplines.

Material is also in demand from scientists in universities and other institutes, both in the United Kingdom and overseas. Orchid leaves and roots can be supplied fairly easily and quickly, but it may be a year or more before flowers or their pollinia become available, and seeds take even longer.

Cut sprays of flowers are also required as decoration for special functions at Kew and for occasions such as Remembrance Day when Kew orchids, usually *Cattleya bowringiana*, adorn the wreath laid at the Cenotaph by the Foreign Secretary in remembrance of armed forces from the Dependent Territories. The Orchid Supervisor maintains a list of requests for orchid material and tries to fulfil all those which merit attention. In 1985 the Sainsbury Orchid Fellow was appointed to co-ordinate the use of the collection for research, conservation, education and display.

The Sainsbury Orchid Fellow also supervises the Sainsbury Orchid Conservation Project which was set up in 1983 (see chapter 15). This project was the brainchild of Phillip Cribb, who has been advisor to several conservation organisations in Britain on various aspects of orchid conservation. Finding ways to grow some of the rare British orchids from seeds, especially *Cypripedium calceolus*, which was reduced to a single wild plant, seemed to him an urgent necessity. In 1981 he was in Durban for the 10th World Orchid Conference where he heard a paper presented by Mark Clements, an Australian orchid biologist from Canberra, who had succeeded in growing some of the rare Australian terrestrial orchids from seeds and in introducing the seed-raised plants to the wild. Returning to Kew, Cribb approached the Director and Curator about the possibilities of a similar project here, in conjunction with the Nature Conservancy Council. Orchid enthusiasts Lisa Sainsbury and her husband Sir Robert Sainsbury provided the finance and Mark Clements was seconded to Kew for 18 months to initiate the project. With continued funding for staff and a glasshouse to hold the research collection and seedlings produced, the project has become increasingly successful. In 1989, Sir Robert and Lady Sainsbury provided an endowment to ensure the future of both the project and the Sainsbury Orchid Fellowship at Kew.

Overleaf: *Cattleya aclandiae.* Joyce Stewart

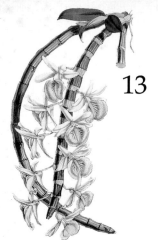

The Jodrell Laboratory

TO THE ORCHID ENTHUSIAST who is enthralled by the complexity and beauty of orchid flowers, and to conservationists trying to protect the ever-decreasing numbers of rare plants, the detailed study of the structure and function of individual orchid cells, minute parts of the plant, may seem irrelevant. But to the serious student of the orchids, these scientific disciplines, and others, are very important, and all can add information to the complex of knowledge that is being gradually accumulated at Kew.

Several sections of the Jodrell Laboratory have, over the years, incorporated orchid studies into their routine work. Cytology, especially work on chromosomes, anatomy of leaves and roots, and studies on the physiology of seed germination and storage have been carried out for many years. More recently, studies of the reproductive biology of certain orchids have begun, combined with investigations of the morphology and anatomy of the stigma, style and ovary of the flowers. The surface topography of pollen grains and pollinia and the storage of pollen for future use has also been investigated in recent years.

Some of the information that has emerged is of great interest to the herbarium botanist, and when allied to morphological and biological studies may lead to the development of a more useful system of classification. Other details will be of particular value to the breeder or hybridist of cultivated plants, and to the conservationist trying to save a rare plant on the brink of extinction. To the specialised scientists who carry out these investigations, the information they yield is of interest not only for its own sake but also for the interesting comparisons that can be made between orchids and other flowering plants.

Anatomical Research

The orchid family presents a daunting prospect to the plant anatomist. Not only are there so many species, worldwide, but many of them are rare, so good material for anatomical work is hard to obtain. Because anatomists prefer to work with live material, they are generally not welcomed in glasshouses with valuable collections. However, at Kew, the collections are principally for scientific study, and providing the

requests are not excessive, leaves, stems and roots are usually made available. No permanent damage is inflicted on the plants by their removal.

In the orchids, leaf anatomy is often typical of the genus rather than the species and there are rather large groups of genera that share quite similar leaf structure. At first sight this would appear disappointing, since it would seem to reduce the chances of using leaf anatomy as an indicator of relationships, and hence of evolution. However, the immediate appearance is rather misleading, and when detailed studies are made, involving both leaf surface and sections, a useful range of character syndromes, or sets, emerges. Silica bodies, often found in orchid leaves, are small opals which generally have a characteristic shape. Their function is uncertain, but they are very hard, and may damage the mouthparts of animals that try to eat the leaves.

The flower stems of orchids do not vary as much in their structure as those of some other monocotyledons. However, on the large scale, trends in evolution can be seen, and close relationships can be detected.

Unlike the stems, it is the roots that have provided a large range in variation, which is unusual among the monocotyledons. This is due partly to the fact that so many orchids are epiphytes, and thus have interesting adaptations in their aerial roots for water capture and retention. The fine details of the velamen (a multiple-layered epidermis) and the nature of the exodermis (a layer or layers of thick-walled cells bordering the cortical parenchyma), provide useful characters for the taxonomist.

Plants that have to withstand drought on a regular basis often show xeromorphic characters in addition to a thick, sculptured cuticle. If the leaves are retained, they are usually adapted so that they do not readily lose scarce water. In the orchids, as in other plant families, it is the xerophytes that show the widest range of anatomical variation, since there are many different tissues involved to a greater or lesser extent in the job of conserving water. For example, the cell walls of the epidermis may become thickened in a characteristic way. The stomata (pores through which water vapour moves from the leaf into the air during transpiration) must be able to close tightly at times of water shortage and are often protected by over-arching flanges, or may be sunken into the leaf surface. The leaves may be very fleshy, and contain water-storing cells, or they may be tough and reinforced with strong fibres and sclereids (cells that are shorter than fibres but have thick, strengthened walls). The chlorenchyma cells, which contain the chloroplasts, may become modified into upright, closely packed, narrow cells. The vascular bundles (veins), which have special cells for transporting water (xylem) and others for transporting soluble food material (phloem), can also be modified in xerophytes, and may be sheathed by one or more layers of cells with thick or thin walls.

With the various permutations and combinations of these different tissue types, it is easy to see how individual species or genera may have a particular set of characteristic features.

Leaf surfaces also have many interesting characters. These may be of taxonomic importance, but they also provide information about the normal habitat in which the plants occur. The shapes of the epidermal cells and the sorts of stomata (pores) are typical for a species. Often the cuticle, the outer waterproof layer of the leaf, has very fine surface sculpturing. This can be seen with the light microscope, but is easier to understand using the scanning electron microscope. This outer layer plays an important part in the survival of the orchid. Different habitat preferences are often reflected in the different sorts of surface sculpturing on the cuticle. Plants that grow in dry, or periodically dry conditions, such as epiphytic orchids, often have very thick cuticles. In plants that grow in moist, humid conditions the cuticle is often thin and smooth.

As preparation for anatomical study, comparable parts of leaf, stem, pseudobulb and the various root types are removed from the plants and fixed, or pickled, in a noxious mixture of formalin, acetic acid and alcohol – FAA. It is best to use fresh material, so that the resulting specimens are as lifelike and unwrinkled or unshrunken as possible. If it is absolutely impossible to obtain live material, particularly of very rare plants, then a technique known as reviving herbarium specimens may be necessary. The dried plant parts have to be gently boiled in water, to try and make them regain the shape they had in life, but not boiled for too long so they cook. As soon as they appear reasonably expanded, they are cooled, drained and transferred to FAA. Often the material has been damaged by drying, and only rather poor sections can be made from it.

After a minimum of 48 hours in the fixative, the material can be removed and thoroughly washed in running water, prior to sectioning. Because the sections have to be drawn or photographed and fine details studied the sectioning is carried out mechanically. Two methods are used. The easiest, which produces good although fairly thick (20–25 μm) sections from firm material, involves the use of a sliding, or sledge

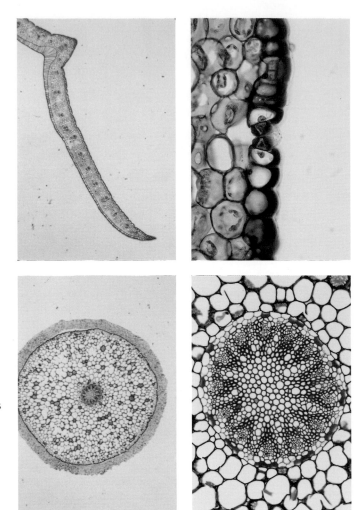

Thin sections of orchid leaves and roots reveal a wealth of patterns and details: top left, transverse section of the leaf of *Phragmipedium longifolium*; top right, transverse section of a small part of the leaf of *Eulophia petersii* showing a stoma; bottom, left and right, two transverse sections of the root of *Paphiopedilum dayanum* at different magnifications.
David Cutler

microtome. The leaf, stem or root is carefully supported in a clamp in the microtome, and slices are cut with a very sharp blade fixed to a head which runs smoothly along tracks. After each section is cut, returning the knife to its start position raises the specimen by a pre-set amount, ready for the next cut.

The second sectioning method involves infiltrating the delicate tissues with wax, or a wax-like substitute in a solvent, and gradually adding more and more wax, eventually allowing it to set. The wax supports the tissues, and slices of the embedded material can be cut on a rotary microtome. This produces thinner sections (about 10–15 μm thick). It can also produce a series of sections in sequence. One limitation is that the plant material to be sectioned should be reasonably soft, or at least of uniform texture. Unfortunately, many orchid leaves have rather hard fibres set in the middle of very soft tissues, so they tend to tear rather than cut evenly.

When sections have been cut they can be looked at immediately, particularly for the examination of cell contents. Usually, however, it is the types of cells and their arrangements within the tissues that are of most interest. So the cell contents are flushed out with domestic bleach solution. Then the sections are washed thoroughly to remove all traces of the bleach. Finally the sections are put in special dyes or stains that colour the different sorts of cell walls in distinctive ways. Nowadays the dye Alcian blue, mixed with the red stain, safranin, is mainly used. The blue goes into the thin cellulose walls of the chlorenchyma, parenchyma and phloem, while the safranin stains the thicker, lignified cell walls of fibres, stone cells and xylem.

After staining, the sections are carefully dehydrated and then mounted on microscope slides under coverslips, in a medium which sets hard when fully dry. The sections retain their colours for many years if the slides are stored in the dark.

Rather like fingerprints, sections can be used to help in identification. They contain a lot of microscopical information, which, taken as a whole, provides a unique story for each of the species from which they are prepared. It is true that the structure of plants that have grown in different conditions shows some minor variability, but this is slight. Anatomists have learned which features may be unreliable indicators of identity or relationship, and these are avoided. Consequently, a section can provide a good set of characters to the tutored eye.

When these are added to those details of flowers, fruits, seeds and leaves which are commonly significant in taxonomy, or evolution, a complete picture of each plant begins to emerge.

The main involvement of the Kew plant anatomy staff in the orchids is currently in co-ordinating the preparation work and editing of the major volume on Orchidaceae in the series *Anatomy of the Monocotyledons*. This will be a major contribution to a series of important volumes recording anatomical features of monocotyledonous plants which was initiated by a former Keeper of the Jodrell Laboratory, Dr C R Metcalfe. His monumental work on the grasses, *Gramineae*, appeared in 1960, and other volumes have followed so that there are now seven in the series. Two of the present Kew anatomists, David Cutler and Mary Gregory, have succeeded Dr Metcalfe on the editorial board. Preparatory studies for the Orchidaceae volume were started by Edward Ayensu and are now being continued by William Stern and his staff at the University of Florida, with help from Alec Pridgeon. Work will probably take at least another three years, as many species still remain to be studied and described anatomically in order to provide even an overview of this vast family. Clearly it would be the task of a lifetime to study representatives of all the genera thoroughly. A careful, considered selection has to be made, based on information from other sources, and then the manuscript must be edited so that it conforms with the style of the rest of the series.

Staff in the Anatomy Laboratory also maintain, on computer, the world's most comprehensive set of literature references to the anatomy of the Orchidaceae. This is invaluable in the editorial work and is added to on a weekly basis. When the Orchidaceae volume is complete, a set of all the slides described will be housed in the Jodrell Laboratory for future reference.

Cytology

Like other plants and animals, orchids are made up of millions of cells. In a mature plant there is a variety of dead cells, which often provide supporting tissue, and many living cells, some of which are actively dividing. Although these are usually transparent or translucent, and difficult to see except with a microscope, their study has become a fascinating and complex subject known as cytology. It is made easier by the technique of killing and preserving the cells at certain stages of development and then staining them with particular dyes before examining them microscopically.

To those who study orchid cells, the structures of greatest interest are the chromosomes, so called because they are bodies which take up certain dyes very readily. They are important to all living organisms because they carry genes, or hereditary information. They thus control the development of the plant and also its breeding potential.

In a normal, non-dividing cell, the chromosomes are in an expanded state and mass together inside a special membrane to form the nucleus. Just before each cell divides, in a process called mitosis, the chromosomes contract and become more readily visible under the microscope. Thus tissues that are actively growing can be prepared for examination so that the chromosomes can be studied and counted.

Several kinds of tissues can be investigated with relative ease. Epiphytic orchids produce aerial roots which are clean and easily accessible. In many terrestrial orchids, too, the root tips are easily extracted from the loose compost in which the plants are grown because they will often be found in the part of the pot where there is most air, near the edge or bottom of the compost.

Apart from the root tips, there are several parts of the flower worth investigating. These have the advantage

that their removal does no harm to the plant. The
development of the individual pollen grains in an
orchid pollinium takes place synchronously. Provided a
flower bud is harvested at the right moment, many
thousands of dividing cells can be obtained with their
chromosomes suitably presented for counting. Similar
success can be obtained by studying ovary material.
Here, however, the developing ovules need to be
examined some days or even weeks after pollination.
Obviously it is much easier to get results from a long
inflorescence such as an *Oncidium* or *Eulophia*, where
there are many flowers opening successively over a
long period, than from orchids which normally
have only single flowers, such as many of the
paphiopedilums. But with observations and records of
more than one flowering season, and perhaps a little
trial and error, even these will yield their secrets.

Chromosome counts are of particular interest because
closely related species and genera often have the same
number and hence a similar amount of genetic material
in their tissues. They may interbreed easily. Hybrids
made from parents with the same chromosome number
are likely to be fertile, whereas those with widely
different parental numbers are usually not.

The number of chromosome sets a plant contains is
sometimes referred to as its ploidy level. Most wild
orchids are diploid and contain two sets (2n) having
inherited the haploid number (n) from each of its
parents, just as humans do. Diploid plants usually grow
easily and flower well under good cultural conditions.
Sometimes, however, plants can contain four sets of
chromosomes. These tetraploid (4n) orchids usually
grow rather slowly and produce fewer flowers than
diploids, although these may be unusually large and of
superior form. Tetraploids are fertile, however, and
those which have been bred with other tetraploids,
sometimes over several generations, have produced
some superior and famous lines of hybrids. Tetraploids
can also be crossed with diploids to form triploid (3n)
progeny with three sets of chromosomes. Triploids are
often very fine, easy to grow and free-flowering with
larger flowers than the diploids, but they are usually or
almost infertile. Thus a knowledge of chromosome
numbers and how to discover them is often of interest
to the orchid grower and breeder.

The chromosomes of most orchids are small and take
up stains easily, but they are often not easy to count
because their numbers in any one cell can be rather
high. A chromosome number of 2n = 38 is a common

The small chromosomes can be counted in these squashed
single cells: from the top downwards, *Bulbophyllum
minutipetalum* (2n=36), *Coryanthes maculata* (2n=40), *Pleione
coronaria* (2n=40), and *Sarcochilus fitzgeraldii* (2n=76)
(magnification × 70). Peter Brandham

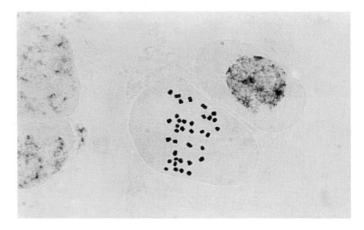
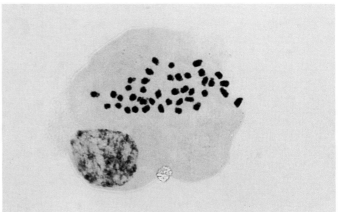
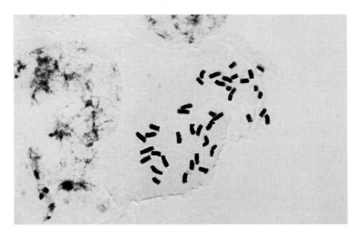
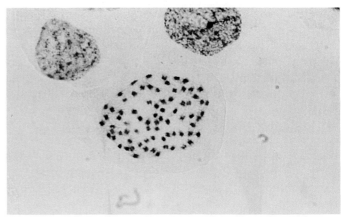

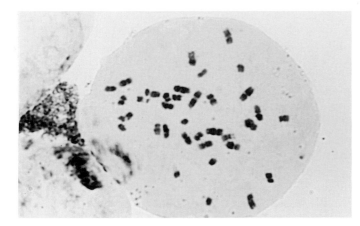

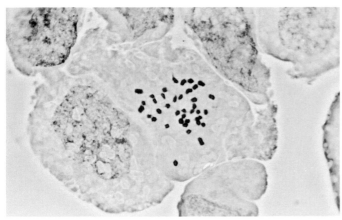

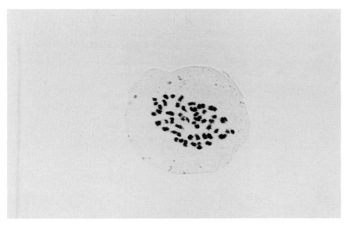

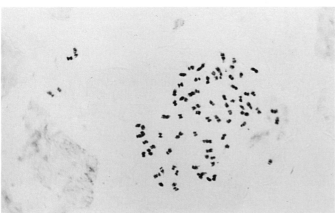

one throughout the orchid family, whereas 2n = 14 is frequent in lilies and grasses. There is also wide variation between species, even in a single genus. The lowest number so far recorded is 2n = 10 in *Psygmorchis pusilla* (formerly known as *Oncidium pusillum*), and numbers over 200 have been recorded in several species. Many of the species of commonly cultivated genera, such as *Cattleya*, *Epidendrum*, *Laelia* and *Cymbidium* have 2n = 40, but the species of *Paphiopedilum* vary between 2n = 25 (*P. fairrieanum*) and 2n = 42 (*P. venustum*).

The techniques for assessing chromosomes used at Kew were developed by Keith Jones, formerly Keeper of the Jodrell Laboratory and Deputy Director, and his co-workers. Root tips are commonly used.

Orchid roots are usually quite bulky and covered on their outer surface with a layer of dead, air-filled cells, the velamen. The tips are usually pale green or yellowish because they are free of mature velamen. The ultimate 1 cm or so of the tip is removed from the plant and placed in a reagent which will disturb the normal phasing of cell division and produce a degree of chromosome contraction. Several different chemical reagents can be used, but the two which have been found most satisfactory are 8-hydroxyquinoline, used at a concentration of 0.002M (0.29g/litre), or a saturated solution of monobromonaphthalene. The roots are immersed for about four hours at room temperature (16°C) or overnight at about 4°C (the usual temperature of a domestic refrigerator). The consequences are that the chromosomes become well spread out throughout the cell and appear compact. The main problem here is to ensure that the reagent is able to penetrate rapidly into the interior of the root tip. To facilitate this, it is the practice at Kew to slit the covering of the root tip along several longitudinal planes, rather like peeling back the skin of a banana. The exposed interior part of the root is then sliced longitudinally.

Following these treatments, the roots are fixed in absolute alcohol and glacial acetic acid, 3 parts to 1, for at least 30 minutes, hydrolyzed in normal hydrochloric acid at 60°C for about 8 minutes, and then placed in Feulgen reagent and left in a dark cupboard. The tips of the roots (which contain the dividing cells) become deep purple, usually within an hour, but are better left for two hours or more. Small pieces of the root are

Counting the chromosomes in these squashed cells reveals differences in ploidy: from the top downwards, *Dendrobium pugioniforme*, a wild species from Australia, diploid (2n=38); *Dendrobium* Cassiope, an early hybrid, diploid (2n=38); *Dendrobium* Plumptonense, a triploid hybrid, (2n=57); and *Dendrobium* Fort Allan 'Lyoth Glory', a modern tetraploid hybrid, (2n=76) (magnification × 70). Peter Brandham

removed to a microscope slide and any velamen that remains is carefully dissected away. The material to be squashed is then covered with a coverslip and firmly squashed with the ball of the thumb. At this stage the preparation can be examined microscopically, or it can be made into a permanent mount after freezing with pressurised CO_2, removing the coverslip, dehydrating in absolute alcohol for 15 seconds and then covering the squashed material in Euparal before replacing the coverslip.

The procedure for making preparations from actively dividing pollen grains is even more simple than examining chromosomes in root tips. Fresh (or fixed) pieces of pollinia are squashed under a coverslip in a 1% solution of orcein or carmine in 45% acetic acid and are gently heated over a spirit flame to aid differentiation. The slide can be made permanent, as outlined above, for later study, or counts can be made immediately.

A wide range of chromosome counts has now been reported in the literature but in taking account of these, two points have to be remembered. First, the attribution of a chromosome number to a species depends on the correct identification of the plant from which the root tip or pollinium was obtained. It is therefore important to preserve voucher specimens of the plant material investigated, which can be checked by a taxonomist if necessary. Secondly, since orchids have such high numbers of chromosomes, and contaminating bodies such as fungal spores or bacteria which stain similarly can be present, it is very important to develop a high standard of preparation and to count only those preparations which are worthy of analysis. Many observations are usually required, from more than one preparation, before one can be reasonably certain that the true number has been determined for any species.

The fascination of work with chromosomes in orchids continues and much more needs to be done. Many species are as yet uninvestigated, and, for those where only single counts have been made, more plants need to be examined. At the same time, a new facet of cytology has begun in the Jodrell Laboratory and orchids are among the first subjects for analysis. This is the technique of DNA 'fingerprinting'.

Sophisticated biochemical techniques, involving the extraction of DNA from a small piece of an orchid leaf and its treatment with various enzymes, will permit the recognition of individual plants. This is intrinsically interesting, and it will be especially important in artificial propagation for conservation.

Where a species has become reduced to a very small number of individuals, it is beneficial, when hand pollinating them for seed production, to breed with individuals that are genetically different. This not only

enhances the gene pool available in the resulting seeds, but usually ensures that a greater quantity of viable seeds is produced.

In Britain, for example, only one plant of the lady's slipper orchid, *Cypripedium calceolus*, can still be found in the wild. Several plants that are said to be of wild origin are still preserved in gardens and flower every year. Some of these are thought to be divisions from one wild source, but no one can be sure. The new technique of DNA 'fingerprinting' is about to be tried out on these plants and may show whether they are clonally related or not. It will then be possible to co-ordinate an improved breeding programme and obtain more seeds that will germinate in the laboratory (see chapter 15).

Pollination and Breeding Systems

In functional terms, orchid flowers could be described as a mechanism to attract a pollinator, usually an insect, who will physically transport many pollen grains from the anther of one flower to the stigma of another in a single journey.

The pollen consists of tetrads of pollen grains held together by fine longitudinal threads to form a more or less globular mass, the pollinium. The lower parts of the sticky threads are fused to form a caudicle by which the pollinium is attached to a sticky base, the viscidium, sometimes with an intervening stalk or stipe. The whole of this unit is called the pollinarium, and it is usually removed *en masse* by a suitable insect visitor. The caudicle or stipe, sometimes both, soon dry out after leaving the flower, and, as described by Charles Darwin more than a hundred years ago, the pollinarium shows characteristic movements on the insect's body

Two-spot burnet moth with pollinia of *Anacamptis pyramidalis*, the pyramidal orchid. RBG, Kew

during flight. These movements change the orientation of the pollinarium on the insect's body, ensuring that it will be in the right position to come in contact with the stigma of another flower. The fact that these movements usually take several minutes for completion may ensure that the next flower visited is on a different plant.

The other peculiar feature of orchid flowers, from the reproductive point of view, is that at the time the flowers open (anthesis) the female reproductive organs, the ovules, are entirely undeveloped. In most orchids the differentiation of ovules occurs after anthesis or even after pollination. It might be regarded as an economical adaptation that energy is not used for the growth of millions of ovules if they are not going to be needed, but it also means there are other hazards, and long delays, in the pathway between pollination and the release of viable seeds to start the next generation.

The study of pollination in both temperate and tropical orchids is a fascinating one, and there is still a great deal to learn about the majority of species. What has been achieved already, by Darwin in Kent in the last century, and by Dodson, Dressler and their co-workers in Central and South America recently, only emphasises how much there is still to do. However, it is work that must be carried out in the field or forest where the orchids grow and the insects live, rather than in the glasshouse. But at Kew, hand pollination of the flowers in the nursery can be followed by careful observations, the keeping of records and the employment of new techniques of microscopy and biochemistry in the laboratory. Thus various stages of the breeding system can be studied in a wide variety of species.

There are several reasons for doing this. It is interesting to know which species will produce viable seed after pollination with their own pollen, i.e. which are self-compatible. With very rare species this may be important for propagation and conservation. Some orchids are well known to be self-incompatible, more than 80% of the species of *Oncidium* for example, and work in the Anatomy Section is being undertaken to discover why this should be so. It would be interesting to identify what it is that is controlling pollen tube growth from the stigma into the ovary and whether fertilisation is successful or not. It would be very useful to discover ways of overcoming such barriers, if they exist. This information could also be of great value to orchid hybridisers who already know that many of their crosses, especially in the more complex modern hybrids, will yield no seeds but do not know why. More knowledge of breeding systems might help them to overcome this difficulty.

Like most plant families, the Orchidaceae exhibit a full range of breeding strategies from the fully self-pollinating and self-fertile species to the fully cross-

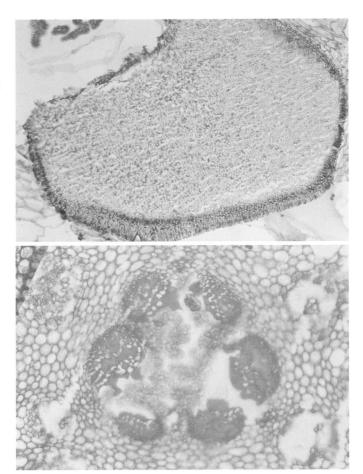

Transverse sections of the ovary of *Oncidium excavatum*: above, section showing 45,000 pollen tubes in one transmitting tract; below, section of whole ovary showing six transmitting tracts. Sean Clifford

pollinating and self-incompatible species. A recent survey of a wide range of genera revealed self-incompatibility in about 40% of the species in the glasshouses at Kew. Many species might be termed intermediate, that is having no self-incompatibility system but promoting outcrossing to variable degree. Orchids are, however, best known for some of the most bizarre examples of breeding systems that exist. The insect-plant relationship is often unique to species and this may mean that the likelihood of successful pollination is infrequent or remote. Perhaps this is why one successful pollination in an orchid flower produces so many seeds, over a million in some cases. Such a massive fertilisation requires massive numbers of pollen tubes and a complex structure to support and enhance their growth down the stylar canal.

Orchids are also unusual in having viable pollinia and receptive stigmas for considerable periods of time – two or three months is by no means extraordinary, and some *Dendrobium* flowers have been known to last for nine to twelve months, still fertile and receptive, until

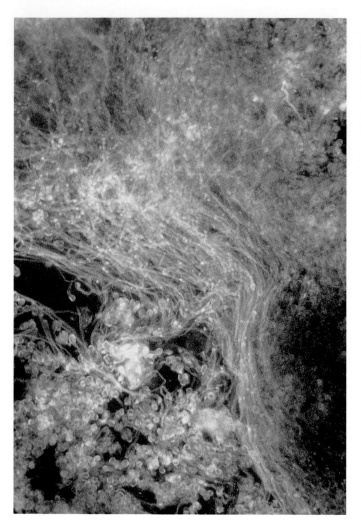 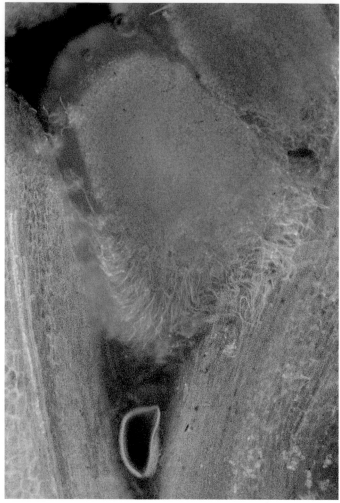

Two views of pollinated orchid styles with pollen tubes fluorescing under ultraviolet light excitation: left, with compatible pollination the pollen tubes grow down into the style; right, with incompatible pollination the pollen tubes stop growing at the entrance to the style. Sean Clifford

they are pollinated. When one considers that a pollen grain of wheat or maize may only be viable for minutes, or at the most a few hours, this once again puts orchids in an exceptional class.

Studies of breeding systems in orchids were started at Kew in 1987, with representatives of the subtribe Oncidiinae. Pollination in these species sets off a series of responses in each flower, some of which appear general while others appear specifically associated with the result of the pollination, incompatible (fail) or compatible (success).

The most obvious are changes in the flower, which may include fading of the bright colour of the lip and petals, other colour changes or wilting of some or all of the floral parts. Less obvious is the closure of the column wings or stigma lobes around the pollinium. This happens within one day of the pollinium being placed on the stigma. Both these responses appear to happen in every pollinated flower and thus might be considered to be general responses. They are not

necessarily always followed by the swelling of the column and ovary which occurs in successful pollinations.

In most other plants the female part is fully formed and ready for fertilisation when the flower opens. Fertilisation follows rather rapidly after pollination. In the orchids there is a hidden response to pollination, which is partially indicated by the swelling of the ovary, and that is the differentiation of its internal tissues. Pollen tubes arriving in the ovary after growing down the column (or its stylar tissue) for six or seven days, may have to wait more than six weeks before fertilisation can take place. It is only during this period, and after pollination has been effected, that the ovules develop and produce the egg cells which the male gamete can fertilise. There are few other plants that have such an economical system, where the female gamete is not developed until the male gamete is already in close proximity. The presence of 45,000 pollen tubes, which were counted by Sean Clifford in the transverse section of a developing ovary of an *Oncidium*, is a remarkable sight and a precursor of the enormous potential for seed development in this and other orchids.

One means of controlling whether a pollination may be successful or not is a breeding system called self-incompatibility. This breeding system appears to be widespread throughout the plant kingdom, and has been recorded for a wide range of species in the Orchidaceae.

In most of the examples that have been thoroughly examined so far, self-incompatibility (SI) is controlled by a gene which has many forms (alleles). Though pollen, stigma, style and ovary are perfectly formed and viable, pollen carrying a form of the SI gene which is the same as that in the style is unable to achieve fertilisation. The pollen grains germinate and a pollen tube is produced, but it is prevented from growing the full distance into the ovary. In the *Oncidium* species examined at Kew, the inhibition of pollen tube growth takes place at the top of the style. Usually this response follows a self-pollination, but it has also been observed when plants of the same clone or some siblings are cross pollinated. Crossing genetically different plants of the same species ensures seed set.

The system, which is not yet understood, thus promotes cross fertilisation and hence genetic diversity. It is also clear that in some interspecific and intergeneric crosses, pollen tubes are able to grow down the style and into the pollen tube guides of the interior wall of the ovary, but fail to stimulate the necessary development of the female. With no egg to fertilise, the pollination is unsuccessful.

The work at Kew is still at an early stage and there is still much to be learned. The most exciting pieces of evidence are just beginning to accumulate. They strongly suggest that chemicals held in the pollen wall, and/or the growing pollen tube, are responsible for stimulating both the incompatibility response of some species and all of the characteristic post-pollination changes.

Seed and Pollen Storage

There has been an interest in research on orchid seed germination and storage since the inception of the Seed Unit at Kew in 1969. The unit, which subsequently became part of the Physiology Section of the Jodrell Laboratory and moved to Wakehurst Place in 1973, was set up to preserve seeds under refrigerated conditions over a number of growing seasons. Today's modern Seed Bank at Wakehurst Place operates at a deep freeze temperature of −20°C and aims to store seeds at around 5% moisture for hundreds of years. In this way, seed-

banking can protect species against the increasing threat of extinction which is brought about by habitat destruction, and, in some orchids, by the over-collecting of plants for study or trade.

Routine germination testing to monitor viability loss is an essential part of seed-banking. However, with orchid seeds, germination testing is far from straightforward. The seeds are usually less than ten-millionths of a gram in weight, and possess an embryo less than 1 mm in length with few nutritive reserves for germination. In the natural environment, the energy resources required for germination and early seedling developments are provided through a symbiotic association with one or more Basiodomycete fungi (often referred to as *Rhizoctonia* species). Reproducing such an association *in vitro* is one way of checking orchid seed viability, and may be the only method of achieving germination in some terrestrial species. Alternatively, germination of most terrestrial and epiphytic orchid species can be induced by sowing the seeds on a complex medium containing inorganic salts, vitamins and amino acids, and a carbohydrate source – the so-called asymbiotic method for germination (see chapter 9).

One limitation of these tests, however, is the relatively slow progress of germination over many weeks. Where there is a need for a quicker assessment of viability, i.e. within 24 hours, it is possible to stain hydrated living orchid seed embryos with a fluorescent dye and observe them under the microscope.

In comparison with seeds of most other families, orchid seeds are short-lived, even when stored dry at −20°C; their longevity apparently being restricted to a few years rather than centuries. The use of ultra-low storage temperatures, i.e. below −150°C, may offer some scope for the improvement of orchid seed storage

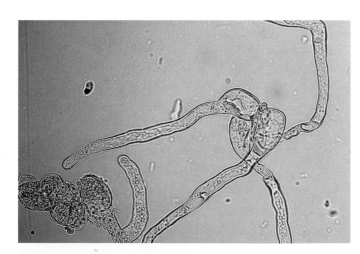

Orchid pollen grains germinating and pollen tubes developing on a simple medium in the laboratory.
Hugh Pritchard

longevity, because the degenerative biochemical processes associated with seed viability loss should be reduced to a negligible rate.

Liquid nitrogen storage (at −196°C) is an economically feasible alternative to conventional freezer storage systems when the seeds to be stored are in short supply or are small in volume. As approximately 50,000 orchid seeds could be stored in a 1-cm vial, this system would appear to be ideal for long-term storage of orchid seeds. To date, orchid seeds have shown no loss in viability after storage in liquid nitrogen at −196°C over a period of a few years.

Orchid pollen storage is of obvious benefit to the hybridist, but also has an important long-term role to play in conservation. For example, several of the rarer British orchid species are at the limits of their natural geographical range. A feature of their relative uncompetitiveness, in an ecological sense, is often the shortage of suitable insect pollinators. The controlled pollination of such populations of orchids, with stored pollen from elsewhere or from an earlier flowering, could ensure a high level of seed set and increase the likelihood of a new generation of plants developing. The orchid pollinia are easily collected and stored.

As with seed storage, pollen viability also needs to be monitored during storage. A simple sugar-agar medium will generally suffice, with the germination process taking between one and two days.

Several experiments with British orchids have shown that pollen viability is at a peak just as the flower opens. To have the maximum chance of obtaining many seeds, pollinia from freshly opened flowers should therefore be used in hand pollinations. Compared with non-orchidaceous species, pollen longevity on the inflorescence is relatively good, however; at ambient temperatures and moisture contents the pollen remains viable for many days.

Short-term storage, of up to three months, may be possible at normal refrigeration temperatures. For longer term storage, of more than one year, −20°C or −196°C storage temperatures should be used. Before storage at sub-zero temperatures, however, some pre-drying of the pollen should be performed, but over-drying, such as using a desiccant like silica gel crystals for about one day, should be avoided, as pollen of some British orchids has been killed at low moisture contents.

Long-term storage of pollen in air-filled gelatine ampoules at sub-zero temperatures is better than storage in the presence of cryoprotectants. Stored in this way pollen of several species has retained its longevity for more than a year.

Bulbophyllum picturatum, an epiphyte from south-east Asia which flowered for the first time at Kew more than a hundred years ago. RBG, Kew

14 The Genus *Cymbidium*

MANY PEOPLE THINK FIRST of a cymbidium flower when they hear the word 'orchid'. Cymbidiums are widely grown by orchid enthusiasts throughout the cooler parts of the world, and they form the basis of a significant cut-flower production. The flowers are long-lasting, both on the plant and when cut, large, attractive and available in a wide range of colours. Smaller plants are now coming into vogue as decorative pot plants. These have smaller flowers but they are as desirable as the standard varieties and often more acceptable in modern homes. In the East a number of wild species are prized for their attractive habit and sweetly scented flowers.

Most of the plants in commerce are hybrids, however. They have been derived, after more than a hundred years of artificial breeding, from only a few of the 44 known species. The search for novelty, which is ever-present in the orchid industry, has stimulated the use of some of the smaller flowered species in new hybridising programmes in the last 30 years with, in some cases, conspicuous success.

The practice of registration of orchid hybrids and their parents, which is managed by the Royal Horticultural Society on behalf of the international orchid community, demands accurate naming of plants. But this can be difficult, for botanists and growers alike, as the species were originally described in a wide variety of books and journals, over a long period of time, and often more than once.

Five years of research by David DuPuy, based on earlier work by Kit Seth and Phillip Cribb, resulted in the publication, in 1988, of *The Genus Cymbidium*. In the course of their work Cribb, Seth and DuPuy examined many hundreds of specimens, both living and preserved. They carried out field work in many of the countries where the species still occur in the wild. Weeks of work were spent in the laboratory making studies of anatomy and cytology. Each species was examined in the same way, in an attempt to gather together as much information as possible before coming to any decisions regarding classification and nomenclature. Illustrations were prepared by the artist Claire Smith when the plants flowered in the Living Collections Department at Kew. Finally, all the information was correlated and compiled into a PhD thesis by David DuPuy and then into an attractive account for publication as a book. It included two species new to science, discovered while the work was under way.

What is a Cymbidium?

In preparing a monograph, one of the tasks of the botanist is to decide what to include and what to leave out. Inevitably, in the past, a number of species have been given the name *Cymbidium* but are now known to be better placed in other genera. Similarly, species which have not yet been transferred to *Cymbidium* may have to be sought in other genera. Before this can be done, the exact characters of the genus, features by which it can always be recognised, need to be elucidated and described. The characters traditionally used are those of vegetative and floral morphology. They are described briefly below.

The cymbidium plant is either epiphytic, lithophytic or terrestrial. Plants which normally grow on trees are sometimes encountered on rocks, and one species, *C. macrorhizon*, is a saprophyte which grows entirely beneath the soil surface except when the flower spike emerges. Most species have thick roots which are covered in a spongy white velamen and have only a thin core of vascular tissue. The erect stems are usually short and swollen to form a prominent pseudobulb which is often slightly flattened. Many species produce a new growth annually. In one section of the genus the pseudobulbs grow and flower for several years before a new shoot is produced, and in *C. mastersii, C. elongatum* and *C. suave*, each shoot grows continuously for many years producing an elongated stem rather than a typical pseudobulb.

Each growth bears three to twelve leaves in two rows. The leaf lamina is articulated from the base by an abscission zone, where it will break after a few years when the leaves are shed. The pseudobulbs remain encased by the leaf bases. The leaves may be thick, rigid and leathery, as in *C. aloifolium* and its allies, but are more often flexible with prominent ribs. The shade-loving species, *C. lancifolium* and *C. devonianum* have broad, elliptic leaves, and many of the forest epiphytes have long, thin and relatively narrow leaves.

Cymbidium parishii is a rare species in Burma, named after the Reverend Charles Parish, who discovered and grew it and prepared this illustration. RBG, Kew

The inflorescence in *Cymbidium* is unbranched and may be erect, arching or pendulous. Each mature pseudobulb usually produces one or two inflorescences from leaf axils near the base. (They are commonly called spikes but this is erroneous: botanically, they are racemes, because each flower has a short pedicel.) In *C. eburneum* and its allies the inflorescences arise from the leaf axils near the apex of the pseudobulb, as they do in *C. suave* and *C. elongatum*. The inflorescences bear up to 50 flowers in *C. canaliculatum* and only one in *C. goeringii* and *C. eburneum*. Most species bear 10–20 flowers.

The flowers are all immediately recognisable as cymbidiums. They comprise a dorsal sepal, two lateral sepals, two free petals and a three lobed lip which is hinged at the base of the column. There is usually a callus of two distinct ridges along the upper surface of the lip. The anther contains two pollinia or four pollinia fused in two pairs.

This brief summary can be applied to all or any of the species. Individually they can be much more precisely defined than this, and some species also vary to quite a large extent. Thus a large part of a monograph will consist of descriptions and illustrations of the individual species and their variation. Their distribution is mapped and habitat preferences recorded.

In attempting to understand the relationship between the various species, or postulate their possible evolution, several other kinds of evidence are assembled and considered.

Leaf Anatomy

Features of the leaf which provide useful anatomical information for classification can usually be discovered by examination of its surface and by making transverse sections of the lamina.

The Scanning Electron Microscope (SEM) allows a picture of the micromorphology of the leaf surface to be produced without destroying it. In this study, the lower

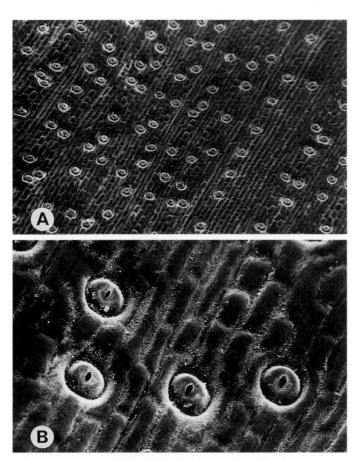

Scanning electron micrographs of the leaf surface of *Cymbidium dayanum*: **A**, the lower epidermis, showing densely crowded stomata (magnification × 80); **B**, stomata (magnification × 380). David DuPuy

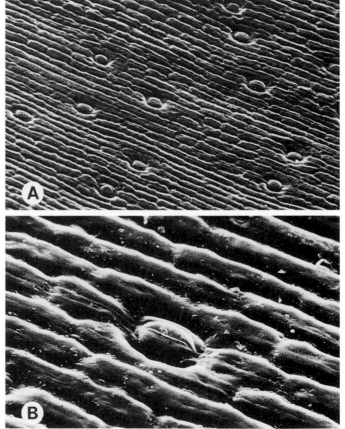

Scanning electron micrographs of the leaf surface of *Cymbidium atropurpureum*: **A**, the lower epidermis, showing scattered stomata (magnification × 125); **B**, single stoma and surrounding cells (magnification × 570). David DuPuy

surface of the leaves was examined closely in order to study the arrangement of the stomata, the shape of the dome of cuticular material formed by their guard cells and the shape of the pore in this dome. Several different patterns of surface morphology were revealed, two of which are shown in the accompanying photographs. The patterns were characteristic of groups of species which seemed to be closely related.

Transverse sections of the leaves also revealed startling differences among the species, particularly in the distribution of the strands of supporting fibrous tissue. In *C. aloifolium* and its allies there is a complete layer of fibres immediately below the epidermis which link the larger bundles of fibres that strengthen the leaf.

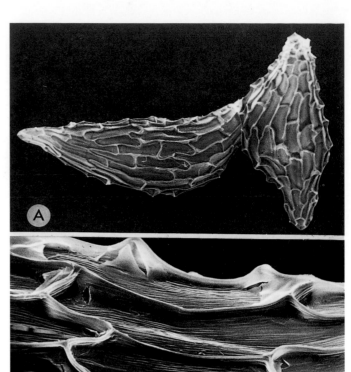

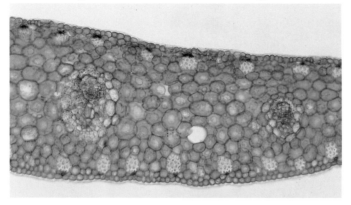

Transverse section of part of the leaf of *Cymbidium whiteae*: fibres are stained red, cells with living contents stained blue. David DuPuy

In the subgenus *Cyperorchis* and in *Cymbidium dayanum*, the subepidermal layer is lacking and the fibrous strands are isolated from each other. These species also have smooth epidermal cells. In subgenus *Jensoa*, however, where the bundles of fibres near the lower surface are also isolated, the epidermal cells have a conspicuous papillose surface. The accompanying photograph shows part of a leaf of a member of the subgenus *Cyperorchis*. The small strands of fibres along the margins and the larger bundles surrounding the vascular tissues of the leaf are similarly arranged in all the species of this subgenus.

Seed Structure

The SEM is also a useful tool for the examination of the tiny seeds of orchids. Photographs can be taken at high magnifications and often reveal significant differences between species or genera.

At first sight the seeds of *Cymbidium* species are quite typical of the majority of orchids. They are minute, 0.5–1.9 mm long, and fusiform or filiform in outline. A spherical embryo, which is not visible in the

Scanning electron micrographs of seeds of *Cymbidium atropurpureum*: **A**, whole seeds, showing the fusiform shape and the network of cells of the seed coat (magnification × 80); **B**, testa cells, showing the junction of cells and striations on their surface (magnification × 360). David DuPuy

photographs, is enclosed in a thin testa which is only one cell layer thick. The cells of the testa are few and large.

Two types of seeds were found among the species examined. Seeds of species in the subgenera *Cymbidium* and *Cyperorchis* are fusiform and 0.5–1.2 mm long. Their testa cells have longitudinal striations along the surface. This type of seed structure was also found in the seeds of several related genera, including *Grammatophyllum*, *Ansellia*, *Eulophiella* and *Cymbidiella*.

In subgenus *Jensoa*, however, the seeds were much narrower and 1.4–1.9 mm long. The striations on the surface of the testa cells in these species were transverse instead of longitudinal. This combination of characters is also found in some Asiatic species of *Eulophia*.

Cytology

The diploid chromosome number in all species of *Cymbidium* was found to be 40. A few exceptions were the triploid or tetraploid, named cultivars of a few species, e.g. *C. insigne* 'Bieri' (2n = 60), *C. floribundum* 'Geshohen' (2n = 80) and *C. floribundum* 'Yoshina' (2n = 60).

Cymbidiums in Cultivation

The beginnings of orchid appreciation and cultivation are found in the Orient. Confucius (551–479 BC) is recorded as saying that acquaintance with good men was like entering a room full of *lan*, or fragrant orchids. The word *lan* is used for a wide variety of fragrant plants, but the *lan hua* that he referred to was almost certainly *Cymbidium ensifolium*. It is still cultivated in China and Japan, today, and displayed there in beautifully decorated containers whether or not it is in flower.

This species was also one of the first cymbidiums to appear in Europe. Linnaeus named it in his *Species Plantarum* in 1753, but under the genus name *Epidendrum*. Live plants were first introduced by Dr John Fothergill, on his return from a visit to China in 1778. They were sent to a relative in Yorkshire and flowered there quite soon afterwards. But they do not seem to have survived long or to have been propagated at that time.

It was the middle of the 19th century before cymbidiums, among many other tropical orchids, were cultivated on a large scale in Europe, and especially in England. The best of the early accounts of them is given by Veitch in his *Manual of Orchidaceous Plants*. In Part IX, published in 1893, he records that about 30 species of *Cymbidium* were then known, distributed from the Indo-Malayan region to tropical Australia and with outlying species in Japan and New Caledonia. *Cymbidium ensifolium* was apparently not cultivated in Europe when he wrote. Most attention was paid to the Indian species with larger flowers and the first hybrid which had been created in 1878 from *C. lowianum* and *C. eburneum*. It took nine years for the resulting

Cymbidium insigne grows in sandy soil in Vietnam, Thailand and China; this species is an ancestor of many modern hybrids. David Menzies

seedlings to reach flowering size, and the Royal Horticultural Society gave its first Award to a *Cymbidium* hybrid, *C.* Eburneolowianum, in March 1889.

The first of the large-flowered cymbidiums to flower in English glasshouses was *C. iridoides* (syn. *C. giganteum*). It was introduced from the tropical parts of the Himalaya range and plants grew well at Chatsworth. The dull greenish brown flowers rarely open fully and are shorter-lived than those of some other species. The plants are relatively large and the combination of these features has made this species less popular with modern growers.

The white-flowered *C. eburneum* was originally discovered in about 1837 and first flowered in an English nursery 10 years later at Loddiges in Hackney. For many years it was highly prized and rather rare in collections, but towards the end of the 19th century plants were imported in great quantity and widely cultivated. The waxy flowers are often scented but only one or two are borne on each peduncle.

Next on the scene was the green-flowered *C. hookerianum* (syn. *C. grandiflorum*). The first plant was seen in flower at Chelsea in the early 1850s and then not again until 1866. It was named by H G Reichenbach in honour of Joseph Hooker. It is an early flowering plant and has been used to breed some beautiful green-flowered hybrids which also flower early in the season. The species is rarely seen today and proves difficult to bring into flower in glasshouses because the buds are sensitive to heat. They stop growing and eventually fall before opening if the spikes are subjected to sudden changes of temperature.

Cymbidium lowianum appeared in flower in Low's nursery at Clapton in the spring of 1879. As a horticultural plant it was immediately welcomed. It proved easy to grow and was very floriferous in cultivation. It produced long arching racemes of brightly coloured, yellowish green flowers, chiefly remarkable for the V-shaped blotch of contrasting red or brownish colour on the lip.

Mixtures of orchid plants were not uncommon in those days of large importations. *Cymbidium tracyanum* first changed hands as a plant of *C. lowianum*, but when it flowered it was immediately recognised as distinct. The enormous flowers with their stripes of red-crimson dots along the sepals and petals, and sprinkling of reddish dots on the white lip, had a remarkable scent and appeared rather earlier in the season than those of other species, always before Christmas in temperate greenhouses.

A white-flowered species with distinctive red coloration on the lip and column is *C. erythrostylum* from Vietnam. First seen in flower in the west at Glasnevin in 1905, it is one of the smaller species but

has large, long-lasting flowers which appear in the autumn. In the last 40 years it has been used to produce some superb hybrids with white, pinkish or light-coloured flowers which are produced readily and in profusion, on plants of compact growth habit.

Pride of place among the species, for its contribution to hybridising, must be given to *C. insigne*. With its long upright spikes which have several white, pale or deep pink flowers near the top, it has been of extraordinary value as a parent in producing a wide colour range of well shaped hybrids. The most well known of these must be *C.* Alexanderi 'Westonbirt' (*C.* Eburneolowianum 'Concolor' × *C. insigne* 'Sanderi'), the first recorded tetraploid clone. It has exerted a tremendous influence in the breeding of shapely hybrids for more than 50 years.

Amongst the smaller growing plants, several species have become important in horticulture and especially in hybridising in recent years. The first to be used on any scale was *C. floribundum* (under the widely used synonym *C. pumilum*). Its erect, multi-flowered spikes of pinkish brown flowers with red markings on the lip are most attractive. Many plants with arching or pendent flower spikes have been bred from *C. devonianum*, an Indian species whose small flowers have a characteristic, dark velvety lip. The true miniature, *C. tigrinum*, has produced some charming hybrids, mainly with pale yellow flowers. *C. ensifolium* has come into favour again, and although the flowers do not last as long as those of other species and hybrids, they are sweetly scented and appear on slender upright spikes during the warm summer months, thereby greatly extending the flowering season for the genus. In China and Japan, selected clones of this and other native species and natural hybrids continue to enjoy great popularity among enthusiasts.

New Classification

The most recent classification of the Orchidaceae which has been accorded wide acceptance among botanists is that of Robert Dressler (1981, and modified in 1986). He recognised six subfamilies in the Orchidaceae, with *Cymbidium* included in the *Epidendroideae*. Within this subfamily there are many tribes, including the *Cymbidieae* which contains all the sympodial vandoid orchids with similar seeds and two pollinia. By this criterion the subgenus *Jensoa*, with four pollinia, should not be included, but this single character seems insufficient to require its removal to another tribe.

Dressler placed *Cymbidium* in a small group of genera within the subtribe *Cyrtopodiinae*. All these plants have pseudobulbs of several internodes, articulated leaves, and usually a lateral inflorescence. The differences in structure of the pollinia and the whole pollinarium in *Cymbidium* and related genera are small but very interesting. The most similar is the African genus *Ansellia*, but that genus has a paniculate inflorescence borne at the apex, not the base, of the greatly elongated pseudobulb.

The genus *Cymbidium* was established by Olof Swartz in 1799, based on *Epidendrum aloifolium* L. (= *C. aloifolium* (L.) Sw.). At that time he included many species which have now been transferred elsewhere, but two of his species, *C. aloifolium* and *C. ensifolium*, are still recognised. Many botanists have described individual species of *Cymbidium* since then, or have removed some of them to other genera, notably the genus *Cyperorchis* Blume. DuPuy and Cribb review this information and then present their own proposal. They propose the division of *Cymbidium* into three subgenera called *Cymbidium*, *Cyperorchis* and *Jensoa* respectively. Each of these contains several sections, in some of which there is only one, rather distinctive species. They distinguish these subgenera according to the formation of the lip and the number of pollinia. In *Cyperorchis* the lip is fused with the column base, while *Jensoa*, with four pollinia, has a free lip, as does *Cymbidium*, with two pollinia.

At the conclusion of their extensive study, DuPuy and Cribb considered that the genus *Cyperorchis*, which was distinguished by the Dutch botanist Blume and others because all the flowers have the lip fused with the base of the column, should be reunited with *Cymbidium* but maintained as a distinct subgenus within it. All the other species they classify in two further subgenera: *Cymbidium*, containing those where the anther bears two pollinia and *Jensoa*, whose species have four pollinia.

Exhaustive details of the 44 species, 7 distinct subspecies and 7 recognised varieties are recorded in the account of this painstaking work. Two new species, *C. borneense* and *C. elongatum*, and several new subspecies are described and illustrated. Some exciting stories have been unravelled concerning the early

Cymbidium iridoides (syn. *C. giganteum*) an epiphyte that is widespread along the Himalaya range but difficult to flower in cultivation. David DuPuy

collections and importations, and the accounts of some of the rivalry betwen enthusiasts and their gardeners for these plants are enthralling reading. Historical difficulties of discovery and description are related and problems solved. Many names are shown to be synonyms, sometimes causing familiar names of widely grown species to be replaced by earlier names which have been neglected up to now.

Above all else this study demonstrates the importance of combining a knowledge of plants in the wild and the glasshouse with careful study in the laboratory, herbarium and library.

Cymbidium hookerianum, a species from high-altitude forests in Nepal, Sikkim, Bhutan, and south-west China. David DuPuy

15 The Sainsbury Orchid Conservation Project

A WIDE RANGE OF EUROPEAN terrestrial orchids have been raised from seeds by the asymbiotic methods of micropropagation that are widely used in horticulture for tropical orchids, especially epiphytes. However, progress is very slow when this technique is used for many of the terrestrial species, and it has proved difficult with others. The transfer of seedlings developed *in vitro* to a soil-based medium in pots is often a particular problem.

The symbiotic methods of seed germination pioneered by the French botanist Bernard at the beginning of this century, and redeveloped in Australia in the last 20 years, more closely resemble what happens in nature. The seeds are invaded by an appropriate fungus which develops a mycorrhizal association in the protocorm and later in the roots of the seedling. Young plants already infected with a symbiont are more easily transferred to pot culture and eventually to the wild.

About 50 species of European orchids are currently recorded in the British Isles, but 10 of these are listed as endangered, and two are reduced to a single locality only. In other parts of Europe a similar situation prevails.

The project initiated in 1983 at the Royal Botanic Gardens, with the co-operation of the Nature Conservancy Council and the generous backing of Sir Robert and Lady Sainsbury, was intended to propagate from seeds those British and European orchids which are threatened in the wild.

The work began with a wide range of orchid species, rare and relatively common, in an attempt to formulate the best methods to follow. Now, seven years after the first attempts at isolating fungi from orchid plants in cultivation, both symbiotic and asymbiotic methods are used.

Since 1985 the project has been supervised by the Sainsbury Orchid Fellow who also liaises with the various conservation bodies which support and take great interest in it. Five orchid species have been re-established in wild situations where they have flowered and set seed; 35 species have been raised and transferred to pots in the greenhouse; and a total of 46 species have germinated in the laboratory where the plantlets are at various stages of growth and development. The techniques learned from Mark Clements and developed by Harriet Muir and Robert Mitchell are used and refined by Margaret Ramsay and Grace Prendergast on an ever-increasing range of species. There is still much to do, but this chapter describes the considerable progress that has been made so far.

Plants of *Dactylorhiza praetermissa* in spring; these are at the best stage of growth for the extraction of mycorrhizal fungi from their roots. Robert Mitchell

Seeds and Fungi

Orchids produce a very large number of minute seeds which are as fine as dust and among the smallest seeds of all flowering plants. Each seed has a tough, transparent testa, or seed coat, and an embryo composed of only 100–200 cells. The cells contain some lipid and starch but there is no food reserve such as endosperm that comprises the bulk of many other seeds. The difficulties of germination and early development of such a small and fragile embryo have been overcome by an intimate symbiosis between the orchid and an appropriate fungus.

Cypripedium calceolus, the last remaining wild plant in Britain. Joyce Stewart

The dispersal of orchid seeds by wind ensures that some will land not too far from the parent plant. These have an excellent chance of encountering the right fungus. Suitable fungi are widespread in the soil, though research has indicated that some orchids are specific in their fungal partner. Others appear to be capable of using various fungi, and several fungi have been isolated which will assist the germination of a variety of orchids.

The fungus penetrates one end of the embryo through its large suspensor cell. As the fungal hypha grows into the inner cells of the embryo it forms coils called pelotons which, in turn, are gradually digested by the orchid plant. As the infection proceeds, the orchid embryo grows rapidly to form a protocorm which, in due course, develops a shoot from which the leaves and roots arise. The fungal hyphae also infect the young roots and form pelotons in the cortical cells of the root.

In wild orchid plants the mycorrhizal fungi are found as pelotons in live and healthy roots which appear cream or yellowish. Usually the coils of hyphae are linked via root hairs to the soil or substratum. It is believed that the fungus digests organic materials in the surrounding medium and the resulting nutrients diffuse into the pelotons from which they are obtained by the orchid.

The underground parts of terrestrial orchids are quite varied, but the fungus is usually present in the roots rather than the tubers or rhizome. The degree of infection varies in different species and it also appears to be somewhat seasonal. In many species there appears to be heightened activity of the fungus while the orchid is at the peak of its vegetative growth. Orchids with tubers usually do not hold the fungal infection through the dormant season, and the new roots of these plants become infected from the soil when vegetative growth resumes each year. Orchids with rhizomatous growth, like *Cypripedium*, seem to harbour fungal activity after the leaves have died down, while for much of the year their roots contain masses of starch but no pelotons. The extent of the dependence of the mature orchid plant on the fungus is still unknown, but it has been interesting to find that the fungal isolates that are more effective for germination have been obtained from the most vigorous orchid plants.

Fungal Isolation

Mycorrhizal fungi have been isolated at Kew from the roots and, rather rarely, the protocorms of European orchid species in cultivation. A few roots have been obtained from wild plants, with the landowner's permission, and from three of the scheduled endangered species under licence from the Nature Conservancy Council. Fungal isolation is not a destructive technique, as a sample of root can be collected with minimal disturbance to the plant.

The root is first washed gently under running water to remove most of the external debris. A soft paint brush is sometimes used to remove the more persistent particles. Pieces about 5–6 mm long are cut from any yellowish regions of the root and transferred to a dissecting microscope.

The epidermis is sliced away from the pieces of root and thin sections are cut from the cortex. These are examined for the presence of pelotons and, if found, the infected tissue is excised and placed in a few drops of sterile distilled water in a Petri dish. With the aid of a fine scalpel and needle, individual pelotons are teased out of the tissue. After all extraneous material has been removed, the pelotons are covered with cool fungal isolating medium (FIM) (table 15:1). The cultures are sealed with laboratory film and maintained at room temperature.

Table 15.1   Fungal isolating medium

	g/l
Calcium nitrate (Ca(NO$_3$)$_2$·4H$_2$O)	0.5
Potassium phosphate (KH$_2$PO$_4$)	0.2
Potassium chloride (KCl)	0.1
Magnesium sulphate (MgSO$_4$·7H$_2$O)	0.1
Yeast extract	0.1
Sucrose	5.0
Agar	8.0
Distilled water to make up to 1 litre of medium	

Within 12–24 hours the fungi that are likely to be mycorrhizal begin to grow. They are removed in blocks of medium and subcultured until free from contamination. This is achieved by the use of 'window' plates. FIM is poured so as to leave an area free from medium in which the blocks of inoculum are placed. As the fungus grows across the plastic surface to reach the new medium, contaminants are left behind in the block, which can be removed later.

The fungal isolates are maintained as cultures in Petri dishes of FIM, which are kept at room temperature.

Stock cultures of fungi growing on FIM are maintained at 4°C in the refrigerator.

So far the fungi have been identified rather tentatively as they have only been seen in the vegetative state. In the past they have all been referred to the genus *Rhizoctonia*, but it appears that at least two different genera of Basidiomycetes are active as mycorrhizal symbionts with the European orchids. For the time being all the fungi at Kew are known by numbers only, and F414, isolated from *Dactylorhiza iberica* growing in the gardens, is the most useful and vigorous that has been isolated.

Media for Seed Sowing and Germination

The major differences between the symbiotic method of raising orchids from seeds and the asymbiotic techniques described in chapter 9 relate to the presence of the fungus in the culture. For symbiotic sowings the medium must contain sufficient nutrients for the fungus as well as the developing orchid seedlings. One

Dactylorhiza iberica, growing in the peat bed at Kew, provided one of the best mycorrhizal fungi for the Sainsbury Orchid Conservation Project. Joyce Stewart

of the best media, which is used most frequently, is the basic oats medium, but it can be enriched with sugar and the salts of FIM medium if required. A small cube of agar from the chosen fungus isolate is added to the surface of the medium (table 15:2). The seeds must be sown thinly, to allow each protocorm space to develop and to ensure that there are sufficient nutrients for both fungus and seedlings. Cultures must be watched carefully so that transfers to new media are made at the optimal time for continued growth.

Table 15.2   Basic oats medium

	g/l
Powdered oats	3.5
Yeast extract	0.1
Agar	6.0
Distilled water to make up to 1 litre of medium	

For asymbiotic sowings, which are often made as a control, the media used for tropical orchids appear to be too rich for the terrestrial species, but some success has been achieved with half and quarter strength of several well-known media. A commercially available medium called TGZ-N is particularly useful. For the immature seeds from green capsules, which has been successful with *Cypripedium calceolus*, a new medium called Kew-A has been devised. It is dilute but complex and contains peptone and potato extract.

Seed Collection and Sowing

The seeds of most terrestrial orchids ripen within a few weeks or months of pollination. At maturity, the capsule usually begins to change colour, from green to yellow or brown. The capsules are taken off the plant before they split and dried in glass vials, covered with muslin or nylon net, in a desiccator containing anhydrous calcium chloride or silica gel. Drying takes place more uniformly like this, and the seeds are less likely to be contaminated by micro-organisms in dry conditions. The vials are sealed and moved to the refrigerator if the seeds cannot be sown at once. At 4°C they may remain viable for two years or more.

For difficult species and asymbiotic sowings, immature seeds are commonly used. In this method, one has to determine the best time to harvest the seeds for each species. Usually about half the usual maturation time is best, and for most European orchids this is six to seven weeks after pollination. The capsules are surface sterilised and opened at the laminar flow bench. The seeds are full-sized, but white, and are

sown immediately. The only difficulty with this method is that the seeds adhere to each other and to the capsule wall. Virus diseases may also be carried over into the medium with the seeds from the tissue of the capsule.

Small quantities of mature seeds are sterilised in paper packets as described in chapter 9. Larger amounts of dry seeds are surface-sterilised for 3–20 minutes in a 2–10% solution of sodium hypochlorite (bleach: 10–14% available chlorine) to which a wetting agent, such as Tween 80 has been added. The seeds are removed by vacuum filtration, rinsed twice in sterile distilled water by suspension and vacuum filtration and then resuspended in sterile water. Small aliquots of this suspension are poured on to filter papers, under vacuum, and sowings are made by inverting these squares on to the surface of the oats medium in Petri dishes. The medium is inoculated at the edge with a cube of agar from an appropriate fungal isolate and the dishes are sealed with laboratory film. The cultures are maintained at 20–22°C in the dark.

Infection and Development

The fungal hyphae grow out from the cube of inoculum across the new medium and very soon reach the seeds. They first enter the seeds through minute gaps in the seed coat called micropores, and, once inside, appear to be attracted to the suspensor region of the embryo where they penetrate the cell wall. When they reach the cortical region of the embryo they begin to form pelotons within the cells. This usually happens within five to six days of sowing and is the first sign that the orchid/fungus pairing is a compatible one and that germination will proceed. Rather little is known of the

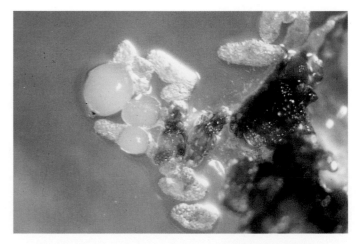

Protocorms of *Cypripedium calceolus* developing in the laboratory from immature seeds. Harriet Muir

Young seedlings of *Cypripedium calceolus* in the laboratory;
each seedling has several roots and a short dormant bud.
Robert Mitchell

Young protocorms of *Orchis militaris* grown in culture with a
symbiotic fungus. RBG, Kew

details of the orchid-fungus symbiosis, but a project in
the Jodrell Laboratory has been started to investigate
the molecular basis of the relationship using fungi and
seeds provided by the project.

The cultures are examined every week and the first
clear sign of success is the swelling embryo that splits
the testa and begins to develop rhizoids on its outer
surface. At this stage it becomes a protocorm. The
protocorms are white or cream, sometimes almost
translucent, and they continue to expand in size
eventually becoming top-shaped and developing a
shoot on the upper surface. The cultures are kept in the
dark for germination and the early stages of protocorm
development. They are moved into the light when the
first leaf forms. This may vary from six to eight weeks
for *Ophrys* and some *Orchis* species, to three to four
months for *Dactylorhiza* species.

The sowing plate is often rather crowded and the
protocorms are best transferred to fresh media as soon
as they are large enough to handle safely. They can also

be sorted at this stage and those of equivalent size
grown on together. They need to be well-spaced,
usually five seedlings per jar.

The asymbiotic sowings develop more slowly and the
plants exhibit a variety of growth patterns. The
Cypripedium calceolus protocorms look like little pearls
after eight to ten weeks of growth and then begin to
elongate into a variety of curious shapes. These
elongated structures become the first roots of the
orchid. When small, yellowish green buds begin to
appear amongst them, the cultures are moved to a
refrigerator where they are kept for 10–12 weeks at
4–5°C. This period of chilling stimulates leaf
development when the cultures are moved into light
and warm conditions again.

Recently the use of a chilling period has proved to be
beneficial with some of the symbiotically grown species
as well. *Orchis militaris* produces a round protocorm
which then appears to require a cold period before
there is any further development. Other species of
Orchis, however, all have round protocorms that
produce their first leaves very readily without a cold
period. These are species which, in nature, are winter-
green, usually producing their rosettes of leaves early in
the winter after a dormant period in autumn. With
several of the *Dactylorhiza* species, chilling appears to
stimulate bud growth and also tuber development
underground.

Weaning the Seedlings

Young orchid seedlings are kept in the controlled
conditions of the growth room until they are large
enough to have a good chance of surviving the
experience of moving to the fluctuating conditions of
the glasshouse. The transfer from agar to a compost
medium, and the move from an atmosphere of 100%
humidity, constant temperature and artificial lighting

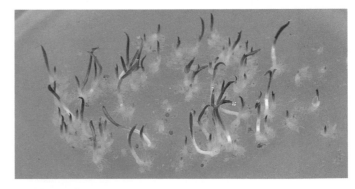

Young seedlings of *Orchis morio* only a few weeks old; the
seeds were sown on a sterile medium together with a culture
of a symbiotic fungus. Robert Mitchell

to the diurnal changes in these environmental factors in the glasshouse can represent disaster to the young plant if it is attempted too early. Nevertheless, it is important to try to move the plants on when they are at the right stage of tuber formation or leaf development.

The easiest stage to transfer terrestrial orchids from the laboratory to the glasshouse is as dormant tubers. This works well with those species that readily produce tubers in culture, including several species of *Orchis* and *Serapias*. Excess agar is removed from the tubers and they are potted into a basic weaning compost (table 15:3) and watered in.

Table 15.3   *Basic weaning compost*

1 part beech/oak leafmould (passed through a 13 mm sieve)
1 part perlite (fine grade)
1 part Terragreen
1 part basic terrestrial compost (Table 15:4)
Base dressing of hoof and horn meal at 0.5 ml per litre

The winter-green species, such as *Ophrys apifera*, are best weaned during the autumn and winter months. The seedlings with two or three leaves are remarkably resistant to cold conditions. The jars containing plants are moved to a shaded position in the glasshouse for one to two weeks and the lids partially removed for a few days more before the plants are potted into sterile weaning compost in seed trays or community pots. It is best to wash away all traces of agar from the roots before potting, especially with the asymbiotic cultures.

The *Dactylorhiza* and *Cypripedium* cultures that benefit from a period of chilling are best weaned as soon as they come out of the refrigerator. The protocorms, or young shoots with their cluster of roots in *Cypripedium*, are potted into sterile weaning compost and covered to a depth of 5–10 mm. The pots or trays are shaded and the compost is kept evenly moist. Symbiotic protocorms of *Dactylorhiza fuchsii* have been planted direct into the open ground at Kew, in spring, after a period of chilling, and their subsequent development and growth was normal and rapid.

The seedling growth room in the Micropropagation Unit is a busy area devoted to the Sainsbury Orchid Conservation Project. RBG, Kew

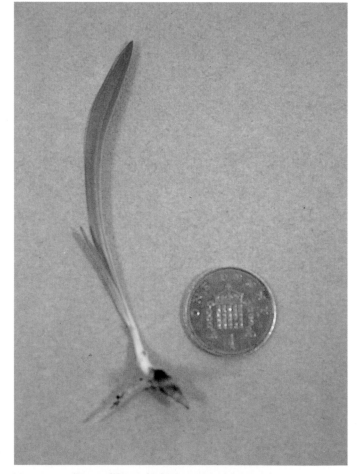

Young seedling of *Dactylorhiza praetermissa* with a well-developed tuber; this is the best size for weaning from the laboratory to the greenhouse. Robert Mitchell

Table 15.4   Basic terrestrial compost

3 parts heat-sterilised loam
3 parts coarse gritty sand or crushed grit (6 mm particle size)
2 parts beech/oak leafmould (passed through a 13 mm sieve)
1 part composted pine bark (6 mm size)
Base dressing of hoof and horn meal at 1 ml per litre

Establishing the Seedlings in the Wild

Several successful attempts have now been carried out to introduce one- and two-year old plants emerging from the dormant period into the wild. The highest survival rates were obtained with plantings made in the late autumn.

The first trial was made at Wakehurst Place in the autumn of 1987 with *Orchis laxiflora*. The lax-flowered, or Jersey orchid, does not occur in mainland Britain, so it was chosen because it would be easily recognised among the *Orchis morio* and *Dactylorhiza* species in the Slips if plants survived the winter. In May 1988, there were seven plants in flower, followed, in 1989, by 35 tall spikes. After two years the plants appear to be strong and well established. The survival rate is excellent, more have been introduced, and a total of 350 plants were present at the end of 1989.

Seventy-five seedlings of *Dactylorhiza fuchsii* were added to the wild flower plantings in the Slips in 1989. These seedlings were derived from seeds collected at Wakehurst Place. *Dactylorhiza praetermissa* seedlings have also been used in the area known as Hanging Meadow where the ecological factors affecting orchid seedlings are being studied. The plants raised at Kew serve as one of the study groups and the monitoring of the plants which will be carried out in the course of these studies will provide further information about restocking and the conditions required for its success.

Meanwhile, a few plantings have been tried in a secluded grassland site at Kew, where, on the generally gravelly soils, conditions for orchids are much less favourable. Several plants of the bee orchid, *Ophrys apifera*, have survived and flowered in 1990, although the first group to be planted, in 1988, was soon disturbed by rabbits. Subsequent plantings have been fenced. The green winged orchid, *Orchis morio*, flowered in its second season and was naturally pollinated. More plants have been added and a colony of 30 plants is now in place. In a damper spot near the edge of a seasonal pond, protocorms of one of the spotted orchids, *Dactylorhiza fuchsii*, were planted out in the winter of 1988. These were also disturbed by rabbits, but they were found and replanted without damage. Most of the plants survived, some one-year old

Ophrys apifera, the bee orchid, was one of the first orchids raised from seed to flower at Kew. David Chesterman

seedlings have been added to them, and protection from rabbits is in place.

A small planting was made in 1988 outside the head office of the Nature Conservancy Council in Peterborough, in what must be the harshest of all conditions for wild orchids. Here a small demonstration garden for rare British plants of various kinds has been established. It has heavy clay soil, but six seedlings of *Orchis morio* flowered there in 1989 and 1990. Three plants of *Ophrys apifera* still survive, two years after planting, but have yet to flower.

In the autumn of 1990, seedlings of these and other species have been distributed more widely to several wild sites and wild flower gardens. These further attempts at introductions of seed-raised orchids will be monitored closely by those who are collaborating with Kew orchidologists.

Future Work

Much remains to be done, but these first results are very encouraging. As might be expected, the rarer orchids are proving the most difficult to raise. Work in the laboratory and glasshouse continues to be carefully co-ordinated with observations of plant growth cycles in the wild and in gardens, at all seasons of the year. New observations may lead to small changes in method which could generate a marked improvement in growth or treatment of seedlings.

There has been tremendous interest in this project since its inception, from a wide variety of sources in the British Isles and Europe; and visitors from Finland, Switzerland, France, Germany, Italy, Sweden, Denmark, Portugal, Canada, the United States of America and Japan have come to the laboratory and glasshouses to learn details of the work. Similar projects have subsequently been established in several of these countries. A special poster describing the work has been used at orchid congresses in Cheltenham, Milan and Geneva, and at the special exhibition 'A Vision of Orchids' at the Sainsbury Centre for the Visual Arts in Norwich. A display of the poster combined with

seedlings at various stages of development, including a few in flower, gained a Silver-Gilt Lindley Medal from the Royal Horticultural Society at the British Orchid Growers' Association Show at Westminster in March 1989.

Perhaps the most significant visitors to the project have been a few dedicated commercial orchid growers who plan to follow the methods Kew has developed and raise hardy orchids for sale. If laboratory-raised plants of European orchids become available in specialist nurseries or garden centres, this will surely be another way of lessening the pressure on the wild plants that still exists despite the legal controls.

Ophrys aesculapii, an attractive bee orchid from the eastern parts of southern Greece, flowers in the cold glasshouse in the Lower Nursery. Joyce Stewart

16 Conservation and Education

THE GROWTH AND DEVELOPMENT of scientific studies of orchids, at Kew and elsewhere, can be traced back through several centuries. It is only relatively recently, however, that the subject of their conservation has commanded serious attention. A respect for the plants in the wild and concern for their continued life there, combined with a wish to promote orchids in horticulture and continue their scientific study, has meant that scientists and horticulturists at Kew have been in the forefront of a number of measures to ensure that orchid conservation is taken seriously. Often this is combined with educational efforts to create greater interest in the problems involved and persuade people to make positive efforts towards their solution. It is encouraging to note the increasing public awareness of the rarity, diversity and beauty of many orchids. Indeed, orchids are often used as flagship plants to attract attention to wider conservation issues.

Meanwhile at Kew many different approaches, botanical, horticultural, legislative and educational, are currently being followed in orchid conservation, and the role of Kew in each of these is considerable.

The Role of the Herbarium

The Orchid Herbarium is a wonderful repository of information on wild orchids and their distributions over the last 150 years. Now that so much of the world is losing its wild vegetation, the stored specimens and their data have an increasing role to play. As the largest family of flowering plants in the world, the orchids offer a good indication, especially in the tropics, of areas of high species diversity. Orchids are among the first plants to suffer when habitats are disturbed or desecrated. They are therefore an ideal barometer of the health of their environments. The study of the past and present orchid flora of many parts of the world can begin in the Herbarium.

Checklists and floras of national parks, mountain ranges, individual countries and even continents can be compiled without ever visiting the areas concerned. With these in hand, it is often beneficial to visit the areas in order to understand better the distributions of species within the habitats, and other features of their biology, before making recommendations for action.

Decisions about areas and regions, and about genera and species that need protection, should only be made when all the data are available for consideration. Recent studies that have been carried out in this way concern the orchids of several Pacific island groups. *Orchids of Vanuatu*, by Beverley Lewis and Phillip Cribb, was published by the Royal Botanic Gardens, Kew, in 1989. A similar project is under way for the Solomon Islands. A Borneo checklist is being produced jointly by Kew with Tony Lamb and co-workers in Sabah. These projects indicate the richness of the orchid flora of these areas of the world and pinpoint areas of species

Dendrobium rarum is an unusual species found only in New Guinea and Vanuatu. Beverley Lewis

131

diversity that might be considered for special protection. In some of these regions the orchids could also be developed as a tourist attraction now that more is known of their diversity and distribution.

Sadly, the herbarium and field studies reveal that an increasing number of orchid species are threatened and some are already extinct in the wild. All that may remain is a dried specimen, or perhaps, if we are lucky, a live plant or two in a living collection. Botanists in the Orchid Herbarium are frequently called upon to provide advice on the status of orchids in various areas by the Worldwide Fund for Nature, the International Union for the Conservation of Nature through its Orchid Specialist Group and through the World

Conservation Monitoring Centre, as well as by many other conservation organisations. The specimens, books and illustrations kept in the Orchid Herbarium, together with the field experience of the staff concerned, provide the basis for this advice – in effect they are a databank on orchid conservation.

The books and illustrations are also an incomparable resource for conservation and education and are consulted frequently by visitors who come by appointment to examine these treasures for a wide variety of reasons. Orchids have become quite popular as subjects for postage stamps. The designers consult Kew staff about the choice of orchids for their particular country and the use of suitable material by their artists.

Dendrobium purpureum is a widespread species throughout the Malay archipelago, extending south to Vanuatu and Fiji. H Bregulla

One such example is a new set for the United Kingdom which will be issued in 1993 when the 14th World Orchid Conference will be held in Glasgow.

The Roles of the Living Collection

By keeping a stock collection of orchid plants, the Royal Botanic Gardens can be seen in some ways as a kind of museum where orchids in cultivation are preserved as living botanical specimens for the future. In the past, it has only sometimes fulfilled this role. Now, however, it is much more dynamic and must remain so if it is to help alleviate the increasing pressures that wild orchids face in many parts of the world. The conservation of orchid habitats is often an economic or political problem, and there is little that orchid growers at Kew or elsewhere can do about it except to bring such problems to the attention of all our visitors.

There will always be a market for attractive, unusual and rare orchid plants. In the past this market has usually been supplied by the collection of plants from the wild, often resulting in the near extinction of already rare species. The day cannot be too far ahead when all collecting will cease, either through increased legislation or because of extinction. An alternative is strongly advocated at Kew, and that is the artificial propagation and distribution of nursery grown plants and seedlings. The vast majority of the more attractive species are probably in cultivation somewhere in the world, and these could provide the seeds required for this work. As a conservation measure, seeds are always preferable to tissue culture techniques, where a single clone is multiplied, although that is of great value for cut-flower or pot-plant production. Seeds provide a greater range of genetic diversity in the progeny and for the future. The artificial propagation of orchid seedlings at Kew has already been described in chapters 9 and 15.

Kew has always responded to requests from many applicants for seeds and pollen and even divisions of plants. Artificial pollinations are undertaken when plants flower, sometimes with donated pollen where we have only a single plant, and seeds or immature capsules are made available to competent growers. Kew also produces modest distribution lists of plants, seedlings, flasks of seedlings and even seeds which are surplus to requirements. The list is sent to other botanic gardens, both in the United Kingdom and worldwide, to nurserymen who specialise in orchid species, and to established amateur growers. It is not part of Kew's role to compete with nurseries who regularly raise orchid seedlings for sale. Many of the species listed are rarities, not available elsewhere, and are in great demand. Small numbers of seedlings are sent out in answer to each

request. It is Kew's hope that the recipients will also propagate from them when the plants mature, and make the species more widely available. In due course the need to collect plants from the wild should disappear completely. Then orchids will have achieved the same status in horticulture as other groups of plants, roses or chrysanthemums for example, where collection from the wild is a very rare event, and, if anything, it is the seeds that are collected.

Research into propagation and cultivation methods is a regular feature of the Orchid Unit's work. New media that appear on the market are always tried. New equipment is tried out in the glasshouses. Advice and information based on the results of this work, and other routine activities, are constantly sought and freely given to visitors in response to many enquiries.

The Orchid Research Newsletter

In 1983 the international *Orchid Research Newsletter* was started as the result of a perceived need to provide better, up-to-date information on current research projects on the family Orchidaceae to workers all over the world. It is sent out every year in January and July,

Paphiopedilum micranthum, a species recently rediscovered in south-west China, is already on the verge of extinction in the wild because of over-collection. Phillip Cribb

and more than 300 names and addresses are now on the mailing list.

Initially, the newsletter (ORN) concentrated on aspects of orchid taxonomy, but it has been expanded in recent years to include all aspects of orchid research and conservation of which we become aware. Since 1986, the newsletter has also been the vehicle for publication of the views of the Orchid Specialist Group of the International Union for the Conservation of Nature/Species Survival Commission (IUCN/SSC). This specialist group has given orchid scientists and growers a forum for the discussion of conservation issues as they affect orchids both in the wild and in trade.

One of the most welcome features of the ORN is a current bibliography of publications of relevance to orchid research and conservation. Hundreds of references to original papers in many languages are listed in every issue. While articles cannot be described fully, the listing of their titles serves to draw attention to work which might otherwise be missed.

The newsletter publishes short reports of readers' activities prepared from the responses they make to each issue and letters from readers on any topic related to orchids. Short reports on new techniques and developments are often incorporated. There are announcements of forthcoming conferences and other events of interest to readers. Advance publicity for books and reviews of books and articles of interest to readers are also published.

The ORN thus informs and co-ordinates and is eagerly awaited in many remote places. The editors benefit by hearing from researchers in so many different avenues of orchid work and are pleased to be able to help them to keep in touch with each other. Any correspondencce should be sent to the Orchid Research Newsletter, Royal Botanic Gardens, Kew, Richmond, Surrey TW9 3AB.

Conservation Legislation

Orchid specialists and other botanists at Kew are inevitably involved in providing information on endangered plants to the Government and its conservation agencies. So far as British orchids are concerned, Schedule 8 of the Wildlife and Countryside Act (1981 and subsequent amendments) lists 10 rare orchids for which a special licence is required to pick or collect any part of the plant, including seeds (table 16:1). All other orchids are treated like other wild flowers: they may not be picked or dug up without the landowner's permission, and they may not be offered for sale. Most landowners in Britain, whether private individuals or corporations, are aware of the law and

The lizard orchid, *Himantoglossum hircinum*, is one of the ten rarest species in Britain. David Chesterman

sensitive to their responsibilities. Thus the future of wild orchid populations is assured. The Sainsbury Orchid Conservation Project at Kew co-operates with the Nature Conservancy Council, its successor bodies, the County Naturalists' Trusts affiliated to the Royal Society for Nature Conservation and others in obtaining seeds and other material for its work on the propagation of British orchids.

Table 16.1   Specially protected British orchids

Species name	Common name
Cephalanthera rubra	Red helleborine
Cypripedium calceolus	Lady's slipper
Epipactis youngiana	Young's helleborine
Epipogium aphyllum	Ghost orchid
Himantoglossum hircinum	Lizard orchid
Liparis loeselii	Fen orchid
Ophrys holoserica	Late spider orchid
Ophrys sphegodes	Early spider orchid
Orchis militaris	Military orchid
Orchis simia	Monkey orchid

CITES

The Convention on International Trade in Endangered Species of Wild Fauna and Flora was concluded in Washington, DC, and signed by 21 states in 1973. It came into force in 1975 and has since been greatly expanded. More than 100 states are now party to the Convention. The basic principles of CITES – no

Peristeria elata, the dove orchid, is the national flower of Panama and is listed on Appendix I of CITES. AOS Award files

international trade, with a few exceptions, in wild-collected endangered species and a carefully regulated trade in species which are not yet endangered but may become so – have proved widely acceptable. 'International trade' so far as CITES is concerned means movement of plants across national borders and is controlled and regulated by a licensing system. Most states recognise that the regulation of international trade requires the co-operation of both producer and consumer countries.

Species controlled by the Convention are listed in three Appendices to the Convention. Those species of animals and plants considered to be threatened with extinction are listed in Appendix I. International trade in wild specimens of these species is generally prohibited, but in exceptional circumstances may be allowed if the parties concerned consider such trade is not detrimental to the survival of the species in question and is not for primarily commercial purposes. More than 100 orchids are now included in Appendix I (table 16:2). Species which are not yet threatened but may become so unless trade is regulated are listed in Appendix II. This includes all other orchid species.

(Specimens in Appendix I which are artificially propagated are treated for permitting purposes as if they are in Appendix II.) Appendix III is irrelevant for orchids.

The administrative structure established by CITES for its operation can be grouped in three recognisable units. These are the Secretariat, the Conference of the Parties and the Management and Scientific Authorities. All parties (countries signatory to the Convention) are required to designate Management and Scientific Authorities to implement the Convention which is operated by a permit system.

The Secretariat, based in Lausanne, Switzerland, ensures that the system is being correctly implemented internationally. The Conference of the Parties meets every two years to review the implementation of the Convention and discuss recommendations for amendments to the Appendices.

In the United Kingdom the principal designated Management Authority is the Endangered Species Branch of the Department of the Environment, and since 1976 the Royal Botanic Gardens has been the Scientific Authority for Plants. The Scientific Authority

Phragmipedium besseae is one of the South American slipper orchids that are threatened by over-collection and listed on Appendix I of CITES. AOS Award files

advises the Management Authority on all applications to import and export species covered by the Convention.

The Management Authority of each party controls the issuing of permits to import and export plants, and the Convention requires that each consignment of specimens is accompanied by a separate permit or certificate.

In terms of the Convention, trade in wild-collected Appendix I material is allowed in very exceptional circumstances only. If permitted, import and export permits are required to accompany the plants.

Trade in artificially propagated Appendix I plants and their hybrids *is* allowed subject to licensing. Such artificially propagated material requires an export permit or certificate as appropriate. The material is listed on the relevant permit as Appendix I and there are *no* exceptions. Flasked seedlings, tissue cultures, seeds and cut flowers of orchids in Appendix I all need a permit at present.

International trade in both artificially propagated and wild-collected material of Appendix II specimens is allowed subject to licensing. Here an export permit or certificate is required. However, certain exceptions have been made for parts of Appendix II orchids. No licence is required for seeds, pollen (or pollinia), tissue cultures and flasked seedling cultures, cut flowers of artificially propagated plants and 'fruits and parts and derivatives thereof of artificially propagated *Vanilla* spp.'.

In the United Kingdom enforcement of the Convention is undertaken by HM Customs and Excise in conjunction with the Department of the Environment. Conservation controls on the import and export of CITES species are applied in this country under the provision of the European Community CITES Regulations which are stricter than the basic Convention, requiring import licences for all Convention material. All orchids brought into the European Community therefore require both an export document and an import document. In addition, the Community has elected to treat all European orchids as if they are in Appendix I of the Convention so that wild populations will also receive the protection gained from an absence of international trade.

Illegally imported plants that are confiscated by HM Customs may be returned to the country of origin or sent to a recognised rescue centre within the country. The Royal Botanic Gardens receive such material, and since 1984 over 20 confiscated consignments of orchids have been added to the collection. These must be kept alive and cared for until any possible legal proceedings have been completed. If the plants are officially given to Kew when the proceedings are finalised, they may then be used in ways that further the purposes of the Convention, such as artificial propagation, conservation, education and scientific study.

Table 16.2   *Orchids included in Appendix I of CITES*

Cattleya skinneri
Cattleya trianaei
Didiciea cunninghamii
Laelia jongheana
Laelia lobata
Lycaste virginalis var. *alba*
Paphiopedilum
Phragmipedium
Peristeria elata
Renanthera imschootiana
Vanda coerulea

Note: Appendix I listing covers all species and their parts and derivatives

The European regulations implementing CITES are presently under review. Anyone intending to import or export must check the licensing requirements in force at the time by contacting: The UK CITES Management Authority, Department of the Environment, Endangered Species Branch, Tollgate House, Houlton Street, Bristol BS2 9DJ (Telephone 0272 218202).

The Role of Education

Education, particularly of young people, is undoubtedly an important key to an improved understanding of the need for conservation.

Each year there are many visitors, by appointment, to see the orchid collection. They include professional scientists, members of orchid societies and parties of school children. Members of the public can enjoy orchids in the Princess of Wales Conservatory and in the Alpine House, where there is always some interpretive material to read.

For the students who may become tomorrow's conservationists, Kew also fulfils a role. The Orchid Unit regularly hosts a horticultural student, for three to six months at a time, as part of the Kew Diploma in Horticulture. Ex-Kew students are scattered throughout the world in a variety of important posts, for example, in Bermuda, Singapore, New Zealand, Chile, Canada, the Solomon Islands, France and Japan, many of them involved in conservation activities. International trainees who come from a wide variety of countries also come to work in the Orchid Unit, for a day or for periods of up to six months. They are able to take newly acquired skills back to their own countries, and pass them on to other students, and so the chain of conservationists who are horticulturists continues.

There is an increasing number and range of lectures and courses at Kew on many different topics, both for specialised groups and for members of the public. Every year in May, some of the botanists and horticulturists who have contributed to this book combine to present an Orchid Workshop for the members of the County Naturalists' Trusts and others who are involved in orchid conservation in Britain. Lectures on British orchids, their distribution and ecology, pollination and seed storage are followed by practical demonstrations in the glasshouses and laboratory. Usually there is an opportunity to practise artificial pollination on some of the potted plants, and this is a useful introduction for those who will be trying to do it in the field later in the summer.

Several years ago, Kew became a member of the British Orchid Council, an 'association of organisations involved in the study and cultivation of orchids and the promulgation of information relating to orchids.' Two members of staff represent Kew at the quarterly meetings which co-ordinate activities related to shows and other aspects of orchid growing throughout the country. More recently, a number of specialist groups have been started under the umbrella organisation. The Royal Botanic Gardens acted as host at the inaugural meeting of the Species Group at which Kew orchidologists gave lectures and arranged a tour of the unique species collection which is normally open to only small groups of visitors by prior appointment. Kew has also contributed plants to the Species Group, by providing seedlings of unusual species that were surplus to requirements for distribution to members on an annual basis.

Staff at Kew regularly lecture to orchid societies on orchid conservation, cultivation, taxonomy and travels associated with studying orchids in the wild. They contribute to National and International Orchid Congresses in various ways, giving lectures, seminars and taking part in a variety of committees and working groups. The results of scientific studies are presented at scientific meetings and conferences in many parts of the world.

The Sainsbury Orchid Fellow represents Kew and the British Orchid Council at the European Orchid Committee which holds regular meetings and organises a triennial Congress. The present Fellow is Chairman of the International Orchid Commission which meets regularly at World Orchid Conferences and is responsible for several scientific and technical aspects relating to orchids and orchid culture which are of interest worldwide, including orchid nomenclature, hybrid registration and conservation. The present Fellow has also served as Secretary and Deputy Chairman of the Orchid Specialist Group of the Species Survival Commission of the IUCN until recently and is still a member of the group.

Future Work

Orchids are just one of the many groups of plants that form part of the special collections at Kew. Learning more about them and sharing that knowledge with others, particularly those who will become enthused to carry on the work in future years, is a vital part of Kew's activities. It is part of the mission of the Royal Botanic Gardens to ensure better management of the world's environment by increasing knowledge and understanding of the plant kingdom – the basis of life on earth. Whenever possible, the Royal Botanic Gardens will endeavour to reduce and reverse the rate of destruction of the world's plant species and their habitats. In the words of the Kew 'Mission' statement: 'Our mission will be achieved through worldwide research into plants and the ecosystem, publication, access to all knowledge so gained for the world's scientific community, and through the display and interpretation to the public of the collections at Kew and Wakehurst Place.'

Haraella odorata, a tiny but distinctive epiphyte with large flowers, from Taiwan. George Nicholson

Glossary

The definitions of botanical terms used in the text are given below. They are limited to the sense in which the words have been used in this book, and many of them would have slightly different or broader meanings in a wider botanical context.

Abscission
detachment of a plant part, usually used with reference to a leaf

Accession
a numbered plant in the collections at Kew

Agar
a gelatinous product made from agar-agar derived from various marine algae

Allele
a form in which a gene may occur

Anatomy
structure and arrangement of cells and tissues

Anther
the pollen-bearing part of a stamen

Anther cap
the outer deciduous cap or case which covers the pollinia

Anthesis
the opening of the flower

Apex
the tip of a leaf, bract, stem or tepal

Apical
at the tip

Artificial hybrid
a hybrid produced as a result of the transfer by man of pollen from one plant to another

Artificially propagated
plants produced in cultivation, from cuttings or seeds of a stock maintained for the purpose

Asymbiotic
seedlings grown in sterile culture, not in a symbiotic relationship with a fungus

Autoclave
an apparatus within which very high temperatures are produced by steam under pressure; used to sterilise laboratory equipment and media

Backbulb
old pseudobulb at the back of a plant, away from the growing point, and usually without leaves

Bract
a small leaf, or leaf-like structure, in the axil of which a flower is borne

Callus (sing.), **calli** (pl.)
a solid protuberance caused by a mass of cells

Capsule
a dry fruit that splits open at maturity to release its seeds

Caudicle
a stalk connecting or uniting the pollen masses to the viscidium, or gland

Chlorenchyma
tissues in the leaf which contain chloroplasts

Chloroplast
the plastids or granules in the plant cell which contain chlorophyll

Chlorophyll
any or all of several green pigments found in plants which absorb light energy for photosynthesis

Chromosome
bodies derived from the nucleus which readily take up certain stains and which are the sites of genetic material in the plant

Classification
arrangement in groups

Clonal
derived from a single individual by the growth of buds or divisions

Clone

an individual plant; a population of genetically identical individuals

Column

the central part of the orchid flower, formed by the union of the stamen, style and stigma

Cortical

relating to the cortex

Cortex

usually the ground tissue of a stem or root between the epidermis and the vascular tissue

Crest

a ridge, usually on one of the tepals, often decorated or fringed

Cryoprotectant

a substance used as an anti-freeze

Cultivar

a variant of any species or hybrid that is considered distinct from the horticultural point of view

Cuticle

the outermost layer of waxy material covering a plant

Cytology

the study of cells, their structure, nuclear division and development

Deciduous

falling off at some stage in the life of the flower or plant; not evergreen

Deflask

remove from a flask or other enclosing vessel

Dehisce

split or open spontaneously when ripe, e.g. seed capsules

Desiccator

an air-tight box or jar containing a drying agent

Dimorphism

the occurrence of two different forms in the same species

Diploid

an organism or nucleus containing two haploid sets of chromosomes

Dormant

not in active growth

Dorsal

relating to the back, or outer surface

Dorsal sepal

the intermediate, or odd sepal, usually at the back or upper side of the flower

Elliptic

shaped like an ellipse, narrowly oblong with regular rounded ends

Embryo

the rudimentary plant, still enclosed in the seed

Embryo sac

the structure in an ovule containing the haploid female gamete

Endemic

confined to a region, or country, and not occurring naturally anywhere else

Endosperm

tissue originating in the embryo sac of the seed which contains reserve food material

Epidermal

relating to the epidermis

Epidermis

the outer layer or layers of cells of the plant immediately below the cuticle

Epiphyte

a plant which grows on other plants but not as a parasite

Epiphytic

relating to epiphytes

Evergreen

bearing green foliage all the year

Exodermis

a layer of cells in the root which is the outermost layer of the cortex

Filiform

thread-like

Flora

the plants of a particular area, country or specified environment

Floriferous

producing many flowers

Foliar feeding

the practice of applying dilute solutions of fertiliser to the leaves of plants

Foot

a basal extension of the column

Fusiform
spindle shaped, i.e. thickened at the centre and tapering to each end

Gamete
a small unisexual body which is capable of giving rise to another individual when it has fused with another of the opposite sex

Gene
a unit of inheritance

Generic
relating to a genus or genera

Genus (sing.), **genera** (pl.)
the smallest natural group containing distinct species

Germplasm
that part of a plant or plants from which new individuals can arise or be produced

Grex (sing.), **grexes** (pl.)
a group or groups, applied collectively to the progeny of any cross between two plants

Guard cells
two cells which open or close the stomata by changes in their turgidity

Haploid
the stage of an organism with the smallest base number of chromosomes for the species

Herbarium
a collection of dried plants

Hermaphrodite
containing both the male and female reproductive organs

Heteranthism
having flowers of different forms

Hybrid
a cross between two plants, usually of different species or even different genera, but also between different forms, varieties or cultivars

Hybridisation
the process of obtaining new hybrids by artificial crossing

Hybridising
the act of making new hybrids by artificial crossing, also used for hybrids which occur naturally

Hybridism
having flowers of hybrid origin

Hydroleca
an artificially produced expanded clay aggregate which is used in horticulture for its moisture-retentiveness and for aeration

Hypha (sing.), **hyphae** (pl.)
cylindrical, thread-like branches of the body of a fungus

Inflorescence
the flowering shoot

Inoculum
the small piece of tissue, mycelium, or group of cells, introduced into a medium for culture

Internode
the portion of stem between two nodes

In vitro
literally, in glass; in an artificial environment

Keel
a medium lengthwise ridge

Keiki
a small plant arising from the stem of a mature plant

Labellum
the lip, or lowest petal of an orchid flower; usually held on the lower side of the flower and different in form from the two lateral petals

Lamina
part of a leaf or petal that is expanded, usually thin and flat; the blade

Laminar flow cabinet
an enclosed workspace open on one side with a fine filter at the back allowing sterile air to be forced to flow across a sterile working surface towards the worker

Lateral sepals
the pair of similar sepals arranged at the sides of an orchid flower

Lip
the labellum, or odd petal of an orchid flower; usually held on the lower side of the flower, and different in shape, colour and size from the two lateral petals

Lipid
fat which occurs naturally in plants

Lithophyte
    a plant which lives on a rock

Lithophytic
    living on a rock

Lobe
    a division of an organ, often round but may be of any shape

Longevity
    length of life

Medium (sing.), **media** (pl.)
    a mixture of substances which provide a suitable substrate for germination and early growth of seedlings

Meristem
    unspecialised cells, usually in groups, which are capable of division and becoming specialised to form new tissues of the plant, or a new plant when they have been isolated

Mesophyll
    the internal parenchyma of the leaf, usually photosynthetic

Micromorphology
    the study of small features of plant shape or form

Microclimate
    the climate of a very small habitat or area

Micropropagation
    the propagation, usually *in vitro*, from very small seeds or tissues of a plant

Microtome
    an instrument for cutting very thin sections which can be studied under the microscope

Mid-lobe
    the central part of a lobed structure

Mitosis
    the division of a nucleus to produce cells with the same chromosome number

Monograph
    a systematic account of a particular genus or other group

Monocotyledon
    a flowering plant that has a single cotyledon in the seed

Monopodial
    a stem with a single, continuous axis

Morphology
    the study of plant form and its development

Mycelium
    network of fungal filaments or hyphae

Mycorrhiza
    the symbiotic union of a fungus with the roots of a plant

Natural hybrid
    a hybrid which occurs in natural conditions

Node
    a point on a stem where a leaf is attached

Nomenclature
    the naming of plants

Non-resupinate
    not twisted as in resupinate

Nucleus
    body in the plant cell containing DNA and dissociating into chromosomes during cell division

Ovary
    that part of the flower which contains the ovules; an immature fruit

Ovate
    egg-shaped in outline, usually pointed at the apex, wider towards the base

Ovoid
    solidly egg-shaped

Panicle
    a branching inflorescence on which all the branches bear flowers

Paniculate
    having the form of a panicle

Papilla (sing.), **papillae** (pl.)
    small protuberance on the epidermal cells

Papillose
    bearing papillae

Parenchyma
    tissue composed of cells which are unspecialised, for example the pith and the mesophyll

Pedicel
    the stalk of an individual flower

Peduncle
    the stalk of an inflorescence

Pelorism
the appearance of regular flowers, in orchids, by the suppression of some parts or the production of extra parts, for example flowers whose petals resemble the lip

Peloton
term used for a cluster of fungal hypha which develops within a plant cell which has a mycorrhizal infection

Perennial
a plant that lasts for several years, flowering repeatedly

Perianth
the colourful parts of the flower, in orchids consisting of six tepals which are usually distinguished as three sepals, two petals and the lip

Perlag
an expanded horticultural aggregate of volcanic origin; similar to perlite but denser

Perlite
a variety of volcanic glass consisting of masses of small pearly globules

Petals
in orchid flowers, two of the three inner members of the perianth; the third is different and is known as the lip

Petiole
the stalk of a leaf

Petri dish
a round, shallow, flat-bottomed dish, made of glass or plastic and with a similarly shaped, close-fitting lid, which is frequently used in microbiology and micropropagation

Phloem
term used for the food-conducting cells in plant organs

Photoperiod
the length of the light period in the alternation of light and dark periods that affects the growth of plants

Photosynthesis
the formation of complex carbon compounds from carbon dioxide and water utilising the energy of sunlight, usually in green, chlorophyll-containing tissues of the plant

Plicate
folded like a fan; pleated

Ploidy level
the number of haploid chromosome sets in the nucleus of a plant

Pollen
the powder produced by anthers, consisting of pollen grains

Pollinarium
the unit of the anther that is transported in pollination, usually consisting of one or more pollinia, caudicle or stipe, and viscidium

Pollination
reception of the pollen on to the stigma or stigmatic surface

Pollinium (sing.), **pollinia** (pl.)
a body composed of many pollen grains cohering together

Progeny
offspring

Protocorm
a round or tuber-like structure that is the first stage of growth from the embryo to the adult plant

Provenance
place of origin

Pseudobulb
the thickened stem or stem base of many orchid plants

Raceme
an unbranched inflorescence in which the flowers are borne on short pedicels and usually open in succession from the base upwards

Rachis
the flower-bearing portion of an inflorescence

Reagent
a substance used for a particular chemical reaction

Relict
a species that is usually found in a different kind of vegetation or plant association from that in which it now occurs

Resupinate
having the lip lowermost because the pedicel or ovary is twisted through 180 degrees

Rhizoid
a small outgrowth like a root hair

Rhizomatous
like a rhizome

Rhizome
a root-like stem that creeps under or over the
ground or other surface, sending out roots,
branches, leaves and flowering shoots; always
distinguished from a root by the presence of
leaves or scales and buds

Rosette
a cluster of leaves arranged more or less in a circle

Rostellum
a distinctive structure between the anther and the
stigma in an orchid flower

Saprophyte
a non-photosynthetic plant obtaining its
nourishment from dead organic matter rather than
by photosynthesis

Scape
a leafless floral axis, or peduncle, arising from the
ground

Sclereid
a stone cell; a strongly thickened or lignified cell

Self-compatible
capable of self-fertilisation

Self-incompatible
the controlled failure of fertilisation of genetically
similar plants following pollination

Sepals
the three outermost tepals of the perianth of the
flower

Sessile
without a stalk

Sheath
the lower portion of the leaf, clasping the stem;
also used for bracts which enclose the flowering
stem below those which support the flowers

Silica body
a small body of opaline silica found inside cells,
usually of a particular shape for a species

Somatic
pertaining to the body of a plant

Species
a group of individuals that exhibit the same
distinctive characters; the unit which provides the
basis for classification; (abbreviated as sp. (sing.),
spp. (pl.))

Spike
an unbranched inflorescence bearing sessile
flowers; often used in general terms for any orchid
inflorescence

Spur
a tubular projection from one of the floral parts,
usually the lip

ssp.
see subspecies

Stamen
the male organ of the flower, usually consisting of
anther and filament; only one or two stamens
which lack filaments in flowers of the orchid
family

Staminode
a sterile stamen; a structure appearing in the place
of a stamen but bearing no pollen

Stigma, stigmatic surface
the sticky or smooth area of the column that
receives the pollen or pollinarium

Stipe
the stalk that connects the viscidium with the
caudicles of the pollinia

Stolon
a sucker, runner, or any branch arising from the
base of a plant which roots easily

Stoma (sing.), **stomata** (pl.)
breathing pores or apertures in the surface of
plants

Stylar
relating to the style

Style
the tissue that connects the stigma with the ovary

Sub-epidermal
below the epidermis

Subspecies
a subdivision of a species, usually restricted to one
geographical area and recognised by one or more
characteristic features; (abbreviated as ssp.)

Substratum
the non-living material on which a plant grows

Suspensor cell
a large cell at the extremity of the developed
embryo

Symbiont
an organism that lives in a state of symbiosis

Symbiosis
the living together of dissimilar organisms with benefit to both

Symbiotic
relating to symbiosis

Sympodial
a stem made up of a series of superposed branches; each branch terminates in a leaf or flower, and a new branch arises laterally below it to extend the body of the plant

Synonym
another name for the same species, genus or section, but one which is no longer in general use; (abbreviated as syn.)

Synonymy
relating to synonyms

Taxon (sing.), **taxa** (pl.)
a group or groups, each of which has a distinctive character

Taxonomist
one who practises taxonomy

Taxonomy
classification

Tepal
a division of the perianth; usually used collectively or when the perianth is not markedly differentiated into sepals and petals

Terete
cylindrical, like a pencil; round in cross-section but rather narrow

Terrestrial
growing on or in the ground

Testa
the outer coat of the seed

Tetrad
a group of four similar cells, e.g. pollen grains

Tetraploid
an organism or nucleus containing four haploid sets of chromosomes

Triploid
an organism or nucleus containing three haploid sets of chromosomes

Tuber
i) a thickened branch of an underground stem, which produces buds
ii) a swollen root or branch of a root, which serves as a store of reserve food

Type
the actual specimen described as the original of a new species or genus

Vandaceous
with a habit of growth similar to that of the genus *Vanda*, i.e. monopodial, with the leaves in two rows

Variety
a subdivision of a species that is easily recognised by its different size, colour, or other minor modification; (abbreviated as var.)

Vascular bundle
a strand of specialised conducting tissue with xylem and phloem

Velamen
the absorbent multi-layered epidermis of the roots of many orchids

Viability
the possibility of growth

Viscidium (sing.), **viscidia** (pl.)
the sticky gland attached to the pollinium, usually produced by the rostellum

Voucher
a representative specimen

Weaning
changing from one state of living to another, e.g. establishing in the glasshouse seedlings which have been raised in the laboratory

Xeromorphic
protected from desiccation by special structural devices

Xerophyte
plant which is adapted to dry conditions

Xerophytic
relating to xerophytes

Xylem
the main water-conducting elements in a plant

Further Reading

Introduction

Aiton, W *Hortus Kewensis or A Catalogue of the Plants Cultivated in the Royal Botanic Gardens at Kew.* London, 1789 (2nd edn by W T Aiton, 1811–13).

Allen, M *The Hookers of Kew.* London, Michael Joseph, 1967.

Allen, M *Darwin and his Flowers.* London, Faber and Faber, 1977.

Bean, W J *The Royal Botanic Gardens at Kew: Historical and Descriptive.* London, Cassell, 1908.

Blunt, W *The Art of Botanical Illustration.* London, Collins, 1950.

Blunt, W *In for a Penny: A Prospect of Kew Gardens: their Flora, Fauna and Falballas.* London, Hamish Hamilton, 1978.

Carter, H B *Sir Joseph Banks.* London, British Museum (Natural History), 1988.

Coats, A M *Quest for Plants: A History of Horticultural Explorers.* London, Studio Vista, 1969.

Desmond, R *A Celebration of Flowers.* Royal Botanic Gardens, Kew, in association with Collingridge, 1987.

Hepper, F N *Royal Botanic Gardens, Kew: Gardens for Science and Pleasure.* London, HMSO, 1982.

King, R *Royal Kew.* London, Constable, 1985.

Reinikka, M A *A History of the Orchid.* Coral Gables, University of Miami Press, 1972.

Stearn, W T *Flower Artists of Kew.* London, The Herbert Press in association with The Royal Botanic Gardens, Kew, 1990.

Turrill, W B *The Royal Botanic Gardens, Kew, Past and Present.* London, Herbert Jenkins, 1959.

The Living Collection

Bechtel, H, Cribb, P J, and Launert, E *The Manual of Cultivated Orchid Species.* Poole, Blandford Press, 1981.

Cribb, P J *The Genus Paphiopedilum.* London, Collingridge Books in association with the Royal Botanic Gardens, Kew, 1987.

Cribb, P J, and Bailes, C P *Hardy Orchids.* London, Christopher Helm, 1989.

Cribb, P J, and Butterfield, I *The Genus Pleione.* Royal Botanic Gardens, Kew, in association with Christopher Helm and Timber Press, 1988.

DuPuy, D J, and Cribb, P J *The Genus Cymbidium.* London, Christopher Helm, 1988.

Fast, G *Orchideenkultur.* Stuttgart, Ulmer Verlag, 1980.

Mitchell, R B 'Growing Hardy Orchids from Seeds at Kew'. *The Plantsman*, 11 (3): 152–169, 1989.

Northen, R T *Home Orchid Growing.* 4th edn, New York, Prentice-Hall Press, 1990.

Rittershausen, B, and W *Orchid Growing Illustrated.* Poole, Blandford Press, 1985.

Stewart, J *Kew Gardening Guides: Orchids.* Royal Botanic Gardens, Kew in association with Collingridge, 1988.

Thompson, P *Orchids from Seed.* London, HMSO, 1977.

Watson, W, and Bean, W J *Orchids: their Culture and Management.* London, L Upcott Gill, 1890.

Williams, B (ed.) *Orchids for Everyone.* London, Salamander Books Ltd, 1980.

Williams, B S, and Williams, H *The Orchid Grower's Manual.* 7th edn, London, 1894.

Orchid Taxonomy, the Herbarium and Library

Clements, M A *Catalogue of Australian Orchidaceae.* Canberra, Australian Orchid Foundation, 1989.

Comber, J B *Orchids of Java.* Bentham-Moxon Trust, Royal Botanic Gardens, Kew, 1991.

Cribb, P J *The Genus Paphiopedilum.* London, Collingridge Books in association with the Royal Botanic Gardens, Kew, 1987.

Cribb, P J, and Butterfield, I *The Genus Pleione.* Royal Botanic Gardens, Kew in association with Christopher Helm and Timber Press, 1988.

Dressler, R L *The Orchids: Natural History and Classification.* Cambridge and London, Harvard University Press, 1981.

Dressler, R L 'Recent Advances in Orchid Phylogeny'. *Lindleyana*, 1: 5–20, 1986.

DuPuy, D J, and Cribb, P J *The Genus Cymbidium.* London, Christopher Helm, 1988.

Flora of Tropical East Africa. *Orchidaceae.* Part I V S Summerhayes, ed. E Milne-Redhead and R M Polhill. London, Crown Agents, 1968. Part II P Cribb, ed. R M Polhill. Rotterdam, A Balkema, 1985. Part III P Cribb, ed. R M Polhill. Rotterdam, A Balkema, 1989.

Flora of West Tropical Africa, *Orchidaceae.* 2nd edn, vol. III, Part I V S Summerhayes, ed. F N Hepper. London, Crown Agents, 1968.

Jones, D L *Native Orchids of Australia.* New South Wales, Reed Books Pty. Ltd., 1988.

Lacroix, I F et al. *Malawi Orchids. Volume I. Epiphytic Orchids.* Blantyre, National Fauna Preservation Society of Malawi, 1983.

Lewis, B, and Cribb, P *Orchids of Vanuatu.* Royal Botanic Gardens, Kew, 1989.

Luer, C A *Thesaurus Masdevalliarum: A Monograph of the Genus Masdevallia.* Volume I and continuing, Munchen, Helga Koniger, 1983– .

Luer, C A *Thesaurus Dracularum: A Monograph of the Genus Dracula.* Volume I and continuing, Missouri Botanical Garden, 1988– .

Seidenfaden, G 'Orchid Genera in Thailand', Parts IV–IX in *Dansk Botanisk Arkiv*, Copenhagen, 1976–80; Parts X–XIV in *Opera Botanica*, Copenhagen, 1982–8.

Stewart, J, Linder, H P, Schelpe, E A, and Hall, A V *Wild Orchids of Southern Africa.* Johannesburg, Macmillan, 1982.

Summerhayes, V S *Wild Orchids of Britain.* London, Collins, 1951.

Wood, J J 'Orchidaceae' in *Flora of Cyprus*, vol. 2, ed. R D Meikle. Kew, Bentham Moxon Trust, 1985.

Wood, J J 'Orchidaceae' in *Flora of Turkey and the East Aegean Islands*, vol. 8, ed. P H Davis. Edinburgh, University Press, 1984.

Wood, J J 'Orchidaceae' in *Flora of Iraq*, vol 8, ed. C C Townsend and E Guest. Baghdad, 1985.

Research and Conservation

Arditti, J (ed.) *Orchid Biology: Reviews and Perspectives.* Ithaca and London, Cornell University Press, Part I, 1977, Part II, 1982, Part III, 1984, Part IV, 1987 (to be continued).

Clements, M A, Muir, H, and Cribb, P J 'A Preliminary Report on the Symbiotic Germination of European Terrestrial Orchids'. *Kew Bulletin*, 41 (2): 437–445, 1986.

Darwin, C *The Various Contrivances by which British and Foreign Orchids are Fertilised by Insects.* London, John Murray, 1862.

DuPuy, D J, and Cribb, P J *The Genus Cymbidium.* London, Christopher Helm, 1988.

Mitchell, R B 'Growing Hardy Orchids from Seeds at Kew'. *The Plantsman*, 11 (3): 152–169, 1989.

Pridgeon, A M (ed.) *Lindleyana. The Scientific Journal of the American Orchid Society*. West Palm Beach, American Orchid Society, 1986 and continuing.

Pritchard, H W *Modern Methods in Orchid Conservation: the Role of Physiology, Ecology and Management.* Cambridge, Cambridge University Press, 1989.

Van der Pijl, L, and Dodson, C H *Orchid Flowers: their Pollination and Evolution*. Coral Gables, University of Miami Press, 1966.

Wijnstekers, W *The Evolution of CITES.* 2nd revised edn, Lausanne, Secretariat of CITES, 1990.

Withner, C L *The Orchids: A Scientific Survey*. New York, The Ronald Press Company, 1959.

Withner, C L *The Orchids: Scientific Studies*. New York, John Wiley, 1974.

Index

Page numbers in **bold** refer to illustrations.